A Simpler Guide to Gmail

5th Edition

An Unofficial User Guide to Setting up and Using Gmail,
Including Google Calendar, Google Keep and Google Tasks

Ceri Clark

A Simpler Guide to Gmail 5th Edition: An Unofficial User Guide to Setting up and Using Gmail, Including Google Calendar, Google Keep and Google Tasks

Fifth Edition

Copyright © 2020 Ceri Clark

Published by
Lycan Books
Apt 12199, Chynoweth House
Trevissome Park
Truro
TR4 8UN

Phone: 0845 869 2802

ISBN-10: 1909236144

ISBN-13: 9781909236141

In association with Myrddin Publishing

Contents

12 Email Management

The email management chapter covers strategies for time management including prioritization of emails.

Learn about starring emails, replying to messages, templates (formerly canned responses), the inbox tabs, filters with labels, filter messages like these and how to unsubscribe from unwanted Newsletters.

15 Gmail on Your Mobile Device

If you check your email on your mobile device, this chapter has what you need. It has an overview and discusses how to browse, compose, reply, forward, search and view your emails.

It covers how to add more than one email account and Gmail settings in the app.

13 Chat

Get an overview of chat and find out how to use it in Gmail. Learn how to turn it on, invite contacts, archive or delete conversations and search your chat history.

Find out about the contact 'card', chat settings, video, phone or text chat, and how to block contacts.

16 Advanced Options

Turbo-charge your Gmail experience with Gmail Advanced options (formerly labs). Those covered are: Auto-advance, Custom keyboard shortcuts, Multiple Inboxes, Preview pane, Right-side chat, Templates and Unread message icon.

14 Google Tasks & Google Keep

Discover Google Tasks and Google Keep. Find out where to find it, adding, completing, editing, organizing, removing and viewing notes and tasks as well as emailing and printing task lists.

17 Frequently Asked Questions

Page 211

I have had many questions over the years, and this chapter aims to cover them, these include;

- where to go to login to Gmail,
- what to do if you lose your password,
- how to change your password,
- is a particular browser required to use Gmail?
- how to print email,
- how to remove the 'extra' inboxes like updates, social and promotions,
- how to remove email addresses when replying to all,
- increasing the size of the text in browsers,
- adding images to emails and,
- how to login if someone else is already signed in to Gmail on your browser.

May I ask for a favor?

Hello, my name is Ceri and I love creating useful and fun books. May I ask for a review at your favorite online retailer if you found this book useful? You will have my undying gratitude and you might help someone else take the plunge and give this book a try. Thank you so much for buying this, I hope you enjoy it as much as I did making it!

18 Google Calendar

Page 219

Google Calendar integrates with Gmail. In this chapter find a Calendar overview, how to get there and see how multiple calendars can organize your life,

Learn how to add, configure, create, delete, edit, export, import, share and view calendars. Color-code your calendars to find events quickly, Change the appearance and view of your calendars to make you work more effectively.

Find out how to create, delete (and get them back), and respond to events.

Discover flairs, how to find and use the settings available and even embed your calendar into your website. Find out how to print your calendar, set goals and create reminders and tasks. Finally, see what keyboard shortcuts can be used with Google Calendar.

Introduction

Dear reader, thank you for choosing *A Simpler Guide to Gmail* and welcome to the fifth edition! I never thought I would be giving this book a complete overhaul so soon after the fourth edition was published, but such is life with technology manuals. The new Gmail looks different and has a few new fantastic features which I am sure you will love. If you are ready to explore the new look, then read on, you are in for a treat!

With over a billion users, Gmail is the most popular email service available. This book is all about how you can get the most out of Google's answer to email, the instant online way to communicate over the Internet. It is written to help new users learn the basics and discover features that are far and above better than the closest competition. This book assumes the reader knows the basics of using a computer and has used a browser.

How should I use this book?

If you have never used Gmail before then the first few chapters explain how to set up your account, how to keep your account secure and the basics of sending and receiving email. Following this there are tips on using the excellent tools that will make organizing your email a breeze for the more experienced users. If this is you, the book is designed so that you can dip in at your level. The contents page will give you an overview of what is in the book thematically but if you want to find something specific, the index at the back is a good place to look.

For the purposes of this guide I have made a few assumptions. The first is that you have (or at least have access to) a computer, you are familiar with using a mouse and know what the Internet is. However, if you do not have access to a computer, a lot can still be achieved with your mobile phone.

> **Did you know...**
>
> According to a Lifewire article published in December 2018, there were over 4.4 billion active mailboxes around the world in 2015.
>
> Gmail has over a billion users while Outlook (Hotmail) has over 400 million.

A small disclaimer at this point. Gmail is constantly evolving and while this book is as accurate as could be made possible at the time of publication, Gmail can and will change. Features will be added and others taken away, however the principles will remain the same.

In the e-book version of this book, the images may appear smaller due to restrictions laid down by retailer and/or download costs. I have tried to write the book in such a way that the images illustrate a point rather than show you how to do a task. For example I will tell you where on the screen a button is and the image will be there as a visual clue but you should be able to find it from the written instructions. In some cases in previous editions, the written instructions have stayed the same while the look has changed!

If you have bought this book as a Kindle book, I recommend downloading the Kindle for PC/Mac programs from Amazon (free) to view the book from your computer. You will be able to click on links and the images will be of better quality.

Some of the screenshots in this book may not look exactly as you see on the screen as you do the tasks described. This could be for a few reasons. The first reason is that Google has put so much on to a page that you need to scroll to see everything on there. In this scenario I have done a screenshot of everything on that page and spliced it together to make one image so that you can see everything in one go.

The second reason is that the webpage will change depending on how big you make it. If you press the Ctrl Key and scroll your mouse wheel, it will make your web page bigger or smaller depending on the direction you scroll. When that happens, the elements on the page rearrange so that they don't disappear off your screen. One example is your email list. If you have your browser screen set to 100% view you should see the first screenshot in *figure* 0.1 but the second screenshot in the same figure shows the page zoomed to 175%. You may prefer the zoomed in or out versions but it is good to know that how you view your Gmail account, will change how it looks for you. All the elements will be there but

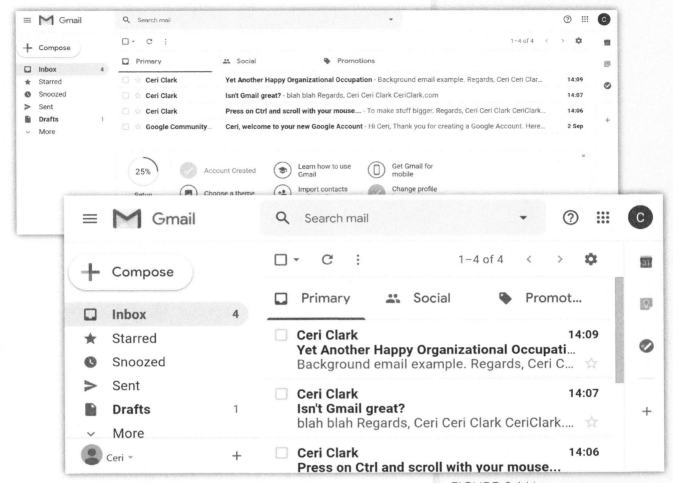

FIGURE 0.1 How a screen may change after changing the size of the page (zooming).

they will be slightly misplaced in the same area of the page.

The final reason that it may look different is that Gmail is regularly upgraded. This means it has got better over time but the look changes when you least expect it. Generally, the old functions will remain the same and the written instructions will remain true but buttons will move around the page and new functions will be added. A case in point is Contacts. The page changed as I was writing the chapter. The screenshots were replaced and were correct at the time of publication but elements were moved around the page as I was writing about them. The instructions in these circumstances are a guide. They will tell you what to look out for and what the buttons look like.

What is Gmail?

Gmail is Google's answer for providing free online email. Email is a way of communicating via text and images sent over the Internet. It is the cheapest way of contacting someone, no stamps or per-minute call charges.

There are a myriad of other email solutions on the Internet, some of them are free, others charge and a few are a combination of the two. Google likes to do things differently and they have improved how I deal with my correspondence. With the use of labels, filters, contacts, labs (now advanced options) and even their calendar, you will find that Gmail can almost be your own personal secretary, and best of all, it is free!

Why Gmail?

In my opinion, Google offers the best service for email because:

- Easy to use
- Nothing to install
- Over 15 gigabytes of space (enough for a lifetime of email, although this total is/can be shared between other Google services)
- Spell Checking
- Address Book (Contacts)
- Mobile and desktop access (there are apps for your iPhone or Android mobile phones, although any phone capable of using a browser can use it)
- Gmail has possibly the best spam (unwanted email) protection in the world!
- Your username and password for Gmail works for all the other free Google services like Calendar, Docs, Sheets and YouTube etc.
- The integration between other services means that if an attachment is too large to send, you can upload it to your Google Drive account and send a link through your email. This effectively means that if you change a document after you have sent your link, then your colleague or friend

X

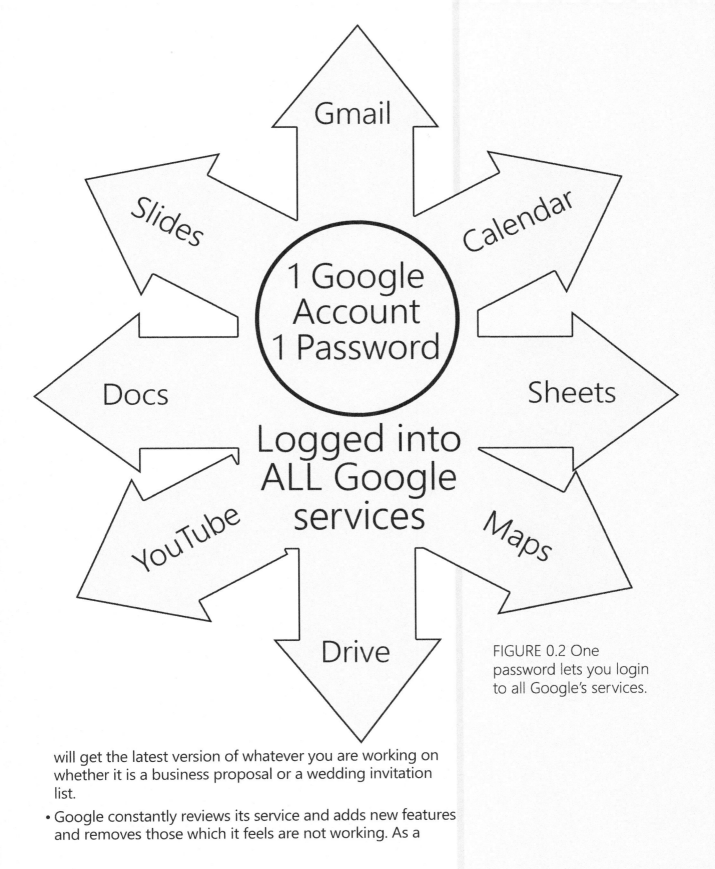

FIGURE 0.2 One password lets you login to all Google's services.

will get the latest version of whatever you are working on whether it is a business proposal or a wedding invitation list.

• Google constantly reviews its service and adds new features and removes those which it feels are not working. As a result Gmail keeps getting better.

• So what are you waiting for, open an account today!

Chapter summary

In this chapter I talk about what is Gmail and why, in my opinion, it is the best email service available. I also discuss how to use this book to get the most of it.

Opening an Account

● ● ● ● ● ● ● ● ● ● ● ● ● ● ● ●

Chapter 01

In order to create your first Gmail account, head over to the account set up page. At the top of your browser, (in your address bar, labeled (**A**) below) type in **gmail.com** or **mail.google.com**. Google will immediately change this and redirect you to the current URL they are using as their homepage (this does change over time). *Figure 1.1* shows what this looks like in the Google Chrome browser which is recommended by Google for use with their products.

Alternatively, search for Google in your favorite browser and when the page loads, click on Gmail on the top right of the page.

Once the new page appears, please click on **Create an account** (**B**) as also shown in *Figure 1.1*.

You will then be taken to the page as illustrated in *Figure 1.2* to open a Google Account:

What to expect in this chapter:

- Where to go to join Gmail
- Filling in the form
- Choosing passwords

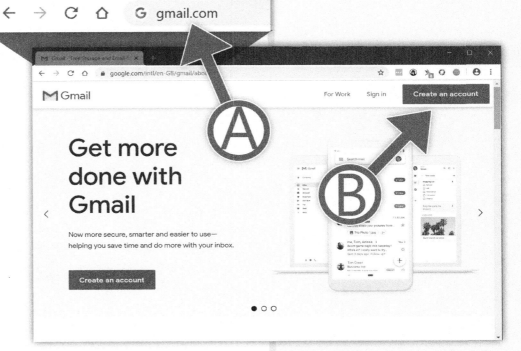

FIGURE 1.1 Creating your account.

Filling in the forms

Please make sure you fill in all the boxes you can in the form. Your mobile number is requested for security reasons. If you cannot get into your account for any reason in the future, Google can send you a text message so you can get back in. The same with your email address. If the one you are creating will be your only email address, don't worry, there are other ways to get into your account, but having a mobile phone or email address registered is the easiest backup.

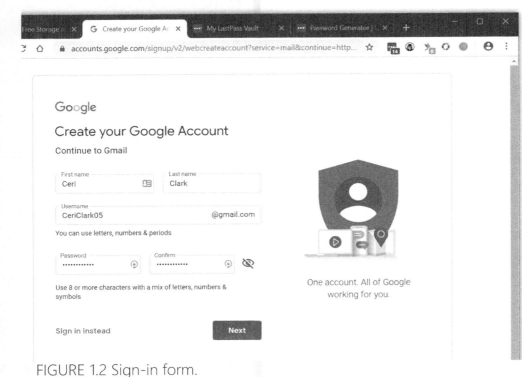

FIGURE 1.2 Sign-in form.

Choosing your username

Your username will be your new email address. The shorter and more memorable it is, the easier it is to login or give out to your contacts. Spelling out your email address over a store counter or over the phone can be annoying when you need to give it to someone.

I recommend choosing something that won't be embarrassing later. You may apply for jobs or be using this email address in your business. Fluffywuffychocolateguzzler may sound funny and may even be free when you type it in but future employers or business contacts may not be so impressed.

The idea is to create an address of the form <username>@gmail.com where you are picking the <username> bit before the @ symbol. You can use letters, numbers and periods (full stops) and it must be between 6 and 30 characters long.

2

When you put in your desired username, Google will automatically check to see if it is available, if not, the following (*figure 1.3*) will appear.

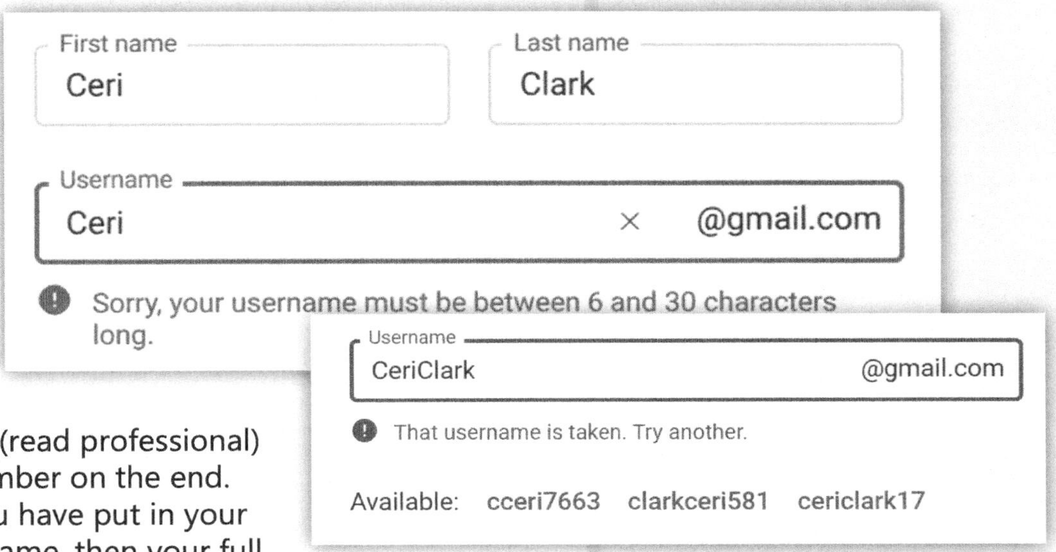

Notice how Google gives you a few pointers below your choices for some names that are available. You can choose one of those but being a bit more creative can look more appropriate (**read professional**) than putting a number on the end. For example, if you have put in your abbreviated first name, then your full first name may be more suitable or even putting in your middle name.

First name	Last name
Ceri	Clark

Username
Ceri   ×   @gmail.com

! Sorry, your username must be between 6 and 30 characters long.

Username
CeriClark   @gmail.com

! That username is taken. Try another.

Available: cceri7663   clarkceri581   cericlark17

FIGURE 1.3 Google will give you suggestions for your usernames if the one you chose is already taken.

Type in different variants or choose one of their suggestions until you find one that you like and is available.

Choosing your password

Next Google will ask you to choose a password. The most important thing to remember is to make it as strong as possible. Alone, passwords can be hacked. Together with two-factor authentication, they are a powerful preventative and will scupper many a would-be opportunist hacker.

Whenever possible passwords should only be *part* of your strategy for keeping your Google account safe. If possible always use 2-factor authentication as well. Please see *Chapter 4 Security* or *A Simpler Guide to Online Security* for more information.

Your password needs to be strong. There are a few schools of thought when it comes to thinking up passwords, so here I am going to cover five ways. Whatever you choose, there should be a minimum of 8 characters in your password. If possible, these should be a mixture of lower and upper-case letters, numbers and special characters such as a $, *, &, @ and punctuation etc.

Option 1:

The simplest one to remember is choosing three random words, which mean something to you but would be impossible to guess for an outsider. For example, if your favorite food is cake, your favorite vacation was in Hawaii and you just love baseball, then as much as my spell check hates it, cakeHawaiibaseball could be considered a reasonable password.

Option 2:

Another way to choose a password is by using a combination of letters, numbers and special characters. Using everyday words can make it easy to remember. For example, Elephantsrock is bad, but El3ph@nt5r0ck is strong. To get El3ph@nt5r0ck, I replaced an e with a three, the a with @ symbol, s with five and o with zero. All the replacement numbers look like their letter counterparts to make it easy to remember.

Option 3:

The third way is to choose a phrase, which you will remember and take the first letters of each word, for example: "The scariest movie I have seen is Omen!" Once you have settled on a phrase just add a special character and number. I saw the film when I was about 9 so that's the number I will choose here. The password in this example would be: TsmihsiO!9

Option 4:

Another way to choose a password is similar to the above method but involves an aid. Those familiar with the 2011 movie *Unknown* starring Liam Neeson may recognize this method. If you have a favorite book then choose a passage and from that passage choose a word. For example, if the word is in the 22nd line on page 150, two words along and the word is mammoth, the word would be 150222mammoth, or any combination of these elements that is easy for you to remember.

Option 5:

Another method to create a highly secure password is to create a spreadsheet on your computer or write them in password books and record all your passwords. The secret here is that you only type half of the password in your file. What you record in the book or database needs to be random with a combination of characters. The reason that this method is secure is that half of the password is *only stored in your head*. It does not matter where you put the memorized half of the password into the complete password (at the beginning, middle or end) as long as it is not written down. An example could be:

Memorized half (only in your head): wind

Recorded half (in book, spreadsheet or database): Hydf54j@#f

For this half you could use a password generator or mash the keyboard. It really doesn't matter as long as it is random.

Full password while logging in: windHydf54j@#f

As you can see this method would make your passwords difficult to guess. You should not store it in a password vault service unless you put it behind something protected by 2-step authentication.

If you are like me and are liable to forget passwords, a good way to cheat is to use a service such as LastPass. Sign up at **lastpass.com** and use their service to either generate passwords for you or to remember passwords you have made. You will need one password to use LastPass but the service will remember all your other login information and can automatically log you in to websites. The service is free and will also work on your mobile devices.

Tip...

> ## Example
>
> **Memorized half (only in your head):**
>
> wind
>
> **Recorded half (in a book or database):**
>
> Hydf54j@#f
>
> **Full password while logging in:**
>
> windHydf54j@#f

Did you know...

Use option 5 with password keepers or online password managers to help keep your passwords safe.

For a large selection of password keepers disguised to look like an ordinary book that you can hide in plain sight on your bookshelf, take a look at:

https://cericlark.com
https://passwordkeeperbooks.com

This way you can have different passwords for all the websites you visit and only have to remember the one to get into LastPass which stores all the impossible to remember ones. The service will also warn you when websites have been known to be compromised and ask you to change your password for them. If you have used a different password (auto-generated) for each website you will only need to change the one password. I highly recommend having a different password for each site so that if a hacker manages to get to a shopping site and steals your password associated with you username or email then they won't be able to use that password for your bank or any other site.

I would like to say a word of warning though. If you use this service make sure that you set up the password recovery options. You will need to install the LastPass plugin and have setup the recovery information. The service is very secure and if you have not done this and you have lost or forgotten your password, then there is no way of getting back the contents of your password database. You can generate a one-time password for emergencies.

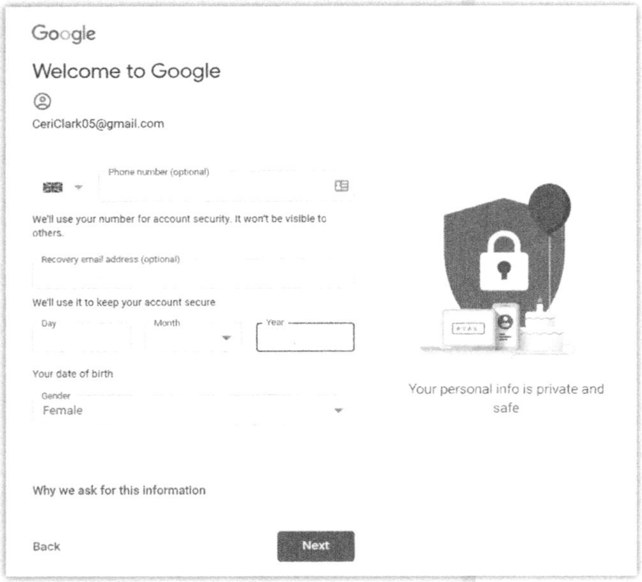

FIGURE 1.4 Security details form.

To be very secure with LastPass, set up two-factor authentication. This means that you will need both a password and your phone (or other physical device) to be able to login. A hacker will not usually have access to your phone and if they do steal it, you will still be protected by the password. If your phone was stolen, you would then automatically change your password and use the recovery information to regain access to Lastpass.

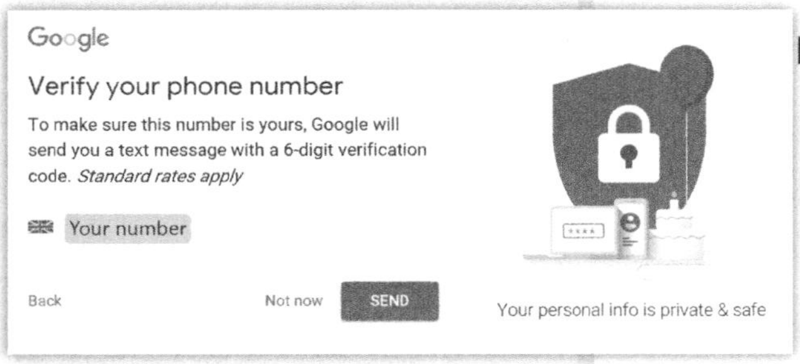

FIGURE 1.5 Verify your number.

Let's get back to making our account.

Phone number, email address, birthday and gender

Your mobile phone is needed so that Google can text you a code to prove who you are when resetting your account in circumstances where you have forgotten your password.

You will also be contacted by your email address if you have a separate one. It is recommended that you give Google an accurate mobile phone and email address when you sign up. You need a way in if you forget your password.

They ask for your birthday for legal purposes. They need to know you are over 13 to get an account but they also use it to verify who you are if you forget your password. I have known people to put a different birthday in here. If you want to do this, remember what you entered!

You can choose whether to say what gender you identify as. Once you have filled in the fields, please click **Next**.

Verify your number

Google needs to check that you are a real person and that your phone umber is real. Type in your number again and click SEND.

Check your phone or wait for the text from Google.

Once you have the verification number add it to the screen that loaded when you clicked on SEND.

If you can't receive a text for any reason, beside the blue VERIFY button you can click on Call instead to get the verification code by a phone call.

As soon as you have typed the code in, click on VERIFY.

Choose how your number is used

The next screen asks you to allow Google to use your

FIGURE 1.6 Type in the code that Google sends you.

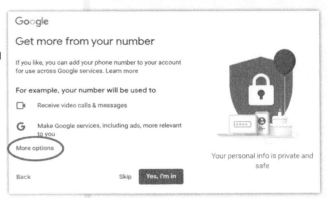

FIGURE 1.7 Click on **More options** for more control over how you phone number is used.

FIGURE 1.8 Your options for how your phone number is used.

phone number in a number of ways. If you are happy for Google to use your number across its services, then click on **Yes, I'm in** (figure 1.7). Alternatively you can choose what they do with your number by click on **More options**.

Here the first choice is to use your number just for security purposes, for example if you get logged out and you need to get back in after forgetting a password.

The second option is if you want to use their video calls service on your computer, smartphone or tablet, as well as security.

The final option is all in. This has all the previous options but also includes targeted ads. Google makes its money from adverts. You will get served ads anyway but it is up to you if they are relevant to you or not.

Another consideration is that Google does add services from time to time. You will have to allow these in the future if you want to use them. By selecting **Yes, I'm in**, you should be automatically allowing your number to be used. This could be a disadvantage as well as an advantage, The decision is yours.

Privacy and Terms

The next section allows you to choose how Google records and keeps your information. This gives you control over your information held by Google. Choose what options you would prefer and after reading the terms and conditions, if you are happy with your choices, check the two boxes at the bottom

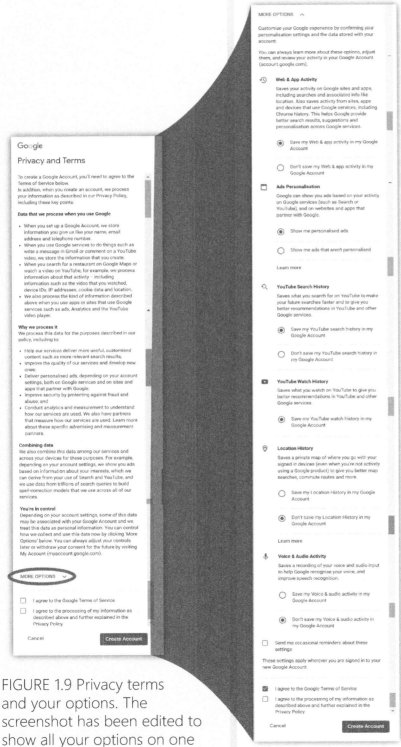

FIGURE 1.9 Privacy terms and your options. The screenshot has been edited to show all your options on one page.

before clicking on CREATE ACCOUNT.

This page also gives you a flavor of what is available through your integrated Google account.

Click on MORE OPTIONS, to find more ways to control your new Google account.

By opening your email account, you are in effect opening a YouTube account, affecting your Google Chrome usability, allowing Google to know your location as well as activating their voice and audio services. You will be able to alter these permissions later so don't worry if it seems daunting. You can click on Create Account without worrying about these settings for now. It is good to know what is available so a quick glance down the list will give you an idea of what is possible.

Congratulations, your Google account is live! Google will show you a welcome screen which can be seen in figure 1.10.

Click on **Next** to choose which view you want. This controls how your emails will look. Your options are **Default**, **Comfortable** or **Compact**. Choose **Default** for now (you can always change it later). Basically, the default view allows you to see the attachment names in the same row, but under the subject, while the comfortable view shows a paper-clip at the end of the row to denote there is an attachment present, Compact allows you to see more emails on one page, but also has the paper clip at the end of the row.

Click on **OK** to get to your new email account. Please take a look at the next chapter for an overview of the page.

If you ever want to add or edit your profile or account details, go to the top and click on the letter (the first initial of your name which will change to your profile picture when you add it). I will be explaining how to set up your account later in this book.

Number 3 in *figure* 1.10 shows how your inbox will look when you first sign up.

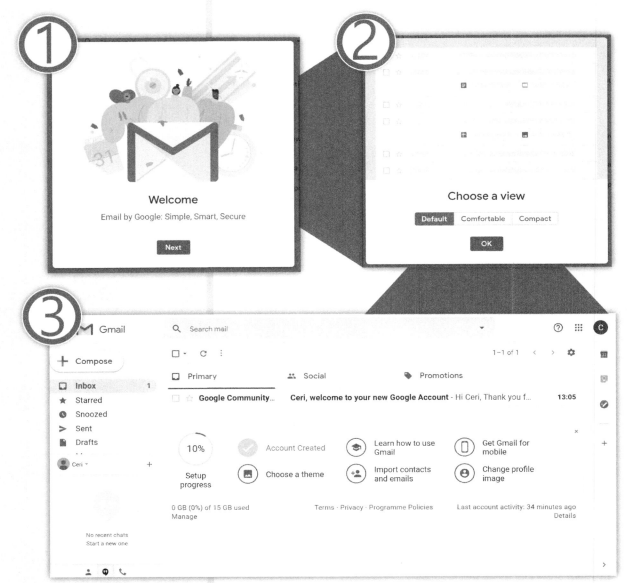

FIGURE 1.10 First look at your new account.

Chapter summary

Google has made it easy to set up a Gmail account. This chapter discussed how to choose a username and password and why Google asks for certain information. Security is important on the Internet and if you can choose a secure password and set up your account so that Google can notify you of any suspicious use of your account then you will go a along way to protecting your information and privacy. *Chapter 4 Security* will go into more detail on how you can secure your account even more.

An Overview

● ● ● ● ● ● ● ● ● ● ● ● ● ● ● ● ●

The Gmail homepage can look a little intimidating when you first look at it. This chapter aims to give you a brief explanation of the main elements on the page to give you a head start.

Navigating Gmail

Navigating Gmail can be done from three places, the top navigation section which includes the search bar, the Gmail specific functions directly underneath the navigation bar and the side navigation panel. Please see the following sections for more information.

The top navigation bars

There are two navigation bars on the top of the screen. I will call the first one, *Account navigation* and the second one the *Gmail-specific top navigation bar*. I have to apologize for the mouthful but it seems the most obvious way to differentiate between the two bars.

Account navigation

Search

Beside the Gmail logo, you will always see the search bar at the top in Gmail. You can search for your emails and it will even search through your attachments for you.

Sometimes you need some more control over searching

Chapter 02

What to expect in this chapter:

- An introduction to the top and dropdown navigation bars
- An overview of the options available from the homepage

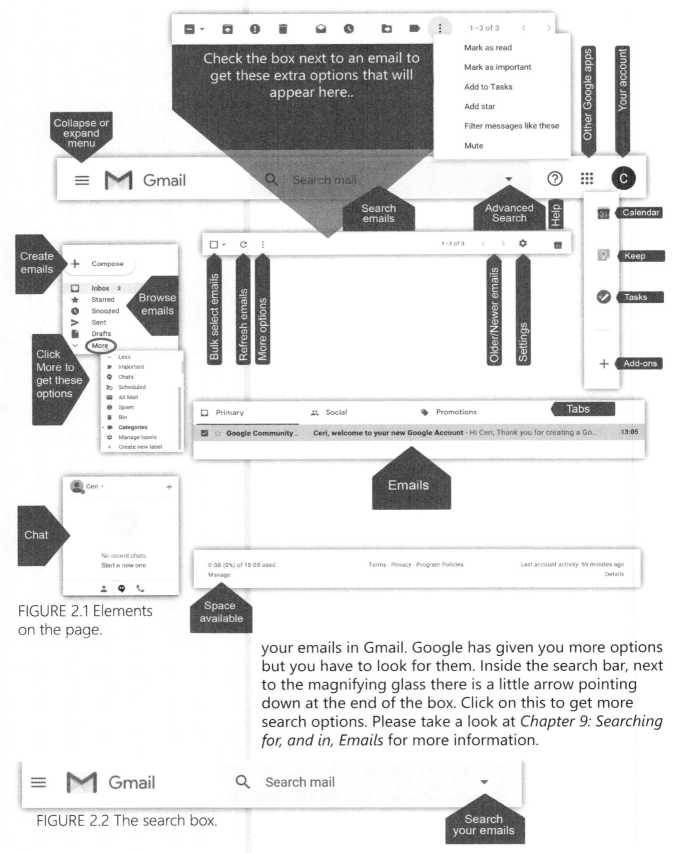

FIGURE 2.1 Elements on the page.

your emails in Gmail. Google has given you more options but you have to look for them. Inside the search bar, next to the magnifying glass there is a little arrow pointing down at the end of the box. Click on this to get more search options. Please take a look at *Chapter 9: Searching for, and in, Emails* for more information.

FIGURE 2.2 The search box.

App launcher

When you press on the squares, also known as a waffle (on the top right of your screen), you will be given the option to go to other Google services like Docs, Slides, Drive and Maps etc. You can add more apps to the initial list and re-arrange them as you prefer them laid out. For example, you may use Gmail and Docs more than any other Google service. The icons can be moved around so they appear at the top.

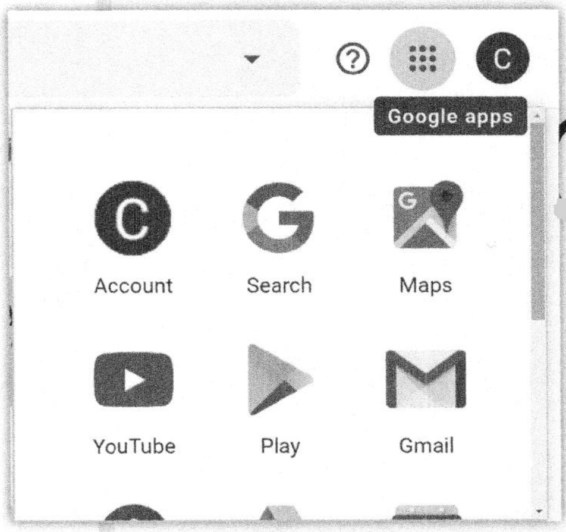

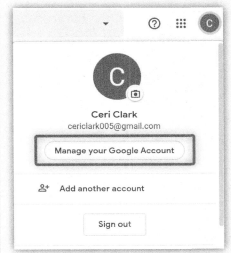

FIGURE 2.3 The Apps button.

Account

Here you can change your account options, find out about Google's privacy policy and update your Google settings. This is where you can add or change your profile picture and manage your security settings for everything in Google, not just for Gmail. Click on the letter inside the circle or your profile picture to get these options.

Gmail-specific top navigation

Bulk select emails

You may want to select more than one email at a time. Possibly to move them to a folder/label, declare them as spam or just delete them. Gmail gives you several options to select a few emails all at the same time. At the time of writing these were, **all**, **none**, **read**, **unread**, **starred** and **unstarred**. If you search for a keyword then you can use these options for even more control. For example if you search for a company name, you can then click on unread to see all the emails you haven't had a chance to read yet.

Refresh emails

Click this button to see if you have any new emails. I do this a lot.

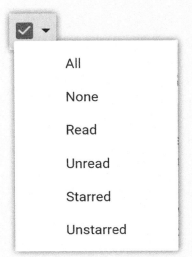

FIGURE 2.4 Your Account.

FIGURE 2.5 Bulk select your emails.

Refresh

FIGURE 2.6 Refresh your email list.

More options

At the top of the overview graphic at the beginning of this chapter you can see another set of options that do not appear unless you have clicked on an email.

When you click on the menu button (three vertical dots) without checking an email, you can mark all as read. However, if you want the other options they will only appear when you check the box of one or more emails.

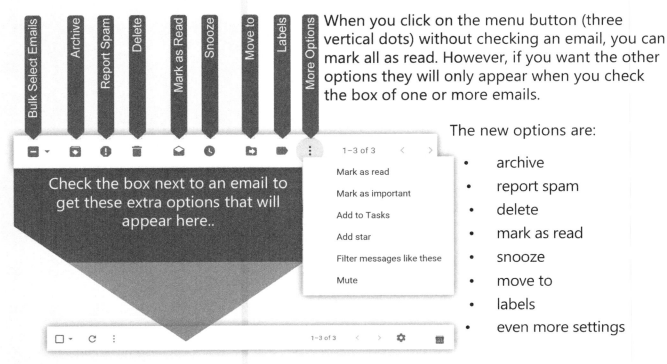

The new options are:

- archive
- report spam
- delete
- mark as read
- snooze
- move to
- labels
- even more settings

FIGURE 2.7 The extra menu button.

The settings when you click on the three vertical dots include:

- Mark as read
- Mark as unread
- Mark as important
- Add to Tasks
- Add Star
- Filter messages like these
- Mute

These settings will be discussed more in-depth later in this book

Older/newer arrows

FIGURE 2.8 Browse by older or newer emails.

Use these arrows to browse pages of your emails in the

order that you receive them whether older or newer. You can set how many emails appear in each page in the settings.

Settings

The Cog Wheel symbol is a short cut to many settings, however you will need to click on Settings again in the drop-down to get to most of them. Please see *Chapter 11: Gmail settings* for more information on these (there are a lot of them)..

The short-cuts are:

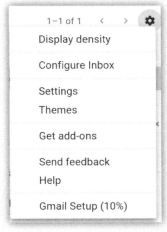

- **Display density**: Change how your emails are laid out on the homepage.
- **Configure Inbox**: Choose what Gmail tabs (if any) you want to add or remove above your emails such as Primary, Social etc.
- **Settings**: Please see Chapter 11.
- **Themes**: Change how your homepage looks by adding backgrounds etc.
- **Get add-on**s: Increase Gmail functionality by adding third-party scripts.
- **Send Feedback**: Let Google know what you think about Gmail or if there are any problems.
- **Help**: Need extra help? Check out Google's official instructions.
- **Gmail Setup**: This shows you how far along you are in the setup process.

FIGURE 2.9 Settings available from the Cog Wheel on the homepage.

Side navigation

The navigation bar on the left, as seen at the beginning of this chapter, holds the main means of finding your emails. If you have made any labels/folders, they will appear in here. If you cannot see them, click on **More** (located in the list under **Drafts**).

Another way to make the labels section bigger is to use your mouse and click on the line directly below the labels you can see, and drag it down to see more. Your mouse will change shape as you hover over the line to show you that it is movable.

The Gmail Logo

Wherever you are on Gmail, if you click on the Gmail logo it will take you to the Gmail homepage.

Contacts (No longer here)

Previously Contacts could be found under the Google email in previous versions of Gmail. If you want to find Contacts now, go to the Waffle (Apps) button on the top right of the Gmail screen and find it in the list.

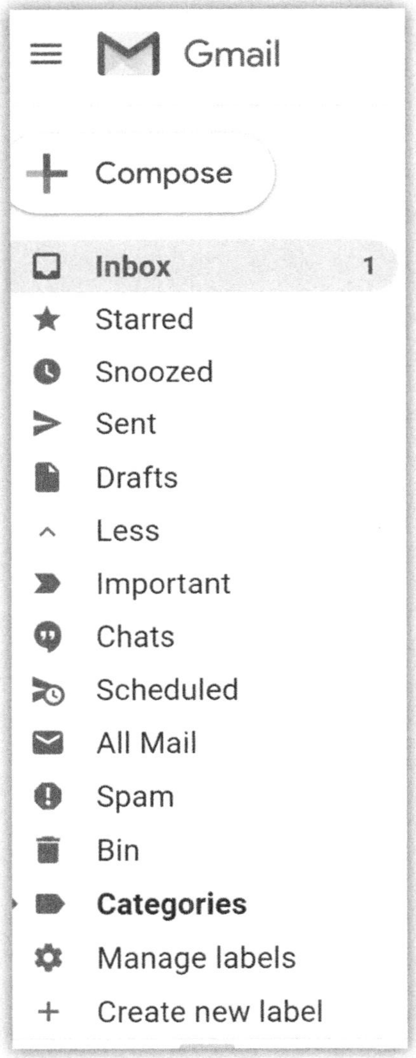

Compose

Click on this button to start a new email. Please take a look at *Chapter 5: Sending and Receiving Emails* for more detail on this.

Inbox

You can choose how you view your emails by clicking on the arrow by **Inbox**. The options are to sort your emails by **Default**, **Important first**, **Unread first**, **Starred first** and **Priority inbox**. The number that appears next to Inbox is the number of *unread* emails you have. If you want the total number of emails in your inbox cast your eyes to the top right under the search bar.

Starred

As you are sorting through your emails, you may add stars or symbols to them so you can file them for later as a strategy for keeping your inbox clear. If you need to find your 'starred' emails, you can find them here ordered by date.

This is useful if you bypass the inbox with a rule that sends certain emails to a label. It can be a quick way to find out

FIGURE 2.10 The side navigation bar.

what is important and new.

Snoozed

Snooze your emails if you need more time to answer them or they are not relevant yet. They will disappear from your inbox for the length of time your specify but you can always find them again here (as long as they are still snoozed).

Sent

This is the place to look for any emails that you have sent to your contacts. Searching for emails in this folder will save you time rather than if you did a general search within the main inbox (there are fewer emails to search and browse).

Drafts

If you are working on an email and you had to leave it, the email will automatically save to your drafts. Check here if you think you have lost an email you are currently working on that hasn't been sent or received.

Important

You can browse your email by what Google considers to be important. This changes based on how you have treated your emails in this past, who sent it to you and other factors.

Chats

This only appears if you have **Chat** enabled. You can find your old conversations using **Chat** here.

Scheduled

Scheduled is a much awaited addition to Gmail. This means that you can write an email and send it but it won't actually be sent until the time you choose. You could be cheeky and write a ton of birthday well-wishes on January 1st and your family will never know they were sent months ago. Just remember that you did it or it could be embarrassing.

All Mail

If you can't find an email, here is the place to look. Everything goes here, from your Inbox to your Sent. If it is still in Gmail then you will find it here.

Spam

Unwanted email should be in here. Google does a really good job but sometimes emails fall through the cracks. This means it is worth having a check to make sure that no important email has found its way to your spam folder. As you re-categorize the erroneously placed emails then it will happen less and less as Gmail learns what you want.

Trash (Bin in the United Kingdom)

This folder will fill up with emails that you have deleted. Remember to empty this folder to delete your emails forever. Your trash folder counts to your email space quota. Even though it empties itself of anything over 30 days old automatically, if you are running out of space, check it out to see if this folder is the culprit.

Categories

When you click on **Categories** in the sidebar, you will be given **Social, Updates, Forums**, and **Promotions**.

Below Categories are **Manage labels** and **Create new label.** For detailed information on how to use labels, *please jump ahead to Chapter 7: Email Organization with Labels.*

Browse your emails with Labels

Your labels will appear under **Categories** but as I have not made any yet, there are not any showing in figure 2.11. To create labels click on **Manage labels** or **Create new labels**.

Once you have selected **Manage labels**, you are taken to the labels area where there are some pre-made 'folders' for you. The options that come 'out of the box' are **Inbox**, **Starred**, **Snoozed**, **Important**, **Chats**, **Sent**, **Scheduled**, **Drafts**, **All Mail**, **Spam**, **Trash** (Bin in the United Kingdom and **More** labels. Under these options are **Categories**.

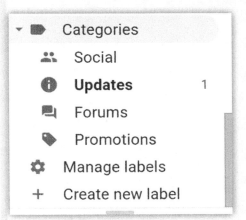

FIGURE 2.11 Click on categories to get to your Social, Promotions, Updates and Forums inboxes.

Tabs

Google has set up five tabs, which are really just labels but they control them. These are Primary, Social, Promotions, Updates and Forums. Google will try to categorize your emails for you if you choose to use these. You can turn these off if you want finer control but if you are starting out, it can be useful to separate your Facebook, Linkedin, or even your Instagram notifications from your usual email. Without categories, you can do this yourself by using filters. See *Chapter 8: Filters and Blocked Addresses* for how to do this.

Emails

Your emails will be in the second pane under Google's tabs. You can select an email by clicking anywhere on it or checking the box next to it. Beside this you will see who the email is from and then what the email is about. The final information you will see is the date you received the email. You will be able to see attachments or a paperclip representing them in different places depending on what density you choose to view your email. You can get to the density options under the Cog Wheel above your emails.

Chat

Use this section to chat to your friends on Gmail. Sometimes it is quicker to get an answer when you send a chat message over an email message. This is a way of keeping a record of your chats in your email as your chats are searchable when you search in Gmail. You can turn this off in the settings.

Space available

Google gives you 15 Gigabytes of space over your whole Google account. This is used up over all their services including Gmail, Drive, Docs, Sheets etc. If you are running out of space, it is a good idea to check your other Google apps such as Google Photos as well as attachments in your email account.

Right Sidebar

The right side bar (please see figure 2.12) houses the icons of Google Calendar, Keep, Tasks and Add-ons which you can see and use without leaving Gmail.

These are widgets. Click on any of these services and they will open a bigger side panel where you can check what events you have organized for the day, write notes and create tasks at the same time as browsing your emails.

For more information on Google Keep and Tasks, check out *Chapter 14: Google Tasks & Google Keep* and for Add-ons, please take a look at *Chapter 16: Advanced Options*.

FIGURE 2.12 The right sidebar is where you can find widgets for Google Calendar, Keep, Tasks and third party add-ons.

Chapter summary

If you are logged in to any Google service, the top-right of your browser window will show you which Google account you are logged in as, a menu to quickly navigate to other Google services and access to your overall account settings such as security and privacy options.

The Gmail specific options in the top navigation include archiving, snoozing, reporting spam and moving your emails into different labels/folders.

Below the main navigation window on the left-hand side is the main navigation which contains your labels. These are like folders but you can have one email in several places without duplication. There is still only one email but you can see it from different places. Be careful if you delete an email, it will be deleted from everywhere!

If you would like to use the chat functionality of Gmail then that is located at the bottom left of the window.

All your emails will be listed in the main window beside the left navigation pane unless you have archived your email. For clarification, if you archive an email, all this does is remove the **Inbox** label from an email. Unless you assign a label/folder to your email it will be in limbo but you can find it again by clicking on **All Mail**.

You can check how much space you have left in your Google account by looking at the bottom of the page.

Getting Started

● ● ● ● ● ● ● ● ● ● ● ● ● ● ● ● ● ●

Now that you have your new Google account, you can set it up so that your profile is up-to-date (handy for when people who have you in their contacts can see who you are) and you can import your mail and contacts from other service providers.

Adding your profile picture

Gmail is only a part of the office applications suite that Google gives you for free. When you create a Google Profile it will be used across all Google services. This means that if you collaborate with someone in Google Docs or Sheets they can see a little picture of you next to changes you make or even when you are currently working on it. You can choose not to make your profile public if you so wish. Your picture can also end up on emails that you send to people who use Gmail and even on your friends' phones in your contact information (when they put your email address into the contact information).

Where to add your profile picture

There are three ways you can add your photo to your account and two places to do it from. These are upload your photo, browse through your photos held in your Google account, and you can take a photo using your web camera. The web camera option is not available at the moment but you can still see the option in some browsers so may become possible again in the future.

The two locations where you can change your profile pictures are either through the account button at the top

What to expect in this chapter:

- First steps in setting up your Google account
- Adding your profile picture
- Importing mail and contacts
- Logging in
- Adding Google and Gmail as your homepage
- Reading emails
- Gmail's category inboxes (tabs)
- Turning chat off

right of the screen, (currently it will have the initial of your first name on but will change to your profile photo once you have added it) and through the Settings.

A quick note about your profile picture. What you choose to have as your photo is of course entirely up to you but if you are using your new email account for business then choosing a business appropriate photo might be the way to go. If you want to be more anonymous on the internet, a lovely picture of your pet, a photo of you in shadow or even an illustration could be more appropriate. Basically think about how you want the profile connected to this account to be viewed by the world.

Adding through your Account button

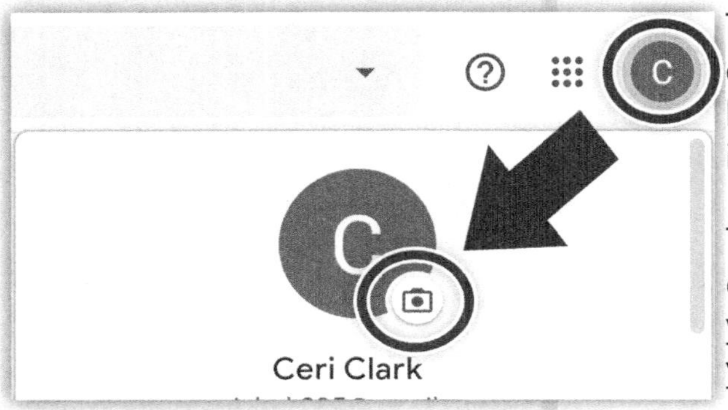

FIGURE 3.1 Where to go to add your profile picture

FIGURE 3.2 The profile photo selection screen showing where the web camera tab appears in some browsers.

To upload a profile picture on to Google, first click on the initial of your name at the top right of your browser. In the box that loads, click on **Change** inside the big circle with your initial in it.

The next screen that will load will look different depending on a couple of factors. The first is if you have Flash installed and secondly whether your browser is set up to use it. Bear in mind that Adobe has pledged to get rid of the Flash player by the end of 2020. This is a reaction to security vulnerabilities and that the main browsers have blocked its use routinely as a result. This really only affects adding your profile photo using your web camera whilst in Gmail. There is nothing stopping you using your web camera to take a photo outside of Gmail and then adding your photos in either of the other two ways.

If you do want to use your web camera I will be providing some brief instructions for using within Gmail later in this chapter but for now, the option will not appear in most browsers. At the time of writing, the tab only appeared in Microsoft Explorer and Firefox. I also tested Microsoft Edge, Chrome and Vivaldi with no success. Given that the software will not be around by the end of 2020, it may not be worth your while to get it working now.

Upload a photo from your computer

- Click on your initial on the top right of the screen
- Click on the camera icon (inside the circle)
- Click on **Select a photo from your computer**
- Browse the files on your computer for a suitable picture or a flattering photo and select it. Click **Open** and the picture will start uploading. You will be given the option to edit your photo before it becomes live
- Reposition and move the squares with your mouse (circled in figure 3.3), until you have the picture how you want it.

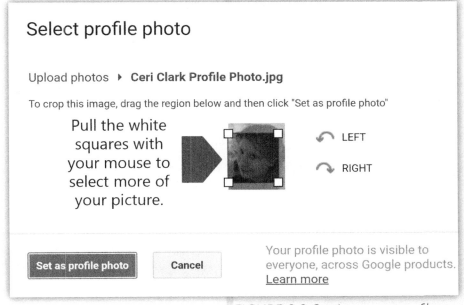

FIGURE 3.3 Setting your profile picture.

The picture will be across all Google services so it has to be standardized. This means that the photo can only be manipulated to a smaller or bigger square. The left and right buttons to the right of your profile picture rotates it left or right

- Click on **Set as profile photo**. You may have to refresh your Gmail page to see the picture you have uploaded when you click on your initial. It may take some time for your initial to be replaced with your picture but it will happen.

Choose a photo from 'Your photos'

- Click on your initial on the top right of the screen
- Click on the camera icon (inside the circle)
- Click on **Your photos**
- Choose from photos linked from Google Photos uploaded from your phone or somewhere else on your Google account

- Click on **Set as profile photo**. If this step does not work, try a different browser. Chrome or Firefox are recommended

Choose a photo using your web camera

Last but not least you can use your web camera to create your profile photo. Currently, at the time of writing, this is a bit hit and miss as it relies on Adobe Flash. Previously other ways to upload profile photos were dependent on the software but have been updated so they no longer need to use it. This means I believe that eventually you will be able to use your web camera from Chrome without Flash in the future.

Do you have Adobe Flash installed?

On some browsers you may need Adobe Flash to be installed to add your profile picture. Some of the elements won't appear on the page. If you are not going to use the web camera to upload you profile photo, you can skip this step. Here is the briefest of guides for adding Adobe Flash to your computer.

- Go to https://get.adobe.com/flashplayer/
- Uncheck the optional offers (unless you really want them)

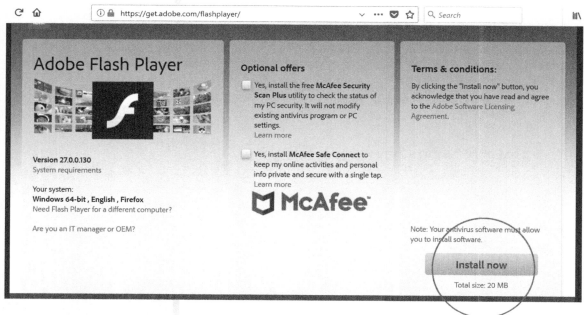

FIGURE 3.4 Installing Adobe Flash.

- Click on **Install now**
- Save the installer file on to your computer
- Run the installer file on your computer (double-left-click on the file and click **OK**)
- Restart your browser

Adding the profile photo

- Click on your initial on the top right of the screen
- Click on the camera icon (inside the circle)
- Click on **Web camera**
- Click on the play button in the middle of the screen
- Allow it to access your camera and microphone. Without allowing this, you can't take a picture with your camera. I *never* choose **Remember** for this kind of thing as I want to know what is using my camera but then I can be known as slightly paranoid!
- Click on the red button with the camera symbol and **Take a snapshot** written on it. You can do this as many times until you get the result you want. Google will keep the last four photos that you take and you can choose from them
- When you have found the perfect picture, click on **Set as profile photo**. If you change your mind and want to finish it later, click on **Cancel**. You can add a profile picture at any time

Importing mail and contacts

If you have another email account you may want to import all your previous email into your brand new Google account. Google can import all your old emails and any new ones that come into your old account. This comes in very handy if you have more than one email account but you want to check them from the one location. They can also import just your old emails, this would be useful if you just want to have Gmail going forward.

Importing you contacts from AOL, Outlook, Yahoo! or any other webmail account is simple with Gmail.

1. From your Gmail homepage, click on the gear wheel on the top right of your screen

Did you know...

Other email providers may stop you from importing information as a security feature. Yahoo is one of these. If you want to import emails and contacts from Yahoo *and it is not working* then you will have to enable a feature to allow this to work. Here's how to do this:

- Login in to Yahoo mail
- Click on your name at the top right of the screen
- Click on **Account info**
- Click on **Account security**
- Enable **Allow apps that use less secure sign-in**

The steps listed should now work. Disable after importing to reduce security vulnerabilities.

2. In the drop-down menu, choose **Settings** which is near the bottom of the list. Please take a look at *figure 3.5* for a visual guide

3. Click on **Accounts and Import** (under **Settings**). This will take you to a page where you can change your password. The second option is **Import mail and contacts**

4. Click on **Import mail and contacts**

5. Type in your email address in the box that loads and click **Continue**

6. You will be asked to sign-in to your other email account to confirm it's actually you trying to import your email and not someone else. Click on **Continue**. You will be taken to your previous email provider such as Yahoo to sign in

7. If the sign-in pop-up that leads to *figure* 3.9 (you won't actually ever see that screen), does not load, you will get a message from Google saying that there was a problem because you are blocking pop-ups. In Google Chrome, click on the icon that can be seen circled in *figure* 3.14 and choose **Always allow pop ups and redirects from https://mail. google.com**. Then click **Done**. The pop-up should then load.

8. Sign in and agree to the transfer of email and contacts (*see figure 3.9*). If you are still happy to do this, click on **Agree**

9. The next window to load will be a confirmation that your two accounts are connected. You will need to close the window to carry on

10. Back in Google, you will be asked what you want to import. There are three options and you can choose to check one or all the boxes. The importing of your data is done by another party so you cannot have your email imported for more than 30 days, however you can have your mail brought into Google indefinitely through the settings which I will explain later. I would therefore not bother with the third option as you might get your emails duplicated

As the Yahoo account was new and created specifically

for this book, my emails and contacts were imported within seconds. The time it takes to import your mail and contacts will vary depending on how many you have to transfer.

Google will create a label using your other email address as the name. Find all imported email in this label from the left navigation bar.

Logging in or Signing in

Say some time has flown by and you haven't checked your email. You click open your browser, probably Edge, Chrome, Firefox, Vivaldi or even Safari. The horror, it's logged you out, how do I check it now?

Going directly there

Depending on if you bought this as a paperback or e-book, you could type in the following website address or highlight and copy it...

https://mail.google.com

...and paste it into the address bar in your internet browser. Press **Enter** on your keyboard (otherwise known as Return) and you will be taken directly there.

Choose your email address from a list as seen in *figure 3.15*. A new box will load inviting you to type in your password. As you type it will be hidden by dots in case there is anyone behind you, having a snoop. Click on **Next**. You will now be logged in.

Adding Google and Gmail as your homepage

If the first thing you do each day is check your Gmail account and maybe do a search in Google, I recommend setting Gmail and Google as two separate tabs as your home pages. This way when you first open your browser

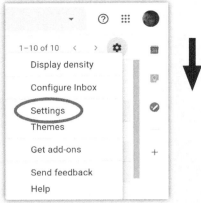

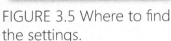

FIGURE 3.5 Where to find the settings.

Visual guide to importing mail and contacts

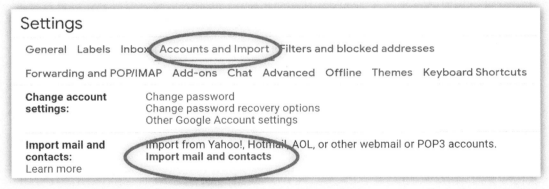

FIGURE 3.6 Where to find Accounts and Import and Import mail and contacts.

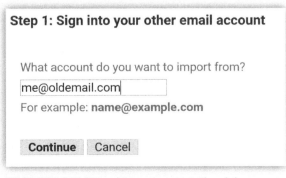

FIGURE 3.7 Type in your email address.

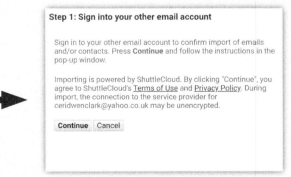

FIGURE 3.8 Login to your Yahoo account.

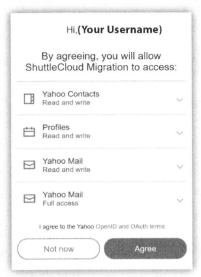

Hi,**(Your Username)**

By agreeing, you will allow ShuttleCloud Migration to access:

☐ Yahoo Contacts
Read and write ⌄

🗓 Profiles
Read and write ⌄

✉ Yahoo Mail
Read and write ⌄

✉ Yahoo Mail
Full access ⌄

I agree to the Yahoo OpenID and OAuth terms

(Not now) (Agree)

FIGURE 3.9 Agree to the transfer.

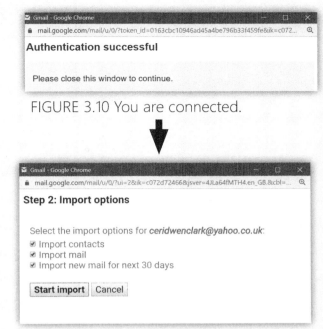

FIGURE 3.10 You are connected.

Step 2: Import options

Select the import options for *ceridwenclark@yahoo.co.uk*:

☑ Import contacts
☑ Import mail
☑ Import new mail for next 30 days

Start import Cancel

FIGURE 3.11 Import options.

Step 3: Finish

Your messages and contacts are being imported.

It may take several hours (sometimes up to 2 days) before you start to see imported messages.

You can close this window and continue using Gmail, or even log out and close your browser – we'll continue importing your mail and/or contacts in the background. To check the status of your import, look under Settings > Accounts and Import.

OK

FIGURE 3.12 Import confirmed.

Troubleshooting...

Browsers are increasingly blocking pop ups by default. In Chrome, you can click the circled icon (*figure* 3.15) to allow the import process to continue.

Pop-ups blocked:
- about:blank#blocked

◉ Always allow pop-ups and redirects from https:// mail.google.com
○ Continue blocking

Manage   Done

FIGURE 3.14 Click on the pop-up blocker at the top of your browser if Google Chrome cannot load the import pop-up.

Settings ⚙

General Labels Inbox │Accounts and Import│ Filters and blocked addresses

Forwarding and POP/IMAP Add-ons Chat Advanced Offline Themes Keyboard Shortcuts

Change account settings:
Change password
Change password recovery options
Other Google Account settings

Import mail and contacts:
Learn more
youraccount@yahoo
Importing – It may take several hours (sometimes up to 2 days) before you start to see imported messages. You can leave this page and the import will continue.
Import from another address
stop

FIGURE 3.13 The import progress can be seen in **Accounts and Import.**

31

FIGURE 3.15 Choose your
email from the list when
you visit mail.google.com.

these pages will load automatically.

On Microsoft Internet Explorer

If you are using Internet Explorer, these are the steps to
follow:

- Open two tabs, one showing Gmail and the other Google
  search, (this will of course work for any website that you
  want to open each time you open your browser)
- Click on the little gear wheel on the top right of your
  browser window
- Choose **Internet Options**
- Choose **Use current** in the Home page section
- Once you have done this click on **Apply** then **OK**

These two pages will be the first pages you see when you
load your browser. Selecting the little house icon on the
top right of your browser will also bring up these pages
from now on.

On Microsoft Edge

If you are using Microsoft Edge, these are the steps to
follow:

- On the top right select the menu button, (three dots)
- Choose **Settings** at the bottom of the list that drops down
- Under **Customize** and **Open Microsoft Edge with**, Select **A
  specific page or pages**.
- Type in the box that says **Enter a URL**: https://mail.google.
  com
- Click on the save icon (as seen circled in *figure 3.16*)
- Click on Add new page if you want to add more pages,
  then repeat from step 4
- Close Microsoft Edge and the settings will take effect

FIGURE 3.16 Adding Gmail to
your tabs whenever you open
Microsoft Edge.

The pages you added will be the first pages you see when

you load your browser.

On Google's Chrome

- Open two tabs, one showing Gmail and the other Google search, (this will of course work for any website that you want to open each time you open your browser)
- Click on the menu button on the top right of your window (three vertical dots)
- Choose **Settings**
- Scroll down to the **On start-up** section and click on **Restore tabs or open specific pages**
- Click on **Use current pages**

The pages will now be set. You can check it by closing and reopening the browser. Every time you open your browser, these two tabs will load, saving you time.

On Firefox

- Open two tabs, one showing Gmail and the other Google search, (this will of course work for any website that you want to open each time you open your browser)
- Click on the menu button on the top right of your window. This looks like three horizontal lines (*see figure 3.17*)
- Choose **Options** and then
- Choose **Current Pages** in the **Home Page** section

The pages will now be set. You can check it by closing and reopening the browser. Every time you open your browser, these two tabs will load, saving you time.

Logging out or Signing Out

If you are on a shared computer, it is a good idea to sign out of your account once you have finished with what you need to do.

To do this, go up to the top right of the screen and click on

FIGURE 3.17 The Menu button in Firefox.

your profile photo (or Initial if you haven't set one up yet). At the bottom right of the drop-down, select **Sign out**.

Reading emails

This is the reason you created the account, right? Well this couldn't be simpler. As with every other email service out there, you just click anywhere on the email. The emails are displayed with who sent it first, the subject (what the email is about) and then the date it arrived. Depending on your display density, any attachments will be indicated at the end of the row or underneath. *Figure* 3.18 shows the default density which shows the attachments underneath.

Images are sometimes blocked by Google. This is done to protect your computer but you can change this by changing the settings. If you would like to always see the images in your emails, got to the **gear wheel** (top right of your screen), **Settings**, then in the **General** tab scroll down to **Images** and choose **Always display external images**.

If you are happier to choose which images you want Google to display then go to the same place as above (**Gear wheel** > **Settings** > **Images**) and choose **Ask before displaying external images**. Whenever Google stops you seeing an image you will get a message underneath the sender's email address that the images have been hidden. Click on **Display images below** to see the email as it was meant to be viewed.

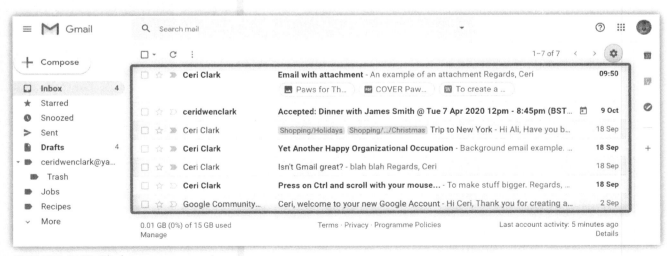

FIGURE 3.18 Click on any row in the box to read that email.

Once you have read the email, you can click on Inbox, the Gmail logo, or Archive or Delete the email to send you right back to the home screen.

Notice that once you have read an email, (*see figure 3.18*) it is no longer bold and will have been grayed out.

To delete the email, click on the small box to the left of the email and then click on the picture of a trash can/bin above it. If you hover your mouse over the pictures, a little message pops up telling you what the picture means. I will go into more detail about archiving, and deleting emails in *Chapter 5: Sending and Receiving Emails.*

Viewing attachments

With Gmail you can look at attachments from right inside your browser. This means that even if you don't have the software on your computer then you can still see most documents. You can view these documents as long as you have a) access to the Internet and b) access to a browser.

In the default view of your Gmail account you can see what attachments you have and download them straight from the message list in your Gmail homepage.

Figure 3.20 shows how Google displays what documents are attached to the email when you are in the email. To view the options available, you will need to hover your mouse over the pictures. As you can see, you can download and save them individually or all of the attachments at the same time. If the document is compatible with Google Docs like Microsoft Word then you will also be given the option to edit the file within Google Docs. This means that you can look at and edit Microsoft Word documents without having Microsoft

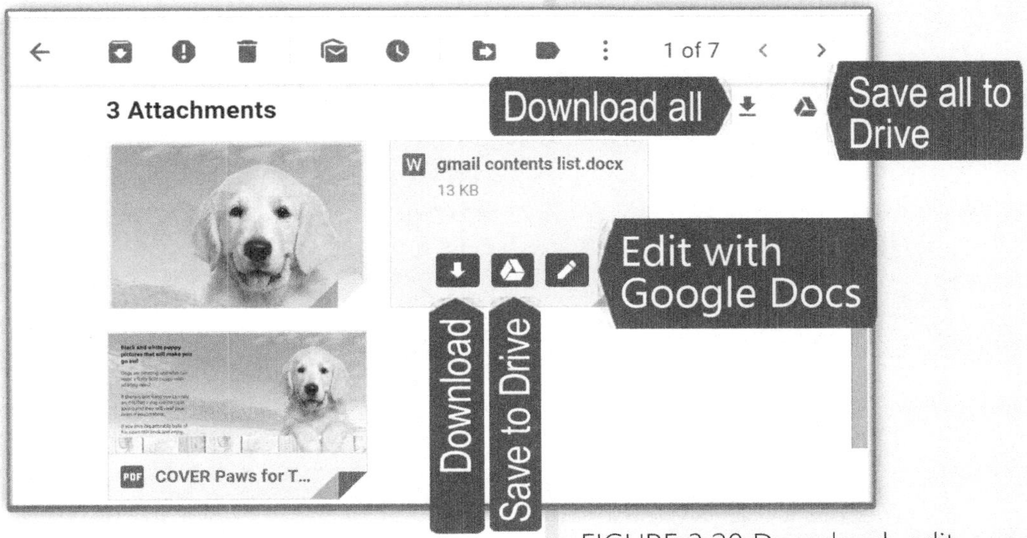

FIGURE 3.19 Trash/bin symbol for deleting emails.

FIGURE 3.20 Download, edit or save emailed documents.

35

Word on your computer.

You can also get a preview of images by clicking on the images and they will load in your browser. If Google does not support the attachment file type, for example, a .mobi file, you can download the file on to your computer and use software from there. In this particular case Kindle for PC or Calibre.

Gmail's category inboxes (tabs)

Google has a set of category inboxes which can be used to automatically categorize your emails as they come in. They will appear above your message list on the homepage and all you need to do is click on the tab to see the emails.

One thing to consider is that when you have the extra Google 'tabs' running, you will have adverts at the top of your messages in each tab. The adverts may take a couple of days to come through after you add the extra tabs to your Google homepage.

This could be a valid price to pay for the organizational benefits but if you absolutely hate ads and don't use an ad blocker then only having the Primary tab activated will mean fewer adverts for now. As ever this advice has the caveat that Google regularly changes their service and they may remove the advertising or put more in at their discretion.

You can activate or remove Gmail category inboxes (which appear as tabs above your message list) from two places:

Location 1. Gear Wheel > **Configure inbox**

Location 2. Gear Wheel > **Settings > Inbox (as long as Default is selected in the first option)**

You can only add or remove inboxes from the first location. If you want to configure them, you will need to go to the Inbox settings as explained in *Chapter 11: Gmail Settings* in the **Inbox** section.

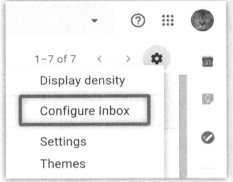

FIGURE 3.21 You can get to the Gmail category inbox settings from the Gear Wheel menu.

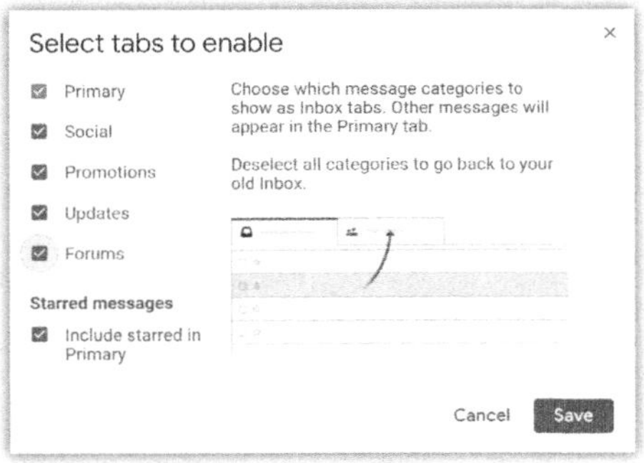

FIGURE 3.22 You can add or remove inboxes/tabs from the Configure Inbox pop up.

The primary tab

Your primary tab is the first tab you will see when you open your inbox. It should have all the emails that you or Google thinks are important to you. If Google cannot classify emails, then they will go into here.

The social tab

Google will put any emails from social networks in this tab to stop them cluttering up your primary inbox. These can be from Facebook and Twitter to Goodreads.

The promotions tab

The promotions tab is for all those emails offering you deals on your favorite stores that you signed up for in the past. If you don't want these but you remember signing up in the first place then you can usually unsubscribe by going to the bottom of the open email and locating and clicking on the word **unsubscribe**. A quick way to do this is to press Ctrl and F together (if you are using an Apple computer use Cmd instead of Ctrl) and type unsubscribe in the search box that appears. The page will jump to the word and will highlight it saving you time. If you didn't sign up for the emails then feel free to mark them as spam. There are instructions for how to do this in the next chapter (*Chapter 4: Security*).

The updates and forums tabs

The emails categorized as updates are usually confirmations, receipts, bills, and statements and emails put into the forums category are usually from mailing lists or forums.

03

Did you know...

Sometimes emails are put into the wrong category. You can easily tell Google the correct place to put these emails by the following two methods:

1. Drag the email from its current location and 'dump' it in the tab (located above the messages list) that you want with your mouse.

2. a) right-click on the offending email

b) then, click on **Move to tab** and choose the correct category. *See figure 3.23.*

In either method, Gmail will confirm that the move has taken place at the top of the web page. Gmail will also ask if you want this to happen to future messages as well. Click **Yes** if you do, **ignore** it if you don't.

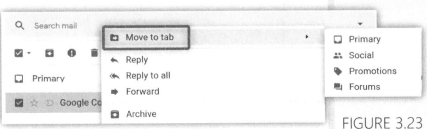

FIGURE 3.23 Move emails to a different tab.

Turn off Chat

If you are new to Google then there is plenty of time to find out more, but to reduce the risk of information overload I recommend you turn off **Chat**.

You can always reactivate it later, but for now there's so much to concentrate on.

First, go to the gear wheel at the top right of the screen, this is the main settings button, and then click on **Settings**.

The Settings page will load when it is clicked on allowing you to choose tabs which run along the top of the screen. Please take a look at *figure 3.24* for where these tabs are and where **Chat** is within these settings.

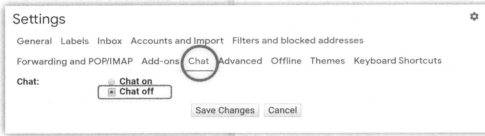

FIGURE 3.24 Where to find Chat in the settings & where to turn it off.

Please be aware that if you make your browser window bigger or smaller then **Chat** may end up appearing on the first or second line but it is fourth or fifth from the end. Keyboard shortcuts appears at the end of the list in the screenshot as it was enabled under **Advanced**. When you first create the account it does not appear until you enable it.

Go to the circled location labeled **Chat** (as seen in *figure 3.24*) to get all the settings relevant to Chat. Turn chat off by choosing **Chat off** and then clicking **Save Changes** at the bottom of the screen.

Reactivating Chat

If you would like to do this later, follow the steps for turning it off but choose **Chat on**.

Chapter summary

This chapter was all about giving you a head start on the basics. How to add your profile picture, importing your mail and contacts from your other email addresses, how to get to Gmail, reading your emails and turning off chat.

There is also a section on using Gmail's category inboxes which appear as tabs above your message lists. This section covered what they are and how to turn them on and off. A tip in the side bar explains how to quickly move an email which has gone into the wrong tab.

While some of these may not be essential, they will make your experience more enjoyable while you learn how to get the most out of what Gmail has to offer.

03

Security

• • • • • • • • • • • • • • • •

Securing your Google account is very important. The sum of all your emails, attachments, photos, contacts and other data can help someone to take advantage of you (and even your friends) or use your details for their own use. Identity theft is a growing problem on the Internet and you need to protect yourself as much as possible.

Passwords

I go into detail about this in *Chapter 2* in the section called *Choosing your password*. Please read this for ways of choosing your password.

Changing your password

To change your password at any time, go to the settings page (the gear icon on the top right of the screen), then click on **Accounts and Import**. The Change Password link is the first item in the page as seen below.

Two-factor authentication

Changing your password regularly is a good way of securing access to your account, but remembering hundreds of passwords, constantly changing, can be impossible. Google uses the one password for all their services to make this easier, and they've added another security feature to really help keep your stuff safe. Google's two-step verification (also known

What to expect in this chapter:

- Passwords
- How to set up 2-step verification
- Spam and phishing
- Downloading your information with Google Takeout
- Deleting your Account

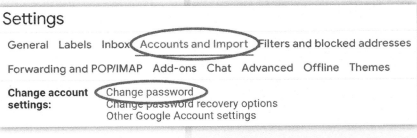

FIGURE 4.1 Where to go to change your password.

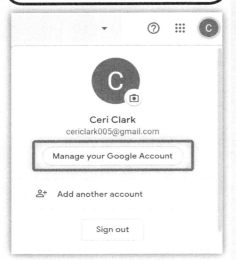

FIGURE 4.2 Your security options are located in **Manage your Google Account**.

as two-factor authentication) can be an elegant solution for access to their website and services.

2-step verification/authentication is an extra step to make sure that access to your information, files and folders is restricted to you. Instead of relying just on passwords (which can be discovered by nefarious means by hackers), a second device is used which you always have on you such as a phone or tablet computer. Any would-be infiltrator, bent on your destruction would need to have your password AND your phone to gain access to your account.

When you setup 2-factor authentication, you can set a computer to be trusted while logging in. This can save you a lot of time but if for any reason you want to reset your access on all your devices, you can go to your 2-step verification page and click on **REVOKE ALL** under **Devices you trust** (at the bottom of the page) for peace of mind.

How to setup 2-step verification on Google

1. Go to your profile picture and click on it followed by **Manage your Google Account**
2. On the next screen, click on **Security** (in the navigation column). See *figure* 4.3
3. In the section labeled **Signing in to Google**, click on **2-Step Verification**.
4. There will be a brief explanation of the benefits of 2-Step Verification and at the bottom of the page click on **GET STARTED**, Google will go through the following steps with you
5. First verify it is you by typing in your password and then click **NEXT**
6. Type in your mobile phone number. You can choose to get this by text message or phone call. Click on **NEXT**
7. Type in the code that Google sends you. If you didn't receive it you can ask for it to be sent again. Click **NEXT**
8. If you are happy with turning this feature on, then

Choosing how to use your second device

There are two options for using your second device. The first is my personal favorite. If you choose this, every time you log in to your account from a new browser or you have been timed out, a message will appear on your

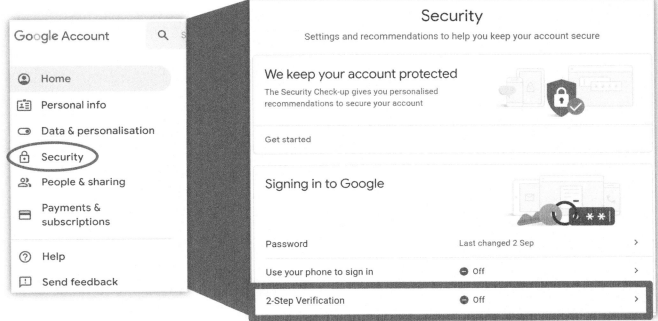

FIGURE 4.3 Choose **Security** then **2-Step Verification**.

mobile phone asking you to click **YES** or **NO**. Obviously if it is you trying to log in then you will press on yes. This is easier than typing in a code. Choose this for an easy life.

Google Prompt

Every time you login to Google from an unknown computer or after a period of time, you will be asked for a verification code that Google will send to your mobile phone. This can be very time-consuming and sometimes, if I'm honest, a little annoying. Google has taken this on board and offered the phone prompt option. Before you do this, make sure you have a screen lock on your mobile phone or

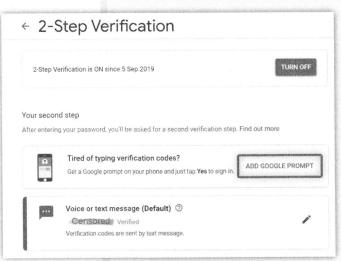

FIGURE 4.4 Choose **Google Prompt** for an easy life.

FIGURE 4.5 Google Prompt in action

anyone will be able to just tap the prompt when you are not looking.

You can do this with an Android phone or an iPhone. The next step is to add your phone. First, choose the type of phone you have. This, at the time of writing, works on Google's Android mobile phones and Apple's iPhone (5S or later). If you don't already have your Google account on your Android phone or the Google app on your iPhone, you will have to set these up before you start. If you have already added your account to your mobile phone, skip the next steps and go straight to Step 9 (after the instructions for adding Google accounts to your phone).

Adding your Google account to Android

- Open the **Settings** section on your mobile phone
- Press on **Accounts (may be called Users and accounts)**
- **Add Account**
- Choose **Google**
- Type in your pin
- Sign in to your Google account

Google will give you a message asking you to prove it is you. Choose to send yourself a code to your phone number.

- Choose **get verification code at ********
- Still on your phone in the **Use this phone to sign in,** choose **Use this phone and my old phone(s)** (you can change this later).
- Agree to the terms and services by pressing on **I agree**

Back at the computer, choose add **Google Prompt**, and it should show your phone. If it doesn't follow the on screen instructions. Once Google has accepted your second device for Google Prompt, *figure* 4.5 shows the screen that you will see when signing in.

Sign-in to Google on your Android mobile phone with phone prompts

Before you start the instructions below, make sure that your new Google account is set up on your mobile phone. If this is not done please look at the section immediately before this one called **Adding your Google account to Android.**

If you have been using Gmail for a while like me, then you might want to switch to phone prompts instead of typing in a code every now and again. It is so much quicker.

- Go to your profile picture and click on it followed by **Manage your Google Account**

- On the next screen, click on **Security** (in the navigation column). See *figure* 4.3

- In the section labeled **Signing in to Google**, click on **2-Step Verification**.

- There will be a brief explanation of the benefits of 2-Step Verification and at the bottom of the page click on **GET STARTED**, Google will go through the following steps with you

- You will be prompted to click **yes** on your device. Don't worry if it suggests a device you don't usually use every day. When I trialled it for this book, it suggested my old tablet but the message appeared on my phone

- You will be asked if you want to use Google Prompt for your device from now on. Click **TURN IT ON**

If you want to turn off phone prompts at any time, you can do this in **Manage your Google Account** > **Security** > **2-Step Verification**.

If the process doesn't work first time, it is worth having another go as the benefits outweigh the inconvenience. There are a few makes of the Android smartphone on sale and it is difficult to provide concise instructions for each one. However if you follow the on-screen instructions and redo them if they don't work first time, the differences are accounted for as they are minor and your **Google Prompt** will be set up. The secret appears to be to add your Google account to your phone *before* you set up the Prompt.

Adding your Google account to your iPhone

a. Visit the App Store
b. Find and install the Google app
c. Open the app and sign in to your Google account

Once your Google account is accessible on your phone, Google should be able to find it. Follow the on-screen instructions from the Gmail website: To get to these:

- Go to your profile picture and click on it followed by **Manage your Google Account**
- On the next screen, click on **Security** (in the navigation column). See *figure* 4.3
- In the section labeled **Signing in to Google**, click on **2-Step Verification**.
- There will be a brief explanation of the benefits of 2-Step Verification and at the bottom of the page click on **GET STARTED**, Google will go through the following steps with you
- You will be prompted to click **yes** on your device. Don't worry if it suggests a device you don't usually use every day. When I trialled it for this book, it suggested my old tablet but the message appeared on my phone
- You will be asked if you want to use Google Prompt for your device from now on. Click **TURN IT ON**

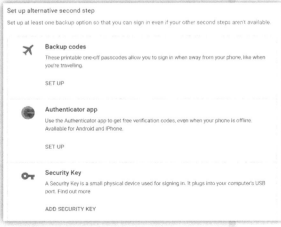

As can be seen in *figure* 4.5, pressing on **YES** or **NO** is a lot easier than having to wait for a code, then type it in to the browser on your computer.

Backup options

Life happens and there may be a time you can't get into your account. You may lose your phone or it might be stolen. You might even forget your password. If you don't choose one of Google's backup or alternative second step options you could

FIGURE 4.6 Backup options.

lose access to your Google account. This wouldn't be just your email but all your documents, spreadsheets, photos. It could be disastrous. Luckily there is a way to solve this but only if you activate the backup options in advance before something goes wrong. You should use at least one of these options.

Backup codes

The most important of these methods is the backup codes. These are one-time codes that you can use to get into your account. Print them out and put them somewhere safe. You may never need them but it's almost guaranteed that if you don't have them you will need them at some point. If you don't do this at setup (you will see this as part of the process) find the codes at:

FIGURE 4.7 Back up codes.

- In any Google Service, click on your account picture on the top right of the screen
- Click on **Manage your Google Account**
- Choose **Security**
- Select **2-step verification**
- Choose **SET UP**.
- Download the codes and save them to your computer or print them out to store or carry with you

When Google asks for a code you can use any of these that you generated once. Cross them out once you've used them so you know they are inactive. You can get new codes by clicking on **GET NEW CODES** at the bottom of the screen above **CLOSE**, **DOWNLOAD** and **PRINT**.

If you lose your backup codes...

If you lose your backup codes you will have to stop them working and get new ones. This is a real security threat. You will need to create new backup codes to invalidate the old ones.

- In any Google Service, click on your account picture on the top right of the screen
- Click on **Manage your Google Account**
- Click on **Security**

47

- Click on **2-Step Verification**
- Prove who you are by tapping in your password
- Type in the code that Google sends you
- In Backup codes and click on **SHOW CODES**
- Click on **GET NEW CODES** at the bottom of the screen above **CLOSE**, **DOWNLOAD** and **PRINT**

By getting new codes, the old codes will stop working automatically. They become invalidated.

Using your Backup Codes

- Have your backup codes ready
- Log into Gmail or any another Google service
- Type in your username and password
- When asked for your verification code, click **More options**
- Choose **Enter one of your 8-digit backup codes**
- Type in your backup code.

The Authenticator App

The Authenticator app is an application that sits on your phone and works even if your phone is offline. It generates a one-time 6 digit code that will 'unlock' your account. You need to be quick though as these codes only last 30 seconds before they expire (text codes usually last for 5 minutes). It is essentially the same as i f you had the code sent by text message (but does not last as long). can be used for other sites as well. I will try to keep this book to within the Google ecosystem as much as I can and although I personally use an app called Authy, these instructions are for Google Authenticator.

- In any Google Service, click on your account picture on the top right of the screen
- Click on **Manage your Google Account**
- Click on **Security**
- Click on **2-Step Verification**
- Look for **Authenticator App** and click on **SET UP**

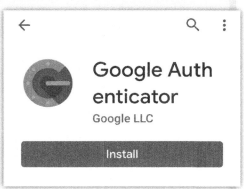

FIGURE 4.8 The Authenticator app on Android.

48

- Let Google know whether you are using an Android device or an iPhone. Once you have selected your phone, a QR code will appear on your computer screen
- Get the Authenticator App from the Play Store for Android or the App Store for Apple on your phone. Look for the logo at the beginning of this section (see *figure* 4.8)
- **In the App,** select **Set up account**
- Choose **Scan a barcode**
- Allow the app to take photos and videos
- Press on **Begin**
- You may need to click on **Scan a barcode** again or the camera will start immediately
- Hold your phone camera up to the screen until you see the QR code (black and white patterned square) using the camera on your phone
- Click **NEXT**
- Type into the website the code that appears on your phone
- Click on **VERIFY**
- Click **DONE**

04

FIGURE 4.9 Activating the Authenticator app

When you want to login to Google, open your app on the phone and type in the code when Google asks for one. While this is great for offline use, the Google Prompt option is faster and easier. You could consider this method as a secure backup of the backup.

Adding a backup phone

This option allows you have codes sent to a different phone. This can a backup phone you own or a friend or family number. If you use someone else's phone make sure that you can trust them and you are happy for them to get into your Google account anytime they wish.

This can be an option if you would like to give your partner access to your account in the event something unfortunate happens, or if you share an account. You can delegate access to your Gmail account so delegation may be a more suitable choice if you just want to give them access to see and answer emails.

FIGURE 4.10 Adding a backup phone.

- In any Google Service, click on your account picture on the top right of the screen
- Click on **Manage your Google Account**
- Click on **Security**
- Click on **2-Step Verification**
- Under voice or text message, you will see your phone number. Underneath this click on **ADD PHONE** (see *figure* 4.4)
- Type in the number of the phone you want to add as a back up to your account. You can choose a text message or a phone call (*figure* 4.10)
- Click **SEND**
- Wait for the phone call or text message to arrive on your chosen phone and then type the code in to the space provided on the next screen, click on **Next**

You now have another backup option set up. If you ever get locked out of your account, codes can now be sent to the alternative phone number.

Security Key

Security keys can be the most secure but be the least convenient. Chrome, Opera, Edge, Safari, and Firefox now all support U2F and FIDO2. If you decide to use a security key, you will have to buy one that works with FIDO Universal 2nd Factor (U2F). You will always need to carry this key with you. The trade off is that it can provide better scam protection as they are encrypted and they won't work on bogus websites. Security keys work similarly to Google Authenticator in that they produce a random code that works to give you access to your Google Account but instead of in your mobile phone, it is a separate device.

If you decide that the better scam protection outweighs the disadvantages then please find the steps below to using one. t.

- Search for *"FIDO2 U2F Security Key"*, "Webauthn" or *"Web authentication dongle"* in your favorite online store to buy one. Make sure that the device states FIDO2 and not just FIDO or it may not work
- In any Google Service, click on your account picture on the top right of the screen
- Click on **Manage your Google Account**
- Click on **Security**
- Click on **2-Step Verification**
- Prove who you are by tapping in your password
- In the **Set up alternative second step** section look for **Security Key** and click on **ADD SECURITY KEY**
- Follow the on-screen instructions

If your key does not have a button on it, then you will need to take the Key out of your USB port and back in again every time you use it.

Turning 2-Step Verification off

Google's 2-step verification is an important step in protecting your account but you may for some reason need to turn it off temporarily. If you feel you want to do this, here are the steps to achieve this.

- In any Google Service, click on your account picture on the top right of the screen
- Click on **Manage your Google Account**
- Click on **Security**
- Click on **2-Step Verification**
- Prove who you are by tapping in your password
- Type in the code that Google sends you
- At the top of the page, click on the button that says, **TURN IT OFF**

Did you know...

FIDO is now also known as *web authentication*.

Browsers with support for FIDO2 are:

- Chrome

- Firefox (latest version)

- Microsoft Edge (from Windows 10 version 1903)

- Opera browser

As of 2019, FIDO2 was renamed WebAuthn but because some Android devices can not be updated to use this standard, Gmail will use FIDO for the foreseeable future.

As ever, this policy may change at Google's discretion.

Spam, Scams and Phishing

Spam, scams and phishing emails can be a security risk. They change all the time as the spammers/phishers get more sophisticated as time goes on. There are however, some things that make these messages stand out. This section includes just some of the things you can look out for and how to deal with them in Gmail.

Recognizing spam, scams and phishing emails

Recognizing the type of emails that are spam, and/or contain scams and phishing attacks is the first step to dealing with them. Here are the top ways to recognize them.

It's too good to be true

If you receive an email from a Nigerian prince/princess letting you know that they are in trouble but they will give you several million but only if you give them your bank details - this can be a good indication.

Another famous email scam is a foreign lottery/ competition letting you know that you have won millions! This would be great, but if you have never bought a ticket, how likely is this actually to be true?

There are variations on these themes but they usually involve offering a large amount of money in unlikely circumstances.

Your friend is on vacation and asks you for money

This is a scam where your friend's email account has been hacked and an email then sent to you stating that s/he is in trouble on vacation and could you send them a couple of thousand to help him/her out? If you get any emails like this, check that they have actually gone on holiday first!

If you get any of these emails, tell your friend that his/her account might have been hacked. The hacker may have deleted all sent emails so it may not be obvious to them that they have a problem. They will need to change their password straight away and maybe enable 2-step verification on their account.

A stranger sob story

A stranger is dying/ill/in trouble. Please send money quickly. I would ignore these emails. How did they even get your address? The sender is probably just sending these emails to random addresses to see if they can get anyone to reply.

An email sent to you by yourself

In the past I have sent emails to myself to remind me to do things. If there is one person I trust it is me! If I am very distracted it is not beyond the bounds of possibility that I could click on one of these emails by mistake. There is a scam where people have faked the email address so it looks like you have sent an email to yourself. Think before clicking on any links!

Bad grammar and spelling

A tell-tale sign of a malicious email is bad grammar and poor spelling. If you get an email with these features, handle with care.

Bank emails

Your bank will never ask you for personal information by email. They will also never give you a link to click on to log in. If you receive emails that ask for this, use a direct link you already have or your bank's mobile app. The web addresses are usually on letters and statements from your bank.

Some of these emails will say your account has been hacked, some money has gone missing or something along these lines. They will encourage you to click on a link in their email which will take you to a special website which will look like your bank's website but will be owned by the scammers. These emails are known as phishing emails. They will ask you to put in your username and password which they will then record. You will be redirected to your actual bank and you will probably not know what has happened until your real bank contacts you by phone or letter.

The way to avoid this is to never click on any link in an email that appears to be from your bank, but to go and have a look at your bank's website (or app) directly.

Reporting spam

Spam is the bane of all email users everywhere. Unwanted emails about medical aids, Nigerian princes needing help to take money from you or fake bank emails bring misery to billions. Spam is unsolicited bulk email, it may or may not be malicious. It can just be annoying. A form of spam is Malspam where you are sent a link to malware in your email. Once clicked the link will download malware on to your computer. This can result in your computer being taken over by the spammer. They can then ransom your computer (ask you for money to give you back control of your computer), or turn your computer into a 'bot' where they can send emails or even mine cryptocurrency in the background and make money from your computer while slowing it down. Fortunately Google has one of the best spam filters on the web.

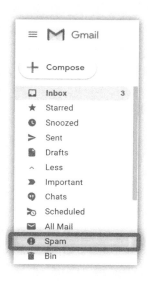

FIGURE 4.11 Location of Spam in left navigation section.

To find emails which may have been erroneously labeled spam, click on **Spam** on the left of the screen in the navigation bar (see *figure* 4.11). Re-label any emails you want to keep using the instructions in *Chapter 7 Email Organization with Labels*.

One of the reasons that Google is so good with spam is that there is a community effort to reduce it.

FIGURE 4.12 Report spam to Google by clicking on this button.

To mark an email as spam, click on the exclamation mark in the octagon symbol (as seen in *figure 4.12*).

54

It is always above your emails so you can let Google know the current email you are reading is spam.

Report phishing

There is another type of email which is sent with the sole intent to cause either harm or take money from you. If you receive an email which you think is trying to trick you into going to a fake bank website that has 'slipped through the net', click on **Report phishing** in the menu that appears when you click on the arrow at the top right of each opened email (*figure 4.13* shows the location).

The unsubscribe link

Most of the time you will receive emails that you have signed up for in the past. You may not want them anymore but they are not spam as you originally asked for them. To stop receiving these, click on the **unsubscribe link** which is usually at the bottom of emails that have them.

Occasionally you will receive offers, promotions and other emails that you don't remember signing up for. If this happens to you, don't use the unsubscribe link. This is because these *are* spam messages used to try and get your details. Sometimes it is just to see if your email address is genuine. A good give-away for this is if your name is in the CC of the email (for example John Smith) but you can also see John A Smith, John B Smith, Jonnie Smith etc. in there. They are trying every combination they can think of to get a hit. Other times it is to get other information such as a username or password. If you have different passwords for every website this is not a problem but a lot of people keep the same password for a lot of sites. Once they get hold of that password, they have access to those websites which could be banks or stores.

Google Takeout

Google Takeout is a way of seeing all the information Google has on you over all Google Services. You can use this to have a look at what they have on you but also

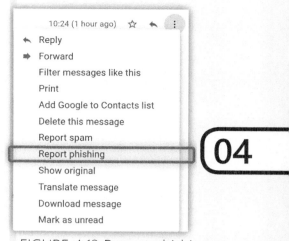

FIGURE 4.13 Report phishing to Google by clicking on this button.

FIGURE 4.14 Google Services covered by Takeout including their logos.

use it as a backup where you can save your information somewhere else. If you ever get locked out you could then upload that information to a new Google account and have everything you had before at your fingertips.

To get to Google Takeout visit:

https://takeout.google.com

The following is a list of Google Products where you can find out what information Google holds on you taken from Google Takeout. It would be worth taking a look at the list just to see the depth and breadth of information they hold on you.

Products

- **Android Device Configuration Service** Android device attributes, performance data, software versions and account identifiers.
- **Arts & Culture** Favorites and galleries that you've created on Google
- **Bookmarks** Your bookmarks stored at www.google.com/ bookmarks
- **Calendar** Your calendar data in iCalendar format.
- **Chrome** Bookmarks, history and other settings from Chrome
- **Contacts** Contacts and contact photos that you added yourself, as well as contacts saved from your interactions in Google products such as Gmail.
- **Crisis User Reports** Information provided to help others during crises
- **Data Shared for Research** Responses saved with your Google Account from your participation in Google research studies and projects.
- **Drive** Files that you own that have been stored in your My Drive and Computers.
- **Fit** Your Google Fit activity data.
- **G Suite Marketplace** Metadata that describes an application published in G Suite Marketplace.
- **Google Help Communities** Your ask and reply contributions to the Google Help Communities including

56

text and images posted.

- **Google Input Tools** Synchronized learned words.
- **Google My Business** All data related to your business.
- **Google Pay** Your saved passes, activity using virtual account numbers and transaction history from Google services such as Play and YouTube and peer-to-peer payments in the Google Pay app.
- **Google Photos** Your photos and videos from Google Photos and from other Google services, such as Google+, Blogger and Hangouts.
- **Google Play Books** The titles and authors of your purchased and uploaded books in Google Play Books, plus notes and bookmarks.
- **Google Play Games Services** Data, including achievements and scores, from games that you play
- **Google Play Movies & TV** Your Google Play Movies & TV preferences, services, watch-list and ratings.
- **Google Play Store** Data about your app installs, ratings and orders
- **Google Shopping** Google Shopping order history, loyalty and addresses.
- **Groups** All posts and memberships of Google Groups that you own
- **Hands-free** Payments transaction data that was processed through Hands-Free.
- **Hangouts** Your conversation history and attachments from Hangouts.
- **Hangouts on Air** Questions that you asked or owned in the Hangouts on Air Q&A app.
- **Home App** Device, room and home information from the Home App.
- **Keep** All notes and media attachments stored in Google Keep.
- **Location History** Your location data collected while opted-in to Location History.
- **Mail** All of the messages and attachments in your Gmail account in MBOX format.
- **Maps** Your preferences and personal places in Maps.
- **Maps (your places)** Records of your starred places and place reviews.
- **My Activity** Records of your activity data, along with

image and audio attachments.

- **News** Data about the magazines, categories and sources in which you are interested.

- **Posts on Google** Your Posts on Google history data including the collections of account, posts, cameos, metrics data and all uploaded images and videos on Posts on Google and Cameos.

- **Profile** Settings and images from your Google profile.

- **Purchases & Reservations** Your transactions, including deliveries, online orders, upcoming and past reservations gathered from Google services like your Assistant and Gmail.

- **Saved** Collections of saved links (images, places, web pages, etc.) from Google Search and Maps.

- **Search contributions** Your ratings, reviews, comments and other contributions to Google Search.

- **Street View** Images and videos that you have uploaded to Google Street View.

- **Tasks** Your open and completed tasks.

- **Textcube** Your images and other files from Textcube.com.

- **YouTube** Watch and search history, videos, comments and other content that you've created on YouTube.

- **YouTube Gaming** Sponsorship badges and emoji that you've uploaded to YouTube Gaming.

Check the box next to each option that you want to download and click on **Next Step**.

The next step will allow you to download the information on to your computer or save it to the cloud (on the Internet in Google or a different service).

Where to store your Download

You can choose for Google to send you a link by email or it can go into Drive, Dropbox, OneDrive or Box. If you choose a non-Google service make sure you have the login details handy.

Export Type

Next choose your export type. This can be as a one time download or a scheduled export every 2 months for a year, (6 archives). If you choose the latter option you will have to come back in a year and redo the options.

File type

The choice here is between a Zip file or a tgz file. Zip files are the most well known and can be opened on almost any computer. The tgz file type is similar to a Zip file but has no file limit. This means if you have a lot of data to download then a tgz file could be more appropriate. The Zip file can still be used but you would have to download several while downloading one file with everything in it can be more convenient.

Archive size

Zips can hold up to 2GB. Google allows you to choose file sizes of 2GB, 4GB, 10GB or 50GB. Archives larger than these sizes will be split into multiple files. If you choose a Zip file you will have multiple files anyway but if you choose tgz be aware that the bigger the file size, the slower the download time. To unpack a tgz file you will also need to get extra software such as 7Zip.

Once you have made your selections, click on **Create archive**. The archive may take a few minutes to a few days to be ready depending on how big it is.

Deleting your account

At some point, you may wish to delete your Google account, including your email. There may be a variety of reasons why you may want to do this, including deleting your old Gmail account to creating a new one if the wrong person (or persons) has got hold of your address.

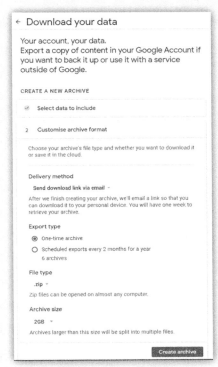

FIGURE 4.15 The next step in downloading your data.

FIGURE 4.16 Choose **Delete a service or your account** under **Download, delete or make a plan for your data**.

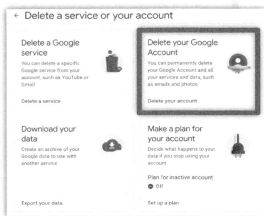

FIGURE 4.17 Click on **Delete your account**.

FIGURE 4.18 To recover your account straight after deletion, click on **Account Support.**

There are a few steps to do this. One of these is to download all the information that Google has on you so you don't lose your photos, contacts and emails using Google Takeout (earlier in this chapter). It might be useful to do this to see how Google is tracking you. Once you know how they are doing this then you can make decisions on whether and how you want to restrict you data on your new account. This could include turning off location services on your phone.

The decision to prioritize privacy over convenience is a personal one and can only be taken by you. It doesn't have to be black and white but it does depend on your personal circumstances and what you need and want.

Deleting your account

- In any Google Service, click on your account picture on the top right of the screen
  - Click on **Manage your Google Account**
- Click on **Data & personalization** (on the left)
- **Select Delete a service or your account**
- **On the next screen look for Delete your Google Account** and then click on **Delete your account**
- Confirm it is you by logging in again.
- You will be warned that you will be deleting everything and Google will remind you what you have on the account. This is your last chance to change your mind. Check the boxes next to **Yes, I acknowledge that I am still responsible for any charges incurred due to any pending financial transaction, and I understand that under certain circumstances my earnings won't be paid out,** and **Yes, I want to permanently delete this Google Account and all its data.**
- Click on **DELETE ACCOUNT** or **CANCEL** if you have changed your mind.

The account is now deleted but you now have one last, *last* chance to get it back for a limited time.

To recover your account immediately after you have deleted it, click on **Account support**, and then follow the on-screen instructions until you see the Success message.

FIGURE 4.19 Type in your email address, password, and your second factor authentication to recover your account.

Chapter summary

It is important to look after your Google account which includes Gmail. Changing your password and enabling 2-step verification are important steps to protecting your account. There are a few options for 2-step verification from the convenient Google Prompt to the super secure Security Key (as long as you don't lose it!).

Recognizing some of the most prevalent scams can also help secure not only your Google account but also any other website you visit online. When you register on websites, emails acknowledging your registration and even password resets all go to your Gmail account. If an unauthorized person gets into your account, they can see what you signed up to and can reset passwords which could allow them to buy things using credit cards stored on retailer sites. Keeping them out with a good strong password, 2-step verification and avoiding scams can stop this happening.

The last sections of this chapter covered Google Takeout and deleting your account. Google Takeout is a great way to keep control of your account. You can see what information Google holds on you which will inform how finely you want to tune your privacy settings or even which Google Services you decide to use. Having the information is the first step to having more control of your account as well as providing a handy backup should a something untoward happen.

Sending and Receiving Emails

●●●●●●●●●●●●●●●●●

Emails are dealt with a little differently in Gmail compared to some other email services. As long as the subject is the same, everything in one conversation is held in one place. No more searching through your Sent folder to find what you said! This section talks about how to send email but also how the discussion threads work.

Discussions

Discussion threads are conversations. Please see *figure 5.1* below for an example. If I have sent the email from this Gmail account then it will appear as '**me**'. Once read, it will go gray as illustrated below.

Notice next to Ceri, the number lets me know how many emails are in the discussion. If anyone sends me an email later, it will revert to white (until I click on it) and the three will become a four. Next to the subject Google has also put some of the first line of the email visible, so I can decide if I want to read it or not.

The date will show you the date (or time if it was sent 'today') that an email was sent to you. If you respond to an email, then the date doesn't change but when you get a reply back it will do.

Click anywhere on the row and it will take you to the conversation.

Once you click on an

What to expect in this chapter:

- What are discussion threads
- How to reply and forward an email
- Composing and formatting emails
- Spell checking
- Confidential Mode
- Deleting emails
- Traditions of communicating over the internet
- What to do with trolls

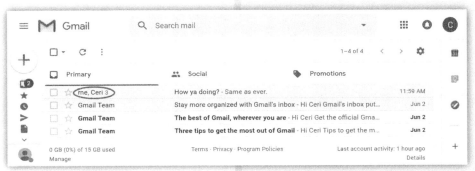

FIGURE 5.1 Example of a discussion thread.

email the thread will look like *figure 5.2*.

If you are not sure which email is the latest, look at the date at the top right of each email, which also tells you how long ago the email was sent. In this discussion thread example the first one arrived on 11:57 AM (46 minutes ago) and the next one was sent at 11:59 AM (44 minutes ago).

If you want to see more of the thread in one long message rather than clicking on each message, you can click on the three horizontal dots under the message you are viewing. You can see its location in *figure 5.2*. This has limited usage as the person who sent you the latest message may have deleted the thread in the email before they sent it to you. Don't rely on this as a complete record of your conversation. Your recipient is able to delete parts of the thread before they email it to you but they cannot delete emails in your email account. So if you are looking for something then it is best to search through your actual email rather than rely on a possibly trimmed discussion thread.

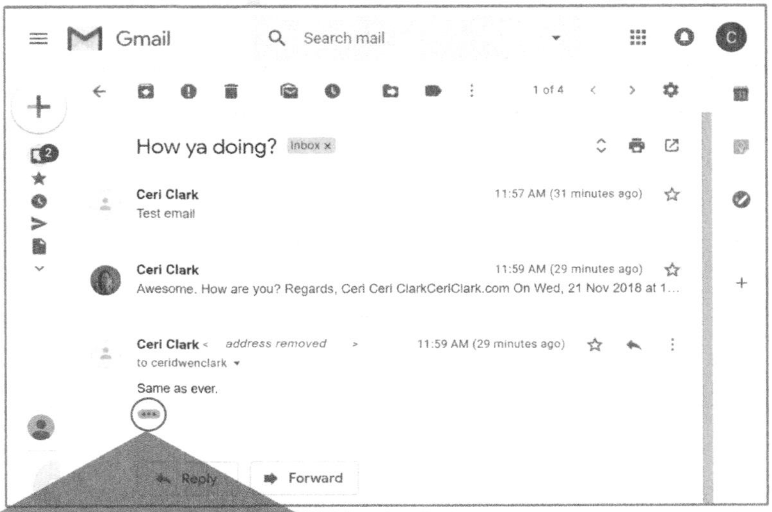

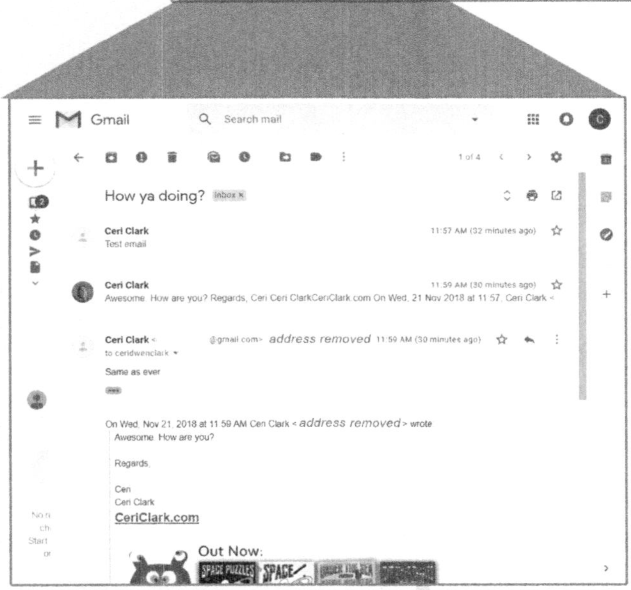

FIGURE 5.2
How to expand
a discussion
thread within
an email.

Replying and forwarding an email

Replying to an email is as simple as clicking on **Reply**! Google has made this extra-easy by giving us two places to use this. At the top of the email on the right hand corner there is a gray box with an arrow in it. As seen in *figure 5.3*, clicking on this will bring up a drop-down list. The top option will be

Reply and of course, there is always the **Reply** at the foot of each email beside **Forward**.

The reply box is illustrated in *figure 5.4*. Type in the white space and then click **Send**. Your email will automatically get saved by Google. If the Internet cuts out or you forget to complete it, you will be able to find it again in **Drafts**, at the left of the screen.

The three dots at the bottom of the white box are previous emails. If you send an email without clicking on the three dots, the old conversation will still be sent to the email recipient. The only time it won't be included is if you click on the three dots and delete the conversations that appear. Remember that the other person will still have access to the actual emails you sent earlier. The only reason to send it is to make life easier for the person who will be reading your email. They can click on the three dots and quickly glance down to reacquaint themselves of the conversation without having to click in and out of older messages.

The box where you reply looks very simple but it is deceptive and once you delve into the buttons, there are a lot of options.

When you reply to an email the convention is to write your message above the email you are replying to. This means that your correspondent does not have to go looking for your answer. If you are replying to a friend then this does not matter as they will love you enough to go looking for your reply, but if you are using your email for business you do not want to annoy your customers/contacts before they have even read your message.

Google has made this easy by automatically putting your reply first. If you click on the three little arrows under your message but above the button marked **Send**, then you can see that the rest of the email thread will appear below your message.

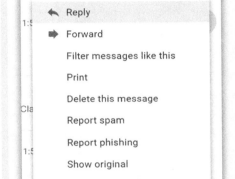

FIGURE 5.3 **Email options from Reply button.**

FIGURE 5.4 **The Reply box.**

FIGURE 5.5 **Where to find Forward**.

If you clicked on **Reply** but you actually wanted **Forward**, you can rectify this easily by clicking on the little downwards pointing arrow by the bigger arrow (pointing left) next to the profile picture as seen circled in *figure 5.5*. You can also edit the subject here but bear in mind that when you change the subject, your message will not only appear as a new thread to your recipient but also in your sent emails (which might be confusing if you are looking for it later).

Did you know...

You can have your friend's profile pictures next to their emails if you add them to your contacts.

If you click on **Pop out reply** (last in the options shown in figure 5.5), you will be able to type in your message above your other emails in a pop up. This will mean you can flip and refer to other emails whilst working on your message.

Once you have clicked on **Send**, you will get a message at the bottom left of your screen to tell you it has been sent.

Forwarding uses the same method as replying but you will have to put in the email address of the person you want it to go to.

The options for formatting an email will appear in the *Composing an email* section below.

Replying to a group

If an email has been sent to more than one person in the

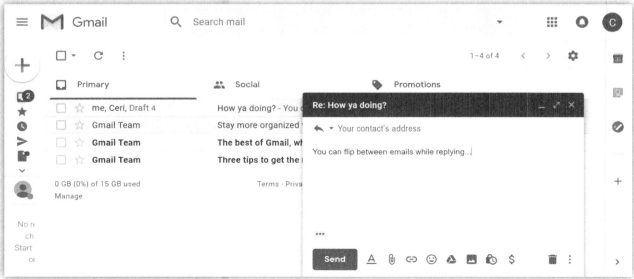

FIGURE 5.6 Using **pop out reply** means you can flip between emails.

To or **CC** part of an email, then you will have the option to **Reply to all**. Don't do this unless you really want everyone to see your message. The only way to stop the email going to everyone is if you just click on **Reply** and manually add people's email address or when you click on **Reply to all**, you have to delete the people you don't want to see your message manually from the email. You can do this by pressing on the **X** to the right of each person's name (please see *figure 5.7*).

Composing an email

Composing an email is a simple process. In the first column of the page, (if the **Compose** button is not visible) click on the plus on the top left of the screen. See *figure 5.8* for what it looks like. If you hover over the plus button you will see the column expand to show the full compose button but you don't need to do this to start an email. Simply clicking on the plus will open the pop-up.

The compose page will load as a pop up on top of your other messages, ready for you to fill in (please see *figure 5.9*).

Clicking on the **To** will bring up your address book but I am assuming you don't have one yet. If you know the email address, just type it into the white box. If you do have your contacts set up, you can start typing your contact's name and Gmail will give you suggestions as you type. Click on the one that you are looking for. This saves you time and means you don't need to memorize their email address, you just need to know their name.

Type in a descriptive subject and what you want to say in the large box. When you are ready, click **Send**. If you have more than one email address setup in Gmail (for example if you own a website domain), you can choose which email address to send from.

Formatting your email

You might think your email is a little boring without formatting. As in a lot of word processors you can change

Did you know...

If you want to reply or forward a particular message rather than the whole thread, open the message from the thread and click the Reply button on that particular message. You can choose not to include the quoted text.

FIGURE 5.7 Click the x to remove email addresses

FIGURE 5.8 Where to find Compose.

FIGURE 5.9 Compose box.

FIGURE 5.10 Formatting options.

the way an email looks and feels by highlighting what you want changed and clicking the **B** for Bold button, **I** for italics etc. Click on the **A** with a red arrow underneath to see these formatting options.

The formatting options are very like those in any standard word processor. If you are familiar with one of these then you will know how to use them. *Figure 5.11* shows what the buttons look like:

- **Undo** - Undo your last action
- **Redo** - Redo the last action
- **Sans Serif** – clicking on this will allow you to change font (Sans Serif is the name of a font as well as a type of font)
- **Two Ts** – Clicking on this button will make your text bigger or smaller
- **B** – Bold your text
- **I** – Italicize your text
- **U underlined** – Underline your text
- **A underlined** – Change the color of your text
- **Six horizontal lines** – How do you want your paragraphs aligned/justified? Click on the arrow in the button to get the options

- **Horizontal lines with numbers** – Bullet your text with numbers
- **Horizontal lines with dots** – Bullet your text with circles (like this list)
- **Horizontal lines with**

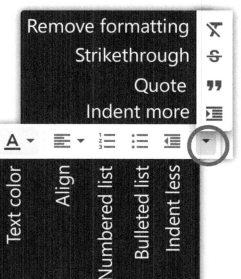

FIGURE 5.11 A closer look at the formatting options.

an arrow pointing left – Indent your text to the left

- **Horizontal lines with arrow pointing right** – Indent your text to the right
- **Quotation mark** – Quote the text
- **Underlined T with cross** – Remove formatting

Other Email Options

FIGURE 5.12 More options under the compose box.

Attach files to your emails

The paperclip icon will allow you to attach files to your emails. You can find it next to the underlined **A**. As seen in *figure* 5.12.

Adding a link to your email

You may find you want to link to an item at your favorite store for a present or to an article you think your friend might find particularly interesting.

To add a link to the main body of text, first highlight some text that you would like your email recipient to click on. Next, click on the little picture that looks like a chain (*figure 5.13*) in the row beginning with the **Send** button (as seen in *figure 5.12*).

Fill in the **Text to display** (this will already be filled in with the text you highlighted but you can change this here) and **To what URL should this link go?** box and click on **OK**.

When you click on the link button, you can also choose to add a link to an email address, in which case Google will ask for the email address when the button is clicked.

Insert Emoji

Spice up your emails with emoji and other graphics. Browse what's available by scrolling through the list or pressing the gray buttons above the emoji as seen in

FIGURE 5.13 <u>A</u> button for more formatting options, paperclip to attach files and link icon toadd lins to your email..

FIGURE 5.14 Link icon.

Did you know...

If you use the left sidebar a lot, click on the menu bar (three horizontal lines at the top left of your screen) to keep it there. If you want it collapsible, just click on the menu button again.

69

FIGURE 5.15 Choose to add a link to a website or an email address when adding the link.

FIGURE 5.16 Choose an emoji.

FIGURE 5.17 'Attach' a file using Google Drive.

figure 5.16. Alternatively you can search for a specific emoji or even a mood. Type in 'sad' after clicking on the magnifying glass and you will be shown a selection of pictures which represent sadness.

Insert files using Drive

To save space in your emails, you can insert an attachment file from your Google Drive account. There is a current limit of 25MB for sending attachments through Gmail. Anything larger than this then Gmail will give you a firm no and kindly suggest that you send your contact a link to your file in Google Drive.

What does this mean? In effect this is really helpful. You have far more control of files in your Drive account than you do once you send them off to the big blue yonder as an attachment. You can restrict your files so that someone can only view it. They won't be able to copy it or delete it by accident and best of all, if you change the file before they have received it but after you have sent the link, they will get the latest version - and they will *always* have the latest version!

Alternatively, you may want to work together on a document. Instead of sending countless attachments to each other you just send the one and you can see immediately when they are editing it.

To attach a document from Drive, whether it is a worksheet, document, picture or anything else, press the button as seen in *figure* 5.17. Browse for your file and then click on **Insert**. Before you click on Insert you can choose to add as a link or an actual attachment. Remember though, if it is more than 25MB you will have to do the link.

Insert Photo

Send your photos to friends and family by clicking the insert photo button as seen in *figure* 5.18. Once clicked

70

you have the choice of adding your photo in four ways; photos, albums, upload or web address (URL).

Photos and albums have photos you have previously uploaded from other Google services. Choosing upload means you can browse your computer for the picture you want to send, and the web address means you can send a link to a picture from the Internet.

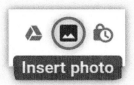

FIGURE 5.18 Insert a photo.

Turn Confidential Mode on or off

Confidential mode is one way of protecting your messages but please don't rely on this if it is very important or potentially embarrassing. There are drawbacks. At first glance, confidential mode protects your email from being forwarded, copied, printed, or downloaded, including any attachment. This seems to be too good to be true. You can set an expiration date so that it will disappear from your contact's email on a certain date, revoke access or insist that an SMS text needs to be sent to your recipient before they can access the email.

However, your recipient can still take screenshots or photos of what you have sent them. There is also software that will allow people to download the attachments. Therefore, still be mindful that whatever you send by email can still be forwarded in some form.

Saying this, it is still a nifty trick and the odds of your friends doing this to you are pretty slim. After all they are your friends, right?

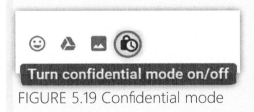

FIGURE 5.19 Confidential mode

Click on the confidential mode button as seen in *figure* 5.19 to see the options shown in *figure* 5.20.

Your contact won't be able to forward, copy, print or download your email as standard but you can set an expiry time of 1 day, 1 week, 1 month, 3 months or 5 years. The final option is to require a SMS passcode. If your contact doesn't have Gmail they will get the code by email. Once you are happy with your selections, click on **Save**.

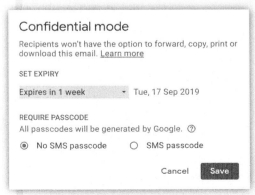

FIGURE 5.20 Confidential mode options.

A message will appear at the bottom of your compose box letting you know that you have set the confidential mode and for what period. It also reminds you that recipients won't have the option to forward, copy, print or download the email. You can click on **Edit** at the far right of this message to change what you have chosen. Click on **Send**.

Your contact will receive the email with the restrictions you have set. Once they open it they will see the same message you did at the bottom of the email.

Revoking access

If the unthinkable happens and you accidentally send an email you *really* did not want to send, you can fix this with confidential mode. Adding the confidential mode while composing your message means you can stop your friend from reading it. If you ever write an email out of anger it might be an idea to enable confidential mode on all of these types of emails!

- Go to your Sent Messages (**Sent** in the left navigation column)
- Locate the specific message that you want to stop your contact from viewing
- Click on **Remove Access**

Your contact will not be able to access the email again. However, your contact will still see that you sent them an email and they will see what the subject line was so you still may have to answer some searching questions if you weren't careful with your subject.

You can let them see the email again by repeating the revoke access instructions but click on **Renew access** instead. The email will appear to them as if you had never revoked it in the first place.

FIGURE 5.21 Email which has had its access revoked.

Even More Options

At the end of the row where the **Send** button is located in your compose box, click on the three vertical dots to get even more options.

72

Default to full-screen

If you choose **Default to full screen**, whenever you start a new message it will take up the whole screen rather than the right corner or popped out for better browsing.

Label

If you choose a label as you are writing your initial email or even replies, it will make it easier to find your messages later. Please take a look at *Chapter 7 Email Organization with Labels* for more information on Labels.

Plain text mode

Choosing plain text mode will remove the formatting buttons from your compose window but you can easily get them back by clicking on the A. To use this write your email as you would normally, then Press on **Plain text mode**. All your formatting will disappear.

Why would you need this?

If you would like your message to be formatted consistently everywhere you send it to then a plain text message will do this. Sometimes a system will not except anything other than a plain text message.

Another way I have used this was when I copied and pasted from a document or a webpage and the formatting just looked weird. Formatting inside Gmail couldn't override the previous formatting, so I had to either copy and paste it into Notepad and then paste it into Gmail or use **Plain text mode**.

To use this, write your message how you want it to look, click on **Plain text mode** and then format the text the way you want it so that your whole message looks consistent.

Print

Select Print to load the message in a new tab and print it

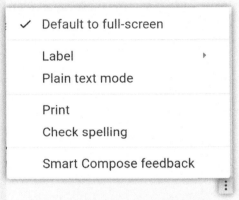

FIGURE 5.22 Even more options.

using your printer.

Check spelling

Spell Check is an amazing tool which Google provides for free. To take advantage of this feature click on the little arrow located in the bottom right corner or the pop up box (as seen highlighted in *figure 5.23*).

Once clicked, the spelling mistakes will be highlighted as also shown in *figure 5.23.*

To see Google's suggestions and correct the spelling mistakes, click on the highlighted text. Once a misspelled word is clicked, a list of options appears. Select which one you think is right and click on it. The word will be replaced and the highlighting will disappear. You can click on **Recheck** by clicking on the little arrow at the bottom right of the compose box. If the highlighting does not disappear after clicking on the correct spelling, **Recheck** will rectify this.

Don't rely completely on spell check. Notice that it didn't pick up on 'yer' instead of 'you'? There is no substitute for giving your messages a quick read before you send them. Reading them out loud can be especially useful for picking up mistakes.

Another problem you might have noticed is that Google's spell check doesn't like my name. You can fix this by adding names you send to regularly (or even your own) to a custom dictionary. This can only be done in the Chrome browser.

FIGURE 5.23 Google will highlight mistakes in yellow.

Right-click on your name (or the word you want to add) and choose **Add to dictionary**, Another way to do this is to go to:

chrome://settings/editDictionary

74

...from your Chrome browser and to add (or delete) names or words there. Theoretically this should work but I have to admit, even though Ceri is in my custom dictionary, Google still does not like it. However, I have found that if you right-click on the highlighted word that Google spell checks for you and click **Ignore**, it does work. If the **Add to dictionary** doesn't work, try **Ignore** instead.

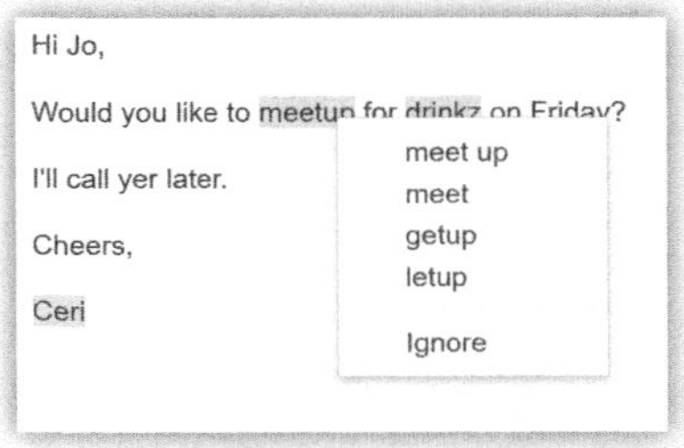

Troubleshooting

If the **Add to dictionary** is not showing up when you right click, try disabling extensions in your Chrome Browser. If this doesn't work then untoggle **Developer mode** that is located at the top right of the extensions window in Chrome.

Smart Compose feedback

The last item in the menu as shown in *figure* 5.22 is Smart Compose feedback. Gmail now offers suggestions for how you might finish a sentence in your email. They are currently asking for feedback on how this works for you. Click on this button for the feedback form.

Deleting emails

Look for the trash can/bin symbol to delete emails. You can select more than one email at a time from the Gmail homepage by checking the boxes next to each email you want to get rid of and choosing the trash symbol at the top of the window.

Deleting draft emails

To delete messages before they are sent, click on the little trash symbol at the bottom right of the window.

To get to your draft emails from the homepage, look for Drafts down the left navigation column. Select it and then select the email or emails you want to remove by checking the box(es) next to it. Click on **Discard drafts** above the email list and they are gone forever. They do not appear in

FIGURE 5.24 Select one of Google's suggestions to replace it.

05

Did you know...

If you receive unwanted email that you never asked for you can report it as spam or phishing to remove it from your Inbox.

For detailed instructions on how to recognise and deal with scams, spam and phishing attacks, take a look at the **Security** chapter near the beginning of this book.

your trash/bin unlike other emails.

Deleting emails sent to you

To delete emails that are sent to you, first go to the message list on the Gmail homepage by clicking on the Gmail logo, then click on the little box to the left of each email that you want to delete. This adds a tick to the box, and then click on the trash can icon which will appear above your emails list.

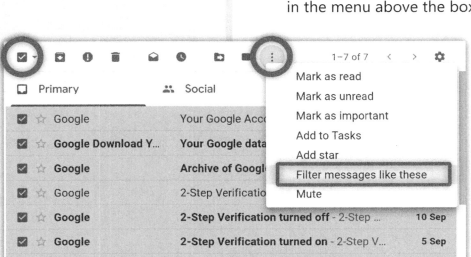

FIGURE 5.25 Discard draft button in the compose window.

Bulk Delete emails

If you would like to delete all emails sent from one address, you can do this by using the '**filter messages like these**' option.

1. First click on the box next to an email or emails which was sent from the address(es) you want to remove
2. Locate the menu button (three vertical dots) at the top of the window and click on it
3. Select **Filter messages like these**
4. Click the **X** at the top of the filter pane
5. Manually check the boxes next to the emails and click on the trash can/bin symbol or check the box in the menu above the boxes next to the emails and press the trash can/bin symbol

This is the quickest way to delete a ton of email.

The way I have shown you is a blunt instrument that will get rid of emails from certain people or organizations but you can fine-tune the **Filter messages like these** to only search for messages with a certain subject or to only have attachments

FIGURE 5.26 Bulk delete process.

or even to have only attachments of a certain size. This method can be as simple or as complicated as you need it to be.

Adding a signature to your emails

A signature can add a personal touch to your emails. It can be used to market your services if you have a business or even just finish off an email if you use the same ending all the time.

You will need to add a signature before you compose your email. This needs to be done in the settings.

First go to the **Gear Wheel** > **Settings** > **General**

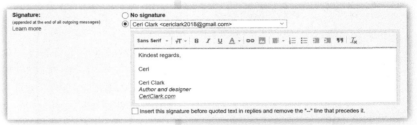

FIGURE 5.27 Adding a signature.

Go down the list until you see **Signature**. If you just want a basic signature, you can start typing and formatting what it looks like using the formatting bar directly above the text box.

Check the box before **Insert this signature before quoted text in replies and remove the "--" line that precedes it** to always have your signature in emails you send out.

If you would like to add a photo to your signature, here are the steps you can follow:

- Click into the text box where you would like the photo to appear
- Click on the **Insert image** button (see figure 5.28)

FIGURE 5.28 Add image button.

From here, there are three ways to add your images. The first is you search through Google Drive, the second you can upload an image from your computer and the third option is to use a picture from the Internet. If you do use an image from the Internet please make sure you have the rights to do that. Any public domain image is fine but most images on the Internet are copyrighted.

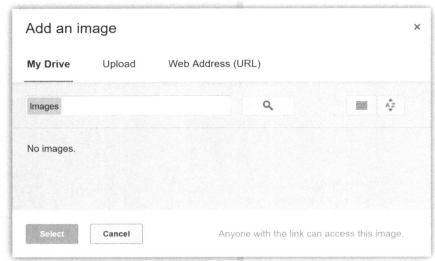

FIGURE 5.29 Options for adding images.

FIGURE 5.30 Change the size of the picture with a click of a button.

If you choose **Drive**, you can search your images within the search box or browse folders and files that you have in your account. Remember to **Save changes** at the bottom of the settings page when you are happy with your signature.

If you do not have anything suitable in your Google account, then you can search your computer by selecting **Upload** at the top of the pop up as can be seen in *figure 5.29*.

Click on **Select a file** from your computer and search for the picture you want to add. Click on **Open**. Your picture will appear in the signature box. If your picture is too big, click on it and choose one of the options that appear.

You can choose four sizes, small, medium and large, original size or remove the image altogether. Choose **Save changes** at the bottom of the page when you are happy with your signature.

If you want to find an image from the Internet, right click on the picture and copy the address. Paste into the box that loads when you click on **Web Address (URL)** when you are choosing how you want to add a picture (*figure 5.29*). Remember to click **Save changes** or the signature won't save.

If you have more than one email linked to your Gmail account then you can have a signature for each email address. Click on the email address that is shown in the email signature section to see the list of addresses drop down so you can select the one you want.

Netiquette

If this is your first email account you may not be familiar with some of the traditions of Netiquette. Here are the top rules of email etiquette.

1. Never type your emails ALL IN CAPS LOCK! IT WILL SEEM TO THE READER THAT YOU ARE SHOUTING AT THEM

2. If you use abbreviations or acronyms, write them out in full during first use. After that you don't need to explain it in the same email

3. Don't remove previous messages from your email thread when replying. The person you are emailing may have deleted your previous emails altogether and if you reply with no history they may have no idea what you are talking about

4. When replying, start your message at the top of the thread. This is so your friends, colleagues and other contacts don't have to scroll down an exceedingly long list just to find out what you have to say

5. If you have a long reply, try to put a summary of the most important items at the beginning of your email. Most people scan-read emails when they are busy and if you want them to do something make sure it is obvious at the beginning of the email

6. Use a meaningful subject. Should I bother to read this email? If it just says "Howdy", the recipient might think it is spam. And in the same vein, try not to send emails with a blank subject

7. Don't forward chain-emails, unless it is a really funny one and you know your friend will appreciate it

8. Read the email before you send it. What sounds perfectly reasonable when you are writing can seem really insulting after ten minutes – and that's when you are not trying to be insulting!

9. Be careful when replying to mailing lists. Remember that email can go to hundreds if not thousands of people

10. Don't make personal remarks about people in jest. The reader can't see the glint in your eye as you are being ironic

11. Don't post your email address on websites unless you want to be sent a lot of spam

12. Be respectful, imagine you are talking to someone you know. Sending an email can seem anonymous, but people's feelings can still be hurt

13. If you don't know the person you are contacting, make

an extra effort to make your emails as clear and concise as possible

14. Keep your fonts and language simple. Make sure you do not use yellow, gray or light colors when emailing people. They are difficult to see, why make life hard for people? You may think it looks cool, but if your contact has to highlight, copy it, then paste it into word, change the color and make it bigger to read it, let's just say your email might go unread

15. If someone comments on one of your posts on social networks and it appears malicious, they are most probably a troll. They are posting to get a response. In this situation, ignore them. Nothing annoys a troll more than if they think someone hasn't noticed a comment designed to infuriate

Chapter summary

Although the compose box looks simple, there are many options that are hidden inside other menus. This chapter covered how to send, receive, format, and delete emails. If you are looking to add links, make your text bold or be in italics or even if you just want to spell check what you have written, you will find that in this chapter.

Confidential mode is explained and how to use it as well as how this could be circumvented by recipients.

A section on your signature explains how to add, format and add pictures to them.

The last section of this chapter dealt with netiquette. Thinking about the person who will be reading your email can go a long way to getting it read. Saving them time reading it will mean that they are more likely to do so and your hit rate for getting things done will explode.

Your Contacts (Address Book)

● ● ● ● ● ● ● ● ● ● ● ● ● ● ● ●

Keeping all your contacts online is a great idea. As well as saving on paper, it also means that you can update your contacts wherever you are, whether at home or on a mobile device when traveling. It is all about convenience. Not only does Contacts keep your friends, acquaintances, business and co-worker details in one place it also integrates with your Android phone so that you can call your friend with a touch of a button.

How to get to Google Contacts

There are two ways to get to Google Contacts.

Google Contacts from the waffle/app launcher

Click on the waffle (the square consisting of squares located on the top right of any Google service you are logged into (including Gmail). Choose **Contacts** from the list that drops down. If you use Contacts a lot, long press on the contacts symbol (see *figure* 6.1) and drag it higher in the list to where you want it to go.

Google Contacts direct address

You can also go directly to your contacts by typing in the following address into the address bar at the top of your browser window. You can bookmark this link as a quick

What to expect in this chapter:

- How to get to Google Contacts
- An overview of the homepage
- How to add and edit contacts
- Deleting contacts
- Restoring contacts
- Organizing your contacts using labels and starring
- Importing and exporting your contacts
- Printing your contacts
- Google Contacts settings

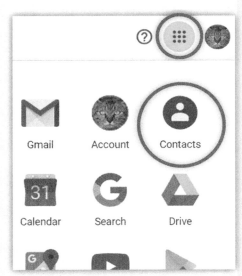

FIGURE 6.1 Where to find Contacts in Gmail.

way of getting there but the waffle does the same thing.

https://contacts.google.com/

Contacts overview

Google contacts is effectively another Google service but which is integrated to Gmail. As such it works similarly to Gmail but looks a little different. This section aims to give you a quick overview of the Contacts homepage.

Top navigation bar

The top navigation bar has a menu button (three vertical lines) on the left which will collapse or expand the side navigation.

The second item is the search bar which enables you to search within your contacts.

The question mark will give you the option to **Send feedback** or go to Google's own **help pages.**

The cog wheel is the new location of settings and this allows you to undo changes or go

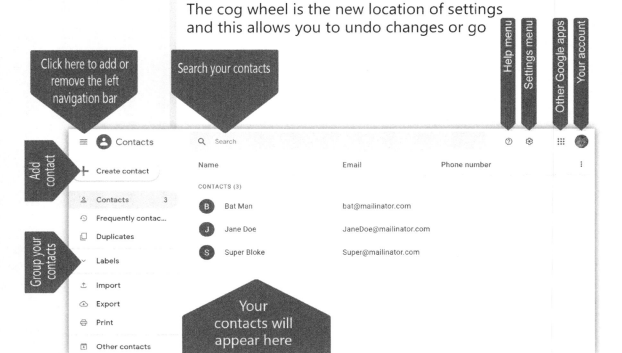

FIGURE 6.2 Google Contacts overview.

to even more settings which are currently; change your language which will apply across all Google services, your country code and whether you want to sort by first or last name.

You can go to any other Google service, including Gmail, Calendar etc. from the square consisting of 9 smaller squares (otherwise known as a waffle or app launcher).

The final item in the top navigation bar is your profile picture. This allows you to get to your Google Account settings which includes privacy, security and account preferences.

Left navigation pane

You will mostly be using the left navigation pane to get around Contacts.

- **Contacts**: Clicking on this will bring up all your contacts
- **Frequently contacted**: This will show you the people you email the most
- **Duplicates**: Google will put any duplicates it finds on this page. You can then choose to merge them if you wish
- **Labels**: This is how you group your contacts into categories and where you can see the labels you have already created
- **Create Labels** Click on **Create label** to add groups such as work, family, friends etc.
- **Import** Import Contacts from other sources
- **Export** Export your contacts for backup or use with other sources.
- **Print** Print a contacts list
- **Other Contacts** These are contacts you have interacted with on other Google Services but you haven't specifically added yourself. You can change how they are saved in the Google Account settings.

Contacts pane

All your contacts will appear here in a list determined by what you choose in **Settings** in the left navigation

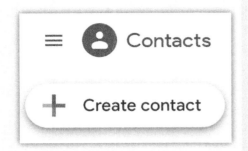

FIGURE 6.3 Create Contact location.

pane. They will appear in alphabetical order. Any starred contacts will appear at the top of the list.

Create contact

You can find **Create Contact** at the top left of the Contacts homepage. Selecting this will bring up the **Create Contact** form.

If for any reason you cannot see this menu, click on the **Menu button** (three horizontal lines) to expand it.

How to add contacts

First click on **Create a Contact** (see *figure* 6.3).

Once the form has loaded (see *figure 6.4)* start filling in the fields (boxes).

Adding a contact using an email address or phone number

If you know the email address or phone number of your contact and they have a public profile with Google, you can automatically add a profile picture and some personal information just by clicking into the email field and adding the email address then **Save**. Once Google has loaded their details you can go back into the contact form to fill in the rest of the details.

Figure 6.5 shows my details filled into a contact just by adding my personal email address. At the time of writing, although I made quite a lot of information public, (my work history for example), only my profile photo was imported. This can be useful in of itself so you know you are writing to the right person. Previously, profile information was obtained through a Google+ profile. Google discontinued this service for consumer users. You may still have it as an organization but for the rest of us it doesn't exist in a meaningful way. Google is still disentangling all the services that previously went through Google+. This means that some elements in Google may not work while they sort this out. This is one of them. When this is fixed the Google profile section will be more substantial, (depending on if your contact has a) filled out the information and b) allowed it to be accessible publicly).

You can find you own profile by going to:

https://aboutme.google.com/

You can choose what is hidden and what people can see about you when they add you to their contacts or email you through Gmail. You can hide everything or only certain elements. It is not possible to only allow contacts to view certain public information. If someone has your email or phone number they will be able to see what you have made public.

Please also bear in mind, because you do not have control over this information, it could be out of date depending on how often your contacts update their profiles.

If you do not already have your contact's details open, click on their name (which may simply be an email address or phone number at this point) on the Contacts homepage.

On the top right of the pane, click on the pencil edit symbol. This is shown circled in *figure* 6.6. These symbols also appear when you hover over your contact's names as well.

You will still need to fill in the details that your

Click **More Fields** to get the complete set of options

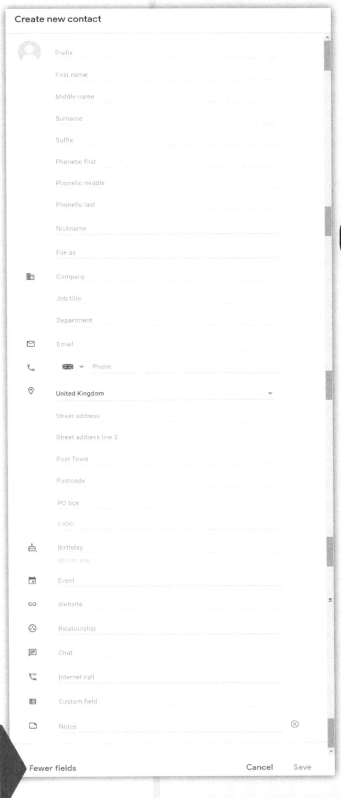

FIGURE 6.4 Click on More fields to get all the options.

FIGURE 6.5 My contact details filled in when you put in my personal email address. My email has been edited out in this graphic!

FIGURE 6.6 Edit contact.

contact has not made public like name, address, email and phone number etc. Most people will keep these details private. The imported information is not editable and you cannot remove it. It is at the bottom of the details though under the heading Google profile so you can avoid it by not scrolling that far in the record!

You won't see all the places to add information until you click on **More fields.** The result can be seen in *figure 6.4*).

Simply type in the boxes (or into the next one) to put in the details. Remember to click **Save** once you have finished.

Filling in the fields

There are a small number of options when you first create a contact. For example, you will not be able to add an address until you click on **More fields**.

- First name
- Surname
- Company
- Job Title
- Email
- Phone
- Notes

When you click on More fields on the bottom left, these extra options appear:

- Prefix
- Middle name
- Suffix
- Phonetic first
- Phonetic middle
- Phonetic last
- Nickname
- File as
- Department
- Address

86

- Label
- Birthday
- Event
- Website
- Relationship
- Chat
- Internet Call
- Custom field
- Notes

The explanations below cover the options in the order in the complete form as they appear when you click More fields.

Name, Phonetic First, Phonetic Last, Nickname, File As, and Company,

These are mostly self-explanatory. The phonetic first and last name options are for names you are unfamiliar with. For example my name is Ceri but you could type it in the **Phonetic first** field as Kerry. This would remind you how my name is pronounced should we ever meet. Android also uses the phonetic name to aid in voice recognition.

The nickname is just the non-formal name you call your contact. In the name you could have Elizabeth Taylor. In the Nickname you could have Lizzie, In the search box, you could search for any of these three things and her information would load.

The full contact name takes priority when you are emailing or when you are looking for someone on your phone. However, typing names in the **Nickname** and **File as** boxes means you can search for these variants and find them easier. This solves the problem of knowing someone by their nickname but having their full details in your Contacts. Put as much information as you can in here and you will be able to find them again.

File as is another way to label your contacts. Like Nickname, it does not appear in your email or the auto-complete when you start typing in a name in the **To** field when composing an email. What it does do is change

FIGURE 6.7 Company icon in Google Contacts.

87

FIGURE 6.8 Email icon in Google Contacts.

FIGURE 6.9 Phone icon in Google Contacts.

FIGURE 6.10 Address icon in Google Contacts.

how your contacts are listed in Google Contacts itself. For example, if your mother's name is Joan Rivers but you put in *Mother* in the **File as** box then in Google Contacts, she will appear as *Mother*. You have three chances to find your contact while searching, their name, Nickname and File As. Type in any of these into the search box and Google will find your contact.

Email, Phone and Address

The Email, Phone and Address fields can all be customized. Type in your friend's email address, and click **DONE** or continue to fill in the fields. (If you know the email address of your contact and they have a public Google profile, all their public details will be filled in by default). If you click on **DONE** straight after you have typed in the email address, you will see a profile photo is added and other information from your contact's Google profile. It will be populated with all the information they have made public in their Google profile. Once this is done, you can go back and fill in the information that is missing.

You can choose to assign the home, work or other label to the email address. This is for informational use and not for organizing. It does not show up under Labels on the navigation panel. This is useful when your contact has a number of email addresses and you want to instantly see which email address applies to what area of their life. If your friend is on holiday, there is no point emailing their work address for example. They may have a work email address, a home address, a club address and so on.

To add an email address, fill in the details then either press the + at the end of the row or click away from the field you are typing in. This could be white space or the email logo beside it.

You can keep on adding email addresses by clicking on the plus that appears at the end of the email address row. Please see *figure 6.11* for where this is located. You can also delete email addresses by clicking on the **x** next to the plus.

FIGURE 6.11 Add or delete email addresses in the contact's details.

88

Phone numbers and addresses are similar. Follow the same steps as above to customize these fields. You could also use the phone labels to call someone. For example, tell your phone "call Jane home" and it will call Jane on her home phone number.

Birthday and Event

Under **Birthday** there is the option of putting your contact's birthday in. Type in the format 05/14/1960 in the United States or 14/05/1960 in the United Kingdom. Make sure that your language settings are correct for your region or Google will interpret the date incorrectly. You can just type anything in here however and it will work. 3rd May 2010 will work but if you type in 03/05/2010 Google will interpret it as March or May depending on where Google thinks you are.

Google gives you the option of adding events. This can be labeled anniversary or any other special date by typing in a date and choosing a label they suggest or typing your own in the label box that appears after you have typed in the date. As with the other details you can delete them or add more events by clicking on the **x** and **plus** icons.

Website

If your contact has a website, put the address next to **Website**. You can add as many websites as you like using the plus icon. Press the **x** if you want to delete them. Google suggests you label the websites Profile, Blog, Homepage or Work but you can just type anything into the field and it will work. If this contact relates to work, this could be your contact's company website.

Relationship

The relationship section of your contact's details used to be important if you wanted to use voice to call them on your Android phone. Calling someone using your nickname used to require filling out the relationship status but testing for this edition showed this is now

FIGURE 6.12 Birthday icon in Google Contacts.

06

FIGURE 6.13 Events icon in Google Contacts.

FIGURE 6.14 Website icon in Google Contacts.

FIGURE 6.15 Relationship icon in Google Contacts.

unnecessary. All I had to say was "OK Google" to the phone and then "Text nickname", or "Call nickname".

However, in case this changes, (Google still has a version of these instructions on their website) I have included the instructions next. Otherwise the relationship field is useful for remembering how you know someone whether they are a friend, family or acquaintance. Typing in here, 'acquaintance 2019 Roswell alien abduction conference' will remind you when and where you met them.

Older instructions:

If you put any relationship in, you can then ask Google to call or text them using your Nickname without touching your phone. It does not matter what you put in the relationship. I typed in 'better half' just to see if it worked and it did. The important information is the nickname but you can literally put anything in the relationship space as long as there is something there.

1. Next to **Relationship** type in your relationship to your contact
2. Make sure the **Nickname** is what you want to tell your phone. Think about how it might sound if you are in public talking to Google
3. Say "OK Google" to your phone
4. Say "Text nickname", or "Call nickname"

Google will ask you to confirm the contact and will then do as you ask.

Chat

Type in your contact's chat ID next to Chat. Google suggests that you can label them Google Talk, AIM, Yahoo, Skype, QQ, MSN, ICQ and Jabber. Use the **+** and **x** to add and delete Chat IDs.

Internet call

Type in your Internet call information in here and label it Home, Work or Other.

FIGURE 6.16 Chat icon in Google Contacts.

FIGURE 6.17 Internet call icon in Google Contacts.

Custom

Like the **Notes** information, you can put anything you like in here. The only difference is that you can label the information to make it easier to find and understand.

Notes

Last but not least there is a big box with **Add a note** to the right. This is invaluable for work or acquaintances. Add as much or as little information as you want here. This could be particularly useful if you can't remember when or where you met someone.

Adding photos to Contacts

If you are syncing your Google Contacts with your phone, then it is always nice to have your friend's picture on your contacts. Even if you are just browsing, seeing a picture can help find your friend quicker than just browsing names down a list.

By clicking on **Set contact photo**, a pop up will appear asking you to browse your computer for a suitable picture. Remember to click **Save** when you are done.

FIGURE 6.18 Custom fields icon in Google Contacts.

FIGURE 6.19 Notes icon in Google Contacts.

06

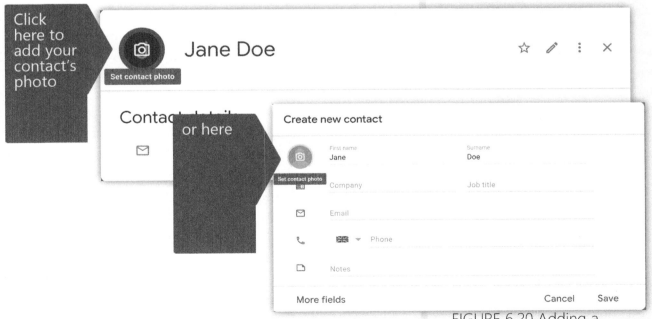

Click here to add your contact's photo

or here

FIGURE 6.20 Adding a contact's photo.

FIGURE 6.21 Upload photos or access your photos in your Google account.

FIGURE 6.22 On an existing contact, click the pen/pencil icon to edit your contact.

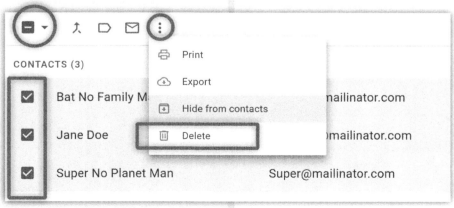

FIGURE 6.23 Deleting multiple contacts.

Browse your computer or click on the photos that Google finds in your account across its services. You will be given the opportunity to edit your picture before you click done. Use the round arrows at the top to rotate the image or left-click on the image and drag down or up to resize it. When you are happy click on **DONE**. The picture will be turned into a circle.

If you want to change the picture later, click on the existing image and choose another or click on **Remove photo**.

Editing Contacts

To change the details on your contacts, click on your contacts name and choose the pencil/pen icon as seen in *figure 6.22*.

Deleting Contacts

There are two easy methods for deleting contacts. Method 1 is best for deleting one contact and the second method is great for deleting multiple contacts at the same time.

Method 1: Deleting one contact

- Click on the contact you want to delete
- Click on the three vertical dots
- Select **delete**
- Confirm you want to remove the contact(s) by clicking on **DELETE** again

Method 2: Deleting multiple contacts

- Click on the profile photo or big letter in a circle next to the name of the contact(s) you want to delete. To select all, click on the

92

arrow next to the check box above **CONTACTS** (*number of contacts selected*) and choose **All**

- Click on the three vertical dots as circled in *figure 6.23*
- Click on the trash can (bin) icon or the word **Delete**
- Confirm you want to remove the contact(s) by clicking on **DELETE** again

You can hide contacts by following the same steps but choosing **hide from contacts** instead of **delete** at the end.

Restoring contacts (Undo changes)

If you have accidentally removed your contacts and you want them back there is a way to get them back by restoring them to a previous time.

- Click on the Cog Wheel denoting the **Settings menu** on the top right of the window
- Click on **Undo changes**
- Choose how far back in time you want to reset your Google Contacts to
- Click on **CONFIRM**

If you chose *Yesterday*, your contacts list and details will revert back to how they were the day before and so on for week etc.

Starring your contacts

You can star your contacts to make them easier to find. When you star a contact it will go to the top of the list. Select your contact and then click on the star icon. It appears next to the pencil symbol as seen in *figure 6.6*.

Grouping your contacts using Labels

With labels you can organize all your contacts into groups. Why should you add labels? If you have hundreds of contacts in a long list, it can be time consuming to find the name you need. Of course you can search for them,

Settings menu

FIGURE 6.24 Settings icon in Contacts

06

Undo changes

Revert your contacts list to any state in the past 30 days. Learn more

Undo changes from

- ○ 10 min ago
- ● 1 hr ago
- ○ Yesterday
- ○ 1 week ago
- ○ Custom

Cancel   Confirm

FIGURE 6.25 Restoring your contacts.

Did you know...

You can have your contacts in more than one label. For example your best friend may work for a certain company and so you might want your friend in your Friends label but also in the Anycompany PLC label.

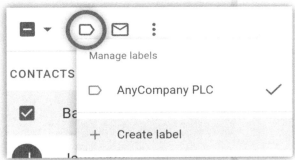

FIGURE 6.26 Manage labels button.

but what if you can't remember how to spell their name or even what their name is?

You may for example have a label for Anycompany PLC. You know you want to talk to the director's PA but can't remember her name. With two thousand contacts (you are very popular), it would be impossible to find him/her just from browsing.

This is where **Labels** comes into its own. When you were putting your contacts from Anycompany PLC into your contacts you created a label of the same name. Now when you go in to your contacts, your groups of people (labels) will appear on the left in the **Labels** section. You just click on Anycompany PLC and a list of contacts at that company will appear in the main window.

Of course you could also search for PA in the search window as long as you put his/her job title in their details.

How to add a label

First either click on **Create label** in the left navigation bar or click on a profile photo and then **Manage labels** symbol/icon (this appears at the top when you select a contact) as illustrated in *figure* 6.26 and click on **Create label** You will not be able to create a new label from the contact page itself only add existing labels. You will need to create a new label from the left navigation bar or from the top of the page when you click in the box that appears when you click on a profile photo.

Adding labels from the Google Contact homepage

- Click on **Manage label** icon above your contacts list which appears after you click on their profile photo or initial (see *figure* 6.26)
- Choose the label
- Click Apply or
- Click on **Create label**
- Type in your label and click **Save**

The labels will appear in their contact information under their name.

Adding Labels from a contact's page

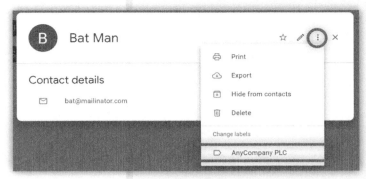

- Go into your contact by clicking on to their name
- Click on the three horizontal dots (see *figure 6.27* for the circled location)
- Choose one or more existing labels by selecting them

FIGURE 6.27 Managing labels from the contact's page.

If you want to check that the right groups have been assigned, go into your contact's page and then look under their name. They will be listed in alphabetical order as seen in *figure 6.28*.

Importing and exporting contacts

FIGURE 6.28 The labels assigned will show under your contact's name.

You may want to either import contacts from another source or export them to share them with colleagues, friends or family. Google makes this easy, Please follow the next steps to add or share your contacts.

Importing Contacts

If someone has sent you a vCard or a spreadsheet with contacts and you want to import it or you want to import your contacts from another email address, Google has made this really easy to do. Export your information from your other service to a CSV or vCard and import it into Google Contacts. Here are some quick instructions on how to do import it. To get your spreadsheet or vCard file, follow your providers instructions. Sometimes this process is done for you as part of the process of importing old email from a different account.

Importing from a CSV or vCard file

A vCard or CSV file is a spreadsheet that can be read by

FIGURE 6.29 Export contacts options.

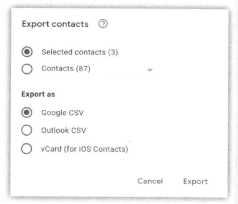

FIGURE 6.30 Further Export contacts options.

different spreadsheet programs such as Google Sheets or Microsoft Excel. You can back this up on your computer or even send them to your friends. If there is anything on there that you do not want your friend to see, edit it in a spreadsheet, save it and then send it to them.

- From the Google Contacts homepage (in the left navigation bar), click on **Import**. A pop up will appear.
- Click on **Select File**
- Browse your computer for the file with your contacts in and click on Open.
- Click on **Import**

Your contacts will appear on the homepage.

Exporting Contacts

If you would like to export your contacts you can do this with a vCard or via CSV which is a spreadsheet that can be read by different spreadsheet programs such as Google Sheets or Microsoft Excel. As with Importing, Google has simplified the process to a few steps.

Before you start, do you want to send a group of contacts (label), a selection or everything? If you want to do a selection, you will need to select the contacts before you click on the Export button.

You may want to create a new label specifically for this import. For example, if you wanted to just send people that know your sister (or brother) to the organizer of a surprise birthday party, you could create a special label for that and put all the pertinent people in there. The option to choose that label will be in the export menu. Side note - You should probably ask the permission of anyone whose details you send on.

- From the Google Contacts homepage (in the left navigation bar), click on **Export**. A pop up will appear.
- If you've already selected a few people then you will have the option to choose just these selected contacts (see *figure* 6.30), otherwise, you can choose to have all your contacts, starred contacts, frequently contacted or any groups/labels that you have made. Please see *figure* 6.29 for how this might look

- Next, choose the file type that you want it exported as. The options are a Google CSV, an Outlook CSV or the IOS Contacts option, a vCard. A vCard also works in Android.

You can preselect just one of your contacts before starting the export process. This allows you to just export that contact.

The options for file types asks you how you want it to be exported. The type of CSV (a type of spreadsheet) that will work with another Google account will be different from a Microsoft Outlook or another application, so you must choose the option for where you want to export to. The third option is a vCard which can be imported into Apple Address books as well as some other applications.

- Click on **Export** and save the file to your computer. The suggested file name is contacts.csv but you can change this if you want to

Printing your contacts list

Again you have granular control over what contacts you can choose. Select certain contacts before you start or choose labels that you have set up.

- From the Google Contacts homepage (in the left navigation bar), click on **Print**. A pop up will appear.
- Make your choice (selected contacts or a label by clicking on the down arrow as illustrated in *figure* 6.31), and click on **Print**. A new page will load with your contents displayed in a list
- In the print dialog box, you can choose to save it as a PDF or send to your printer. Choose **Print** or **Save** depending on your selection.

FIGURE 6.31 Printing options.

Other Contacts

On the left navigation bar, you will see an option for **Other contacts**. These are contacts you didn't add but are found within your Google account. These could be people that emailed you or remnants from the ill-fated Google+.

If you have contacts that you know have emailed you but

you haven't added to Google Contacts, you can add them from the contact's page.

- Click on your contact's name from the Google Contacts homepage
- Click on the **Add to contacts** button. It looks like a + beside a person icon. Please see *figure 6.32* for how this looks

FIGURE 6.32 Click on **Add to contacts** to add them to your main contacts list.

That's it. If you close the pop up and click on Google Contacts on the top of your screen, the contact will now appear in your list of contacts on the homepage.

Google Contacts settings

The settings for Google Contacts are basic but it is worth reviewing them as they can have a big impact on how you use it.

The settings option on the Google Contacts service is located at the top of the page. It looks like a cog wheel.

Language

If you change your language here, it will affect Gmail and all the other Google services that you use, including Google Docs etc. This will affect your spell check.

Phone number country code

Add the country where you live to this section.

Sort by

You can choose to sort your contacts on the homepage by their first name or last name. The **Name** section in your contact's details takes precedence, unless you choose **File as** which will supersede the name you input.

Did you know...

Back up your contacts by exporting them all to a CSV file and saving them on your computer.

In the unlikely event that the **Undo changes** option doesn't work and if you have any problems with your Google Contacts in the future, just delete what is in there and import them again!

Duplicate contacts

If you have duplicate contacts within Google Contacts you can merge them into one contact using **Duplicates**. Google will not always find your duplicate contacts. If the only information your duplicate records share is their name, then it won't find them. However, if two or more records share the same email address or phone number then you should be able to find it by clicking on **Duplicates** on the left hand side of the browser in Google Contacts.

If Google does find any duplicates they will appear in a box. Click on **MERGE** on the bottom right of the box for all the records to be merged into one.

Chapter summary

Google Contacts is an essential service that is integrated into Gmail. It is where all your friends, co-workers, business and other contact details are held. This chapter explains what is available and how to do some important tasks, including:

- How to get to Google Contacts from Gmail, direct by Internet address or from any Google service you are logged into
- A Google contacts homepage overview
- How to add contacts
- Editing contacts
- Deleting one or more contacts
- Restoring your contacts if you accidentally remove them
- Starring your contacts to make them appear at the top of your list
- Grouping your contacts using labels to more easily find your contacts by relationship, work or any other kind of category
- Importing and exporting contacts to and from Google
- How to print your contacts in a list
- Where to find other contacts and how to integrate them into your main list. These could be people who have

emailed you but you haven't manually added them to your account. Google allows you to find them in **Other contacts** and add them from there

• What are the settings available in Google Contacts and what do they mean

Email Organization with Labels

● ● ● ● ● ● ● ● ● ● ● ● ● ● ● ●

Google is second to none as a tool for organizing emails. There are four big guns in the Google arsenal. These are discussions (mentioned in detail in *Chapter 5*), filters (find out more in *chapter 8*), Labels and Spam protection (*Chapter 4 Security*). This chapter will look in depth at labels.

Labels

Labels are what folders were in other programs and that antiquated filing cabinet gathering dust in the corner of your garage (because of course you have a paperless home office now). I used to have folders for everything including folders within folders. I had folders for holidays, work, friends, shopping, advice and many more. The old way was organized but there was always a point where you had to make a choice of where something went in your folder structure. For example if I planned a holiday with my friend to go shopping. Which folder would it go under? I would have chosen holidays in the past. Probably narrowing it down to Holidays > New York or something to that effect.

With Gmail you don't have to make that choice, create the labels and add them all to the one email. If I look in any of the Holidays, New York, Friends or Shopping labels I can now find it easily and quickly. Simply put, you can label your emails with as many 'labels' as you want. Whatever makes it easier to find the information you need. Labels can be described as categories, folders, groups, tags or just labels.

Chapter 07

What to expect in this chapter:

- What are Labels?
- How to create them
- How to customize your labels
- How to apply your labels
- Removing labels

Did you know...

The Inbox is just a label. If you remove the Inbox label (or archive it), you can find the emails again by searching for it or looking in **All Mail**.

Labels

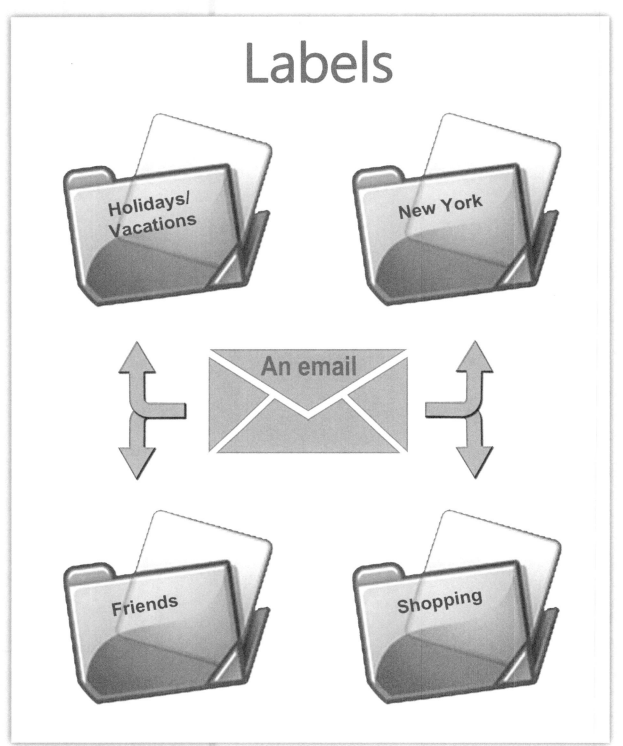

FIGURE 7.1 **Many labels can be given to one email.**

Creating a Label

Making a label is simple. Click on the **gear symbol** at the top right of the webpage (when you hover your mouse over the gear wheel it should confirm that it is the settings function). A drop-down menu will appear - you will need to select **Settings**. The reason you have to select it twice is that Google has put a few extra cosmetic options which they feel you might need to see first, such as how compact you would like the webpage to appear, and a **configure your inbox** option. Click on **Labels** as in number 1 in *figure 7.2*. Scroll down the page, past **System Labels** and **Categories** until you will see just Labels as in the section labeled number 2 in *figure 7.2*.

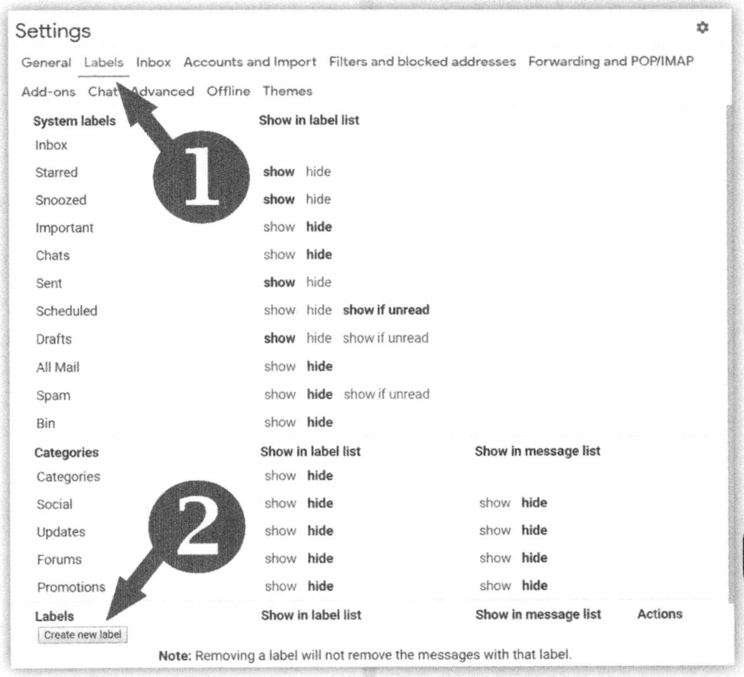

Click on **Create new label** as seen in the next figure (the arrow marked 2). Type in the box the label name you want, for example *Shopping* and think about if you want it to be a nested label.

FIGURE 7.2 How to get to the labels section.

A nested label means that a label will appear under another in the label list. This will require a little forethought if you want to keep your emails organized. You don't want to keep chopping and changing your labels. It could get confusing!

Nesting labels is similar to the file structure you will find in a computer. You have a main category like for example, *Shopping*, then underneath you could have several other categories like, *stores, groceries, electronics* etc.

Underneath these folders/ labels you could have even more labels such as store 1, store 2 under the main stores label. While you can only have one parent label (the top label), remember you can add your email to as many labels as you want.

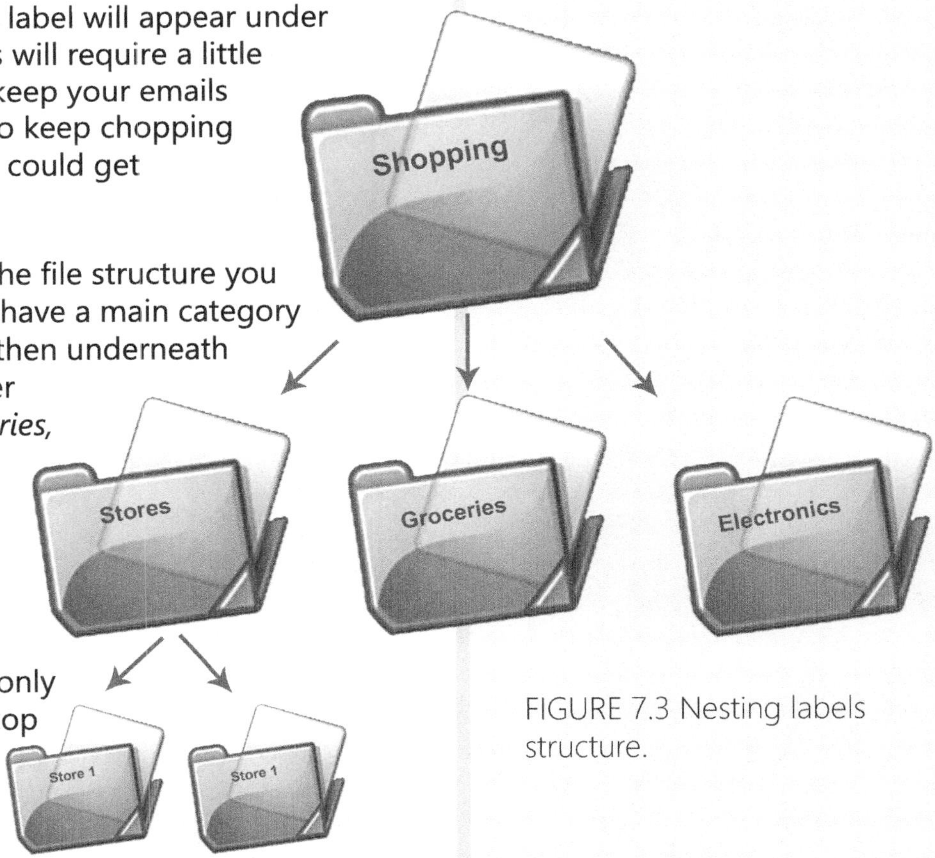

FIGURE 7.3 Nesting labels structure.

To put this in perspective say you shopped at a store called YellowStone where you bought a new laptop for your daughter. Using *figure* 7.3 as an illustration, you could put your email receipt into **Shopping**, **Stores**, **Store 1** (Yellowstone), and also **Electronics**. You could extend this further, if your daughter's name was Petunia, you could have a top level parent label called **Petunia** and maybe another underneath called **Purchases** where you could put the email. This would be 6 places where your email could be found but still only the one email. This maximizes your finding the email you need when browsing in a timely manner.

In *figure 7.4* I am creating a new label called **Groceries** which will be nested under **Shopping**.

Later, I will use a filter that will send all my receipt emails from my grocery stores to the **Groceries** label so I don't have to deal with them as they come in but I can find them later.

Having labels within labels has the effect of cutting down the number of labels that appear in the Gmail sidebar but you still have easy access to the more specific labels. To do this, I have put **Groceries** under **Shopping**. This means I will be able to find it quicker and all similar emails will be in the same place.

The quick steps for doing this are:

1. Go to **Settings**
2. Then **Settings** again (in the drop-down list)
3. Click on **Labels**
4. Select **Create New Label**
5. Type your **Label**
6. Select a parent label (to be nested under)
7. Click **Create**

Your new Label will then appear in the list of Labels below the box.

Groceries now appears under **Shopping**. If you click on the little arrow to the left of the Shopping label (as seen circled in *figure 7.5*), you can show or hide the Groceries label and any other label you have 'nested' under

Shopping.

I would like to sound a note of warning about the use of nested labels. If you label an email with Groceries, even though it will be under Shopping in the list, the email will not appear if you just click on Shopping. Therefore if you want it to be available under the two labels then you must make sure that both labels are assigned on an email. This way the email will appear when you look under each label.

FIGURE 7.4 Nested labels.

Customizing your labels

All the labels can be customized further. There is a little menu button to the right of each label in the left navigation section on the Gmail homepage. This appears when you hover your mouse over the label. Once you click on this, a menu will appear with more options. Please take a look at *figure 7.6* for the list of options.

A particularly useful feature is that you can change the color of the labels. For example if you have an urgent label, you could color it red. If your favorite color is blue why not make your **Friends** label blue?

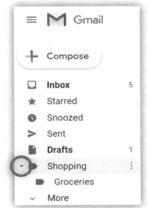

FIGURE 7.5 Nested labels as they will appear in Gmail.

Under the label list, you can have the label only show it if there are unread emails in it or your can hide the label entirely - all from the menu on the left of your Gmail homepage. What you choose will apply to sublabels which is why the option doesn't appear when you click on the menu button for a sublabel. Also the labels will still appear in both read and unread emails, but next to the label in the left hand navigation menu the number of emails indicated changes. This is shown circled in *figure 7.7*. There are actually two emails labeled **Shopping** and **Groceries** but only one is unread. The number in the navigation bar therefore shows one.

There are two options under the message list. This means you can show or hide the label in the row your email appears in the message list on the Gmail homepage. If you have lots of emails, this can make Gmail look cluttered

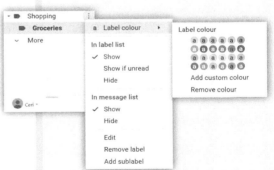

FIGURE 7.6 Click on the arrow to the right of the label that appears when you hover over it to get these options. **Add sublabel** at the bottom of this menu can be a quicker way to make labels.

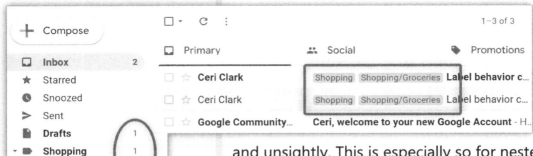

FIGURE 7.7 Show or hide the labels in your message list.

and unsightly. This is especially so for nested labels where they will appear like Shooping/Groceries or Shopping/Groceries/WalStore. These can be quite long and result in you seeing less of the subject which can be less useful depending on how you like to use Gmail. For a more clean and uncluttered look turn off the labels in the email list pane by:

- Hovering your mouse over the label to reveal the menu button (three horizontal dots)
- Clicking the menu button
- Under '**In message list**', click **Hide**

Do this for all your top level labels (parent labels) for a lovely streamlined look.

The other options in the submenu are **Edit**, **Remove label** or **Add sublabel**.

Edit your label

When you choose **Edit**, you can change the name or add/remove a parent label. If you remove the parent label and it is the direct 'child' then it will appear alongside the former parent label in the label list on the homepage.

Remove the label from the submenu

Choosing **Remove label** will delete the label but any emails that were categorized under it will still exist. It will not have a label attached (unless you have categorized it under several labels. If this happens, your emails will become 'orphaned' but you can always find emails under **All mail**. To find **All mail** click on **More** directly under your label list on the homepage.

106

Add a sublabel

The last option in the list allows you to create a new label. It doesn't matter which label you clicked into to get to this option. The box that will appear will allow you to choose any of your labels to nest under.

Applying a Label

Now that you have created a Label you will want to add it to your email.

From the email list

Check the box on the left of the email that you would like to label. Once you have done this, options for organizing your emails will appear above the email list. Choose the icon (picture) that looks like a label you would put on a wrapped gift or a sideways arrow as illustrated in *figure 7.8* by clicking on it. A drop-down list will appear.

Tick the box next to the label you want. You can choose as many as you like. If you have too many labels to appear in the list without scrolling you can save time by searching for the labels by typing a few characters in the search box. You don't need to search for the whole word. **Create new** at the bottom of the list will do exactly as the name suggests and will allow you to create a new label. By clicking on **Manage labels** you will be taken to the Labels page in the settings area of Gmail.

From an opened email

The options are similar to applying labels from the list of emails in the Gmail homepage. Choose the label icon above your emails (see *figure 7.8* to see what this looks like).

At this point you can assign as many Labels as you want to it. Once you click **Apply**, the email will be assigned or 'moved' to the Label 'folder' or category.

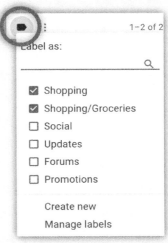

FIGURE 7.8 Click the label icon to get a list of labels to apply.

07

Google has its own set of labels which it calls categories. These are Social, Promotions, Updates and Forums. These are still labels though and can be found in the labels section of the settings.

Applying a label to more than one email

To apply a label to emails, select the boxes next to your emails in the message list and choose the label icon (see *figure* 7.8) ... but what if all your emails are not in your message list?

You can label all emails from the same address at the same time using the **Filter messages like these** option. Here is how to do it.

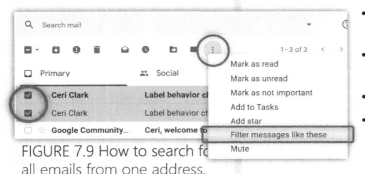

FIGURE 7.9 How to search for all emails from one address.

- Choose an email with the address you want to label

- Click on Menu button (three vertical dots), at the top of your screen

- Choose **Filter messages like these**

- Click on the search button at the bottom of the pop-up that loads. All the emails in the list will be from that email address

- Click on the arrow next to the empty square at the top of your message list (see *figure* 7.10)

- Choose **All**

- If the emails go onto the next page, Gmail will tell you at the top of the page *"All 100 conversations on this page are selected. Select all conversations that match this search"*. Click on **Select all conversations that match this search**

- Click on the label icon (see the top of *figure* 7.8)

- Uncheck the boxes/labels you want to remove. You may have to click more than once to empty the box

- Click on **Apply**

FIGURE 7.10 Select more than one email quickly.

Removing Labels

You can remove labels easily from one email or several email at once. This section will show you how.

Removing labels from one email

To remove a Label from an opened email, click on the **x** next to the Label. Your labels can be found next to or below the subject in your emails.

Removing labels from several emails

If you want to remove a label from several emails in your message list, select the emails you want to remove the labels from and click on the label button (illustrated in the gray circle in *figure* 7.11). Uncheck the boxes and click **Apply**.

If the emails you want to remove the label from are in one label, all the emails can be changed at once.

- Choose the label from the left navigation bar. All the emails will be in that category
- Click on the arrow next to the empty square at the top of your message list
- Choose **All**
- Click on the label icon
- Uncheck the boxes/ labels you want to remove. You may have to click more than once to empty the box
- Click on **Apply**

Deleting labels

FIGURE 7.11 Click on the **x** to remove the label.

You won't be able to delete labels originating from Gmail itself, (you need to click hide in the labels section of settings) but you can delete labels that you make. Here are some quick instructions:

- Go to **Settings**
- Then **Settings** again (in the drop-down list)
- Click on **Labels**
- Scroll to your labels, and under **Actions**, click on **Remove** to the right of the label you want to delete
- Click on **Delete**

FIGURE 7.12 Click on **Remove** to delete your label.

Chapter summary

This chapter is all about labels. It describes how labels are like folders and that more than one label can be assigned to one email. This means you can find an email in more than one place when you are browsing your emails. There are instructions for creating, customizing and applying them, as well as removing labels from one or more emails.

Filters and Blocked Addresses

Applying labels to everything can be a bit of a chore; however Google has come up with an elegant solution with their *Filters* option to save you time.

Filters can allow you to automate the process of adding labels. With this system, if you always want to put all emails from Auntie Flo in a Label called Auntie Flo as soon as they arrive in your inbox without you having to constantly apply labels, then you can get Filters to do this. You can also ask it to treat her emails as very important. It might not mean that you answer her emails any faster but it will mean that you won't lose them amongst the hundreds of other emails you get, or in the spam folder.

Filters also allow you to immediately delete emails from people or companies without ever seeing them or just archive them for later viewing. You can make sure that certain emails never go into spam and that they are marked important or are starred so they are easy to find in the mix of emails you will get daily. Filters are an essential resource for email organization.

What to expect in this chapter:

- What are filters
- Making filters
- Importing filters
- Exporting filters
- Editing filters
- Deleting filters
- Blocked addresses

Creating a Filter

Go to **Settings** on the top right of the screen (the gear symbol) and choose settings from the drop-down. Then select **Filters and Blocked Addresses**.

FIGURE 8.1 How to get to Filters

Please see steps 1-3 in *figure 8.1*.

Click on **Create a new filter**, (Step 4 in the image).

The options that Google offer you in Filters can be seen in *figure 8.2*.

Examples of how to filter:

- To label all emails from a person or mailing list, type the email address into the **From** box. For example, *auntieflo@gmail.com*. If you put the email in the **To** box, it will filter all the emails you send *them*

- If there are specific words in the subject you want to pay attention to, for example if you receive a newsletter from *horse riding weekly* and you want to make sure they all appear together in one place then put *horse riding weekly* into the **Subject** box

- **Has the words** are for general keywords, for example any emails containing a place, name or brand. It is best to use unusual words or you will end up with emails which are not relevant

- The **Doesn't have** is a powerful tool. If you want to label all emails with a word but you are getting too many results and all the wrong results have the same word in them, pop that word into this box and it will ignore those emails with the wrong word in them

- **Size** This is related to the size of the attachment. If you are running out of space or you are looking for an email which you know had an extremely large attachment, you can search for emails with a size greater or less than a size you choose. This isn't just for emails with attachments though as you can search without checking the **Has attachment** box and you can search for MB (Megabytes), KB (kilobytes) or just Bytes

- **Has attachment**. If you want all emails with attachments from a certain person to go in the Trash/Bin then, type in the person's name in

From		
To		
Subject		
Includes the words		
Doesn't have		
Size	greater than ▾	MB ▾
☐ Has attachment ☐ Don't include chats		
	Create filter	**Search**

FIGURE 8.2 Filter options

the **From** box and click the box by **Has attachment** and you will never receive the emails again

Remember you can use one of the filter options or all. You are only limited by your imagination. Once you have put the words you want in the filter, you can choose to just search for emails and they will appear in your messages list or you can create a filter.

If you only want to search, click on the **Search** button (the button will either say **Search** or show a magnifying glass icon) to see if there are any emails already in your account with these options.

To filter, click on **Create filter**.

Figure 8.3 shows the next options available to you. You can archive it, mark it as read, star it, apply the label, and forward those particular emails to an email address and so on.

The most important options are **Apply the Label** and **Always/Never mark it as important**.

After clicking on **Create Filter**, you will get a confirmation screen to say it has been set up. The downside is that you will have to go through the process for each label as it doesn't allow you to choose more than one label at this stage.

If you are tidying up your emails and want to apply the label to all your previous emails then check the box next to **Create filter** which says **Also apply filter to X matching conversations.** If you are deleting all emails from a certain email address then all of the emails will be deleted not just future arrivals. This is a great way of clearing your inbox!

As can be seen above, you can do so much with filters, but what if you want to edit or delete a filter? Better yet, what if you have spent lots of time creating the best filters and you want to share them

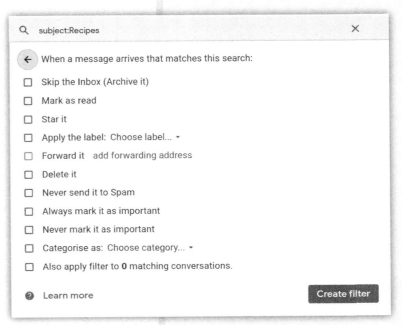

FIGURE 8.3 **The next step in creating a filter**

with a friend or vice-versa? Google has enabled them so that you can share with your friend (export filters) or have your friend share their filters with you (import filters). This section aims to show you how to do this.

Editing/changing a filter

If you think a filter is not appropriate any more you can change the filter by clicking on the **Gear Wheel** > **Settings** > **Filters and Blocked Addresses** and clicking on **edit** next to the filter you want to tweak.

A word of warning, even if you change the filter and apply to all your emails, changes made by the previous filter will have to be dealt with on an email by email basis.

For example I had a filter in my test account which had everything from Ceri Clark go into a Friends/Ceri Clark label. All emails which had this label applied had these words in it. I then realized that the emails from Gmail which stated at the beginning 'Hi Ceri', were all labeled Friends/Ceri Clark. The filter did not discriminate that I wanted the two words together sent to a label. It included emails with just Ceri in. Adding quotation marks to the search had no bearing on the results so "Ceri Clark" still had emails with just Ceri sent to the label. Clearly inaccurate!

I edited the label to have all emails sent from my email address to go to that label and all the right emails were now labeled correctly but of course there were still emails in the label that shouldn't have been there from the previous mistake. I had to manually delete the labels from each email. The moral of this story is to think carefully about what labels to apply!

Deleting a filter

There are two places to delete your filters in the settings. Deleting a filter could not be simpler,

1. Go to the **Gear Wheel**

2. Click on **Settings**
3. Select **Filters and Blocked Addresses**
4. Check the box next to the filter you want to remove
5. Click on **delete** on the far right of the filter you want to remove *or* click on the **Delete** button at the bottom of the Filters page in settings

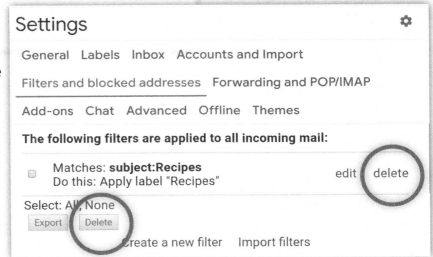

Sharing filters with friends (exporting filters)

FIGURE 8.4 The two places to delete your filters in the **Filters and Blocked Addresses** settings page. **08**

In order to export your filters, go to the filters section in settings (**Gear Wheel > Settings > Filters and Blocked**) and click on **Export** at the bottom of the page. Please see *figure 8.5* to see its location.

Once you have clicked on **Export** you will be asked to save the file on to your computer. The file will be downloaded with the extension of .xml. You can now email this filter to your friend.

FIGURE 8.5 Where to find Export.

Adding filters given to you (importing filters)

First go to **Gear Wheel > Settings > Filters and Blocked Addresses** and click on **Import filters** (*see* 1 in *figure* 8.6). A new section will load at the bottom of the page which will look like the next image.

Click on **Choose file (2)** and find the file with the .xml ending such as **MailFilters.xml** that you were given. Once you have clicked **Open** you will return to Google and you will need to click on **Open File (3)**.

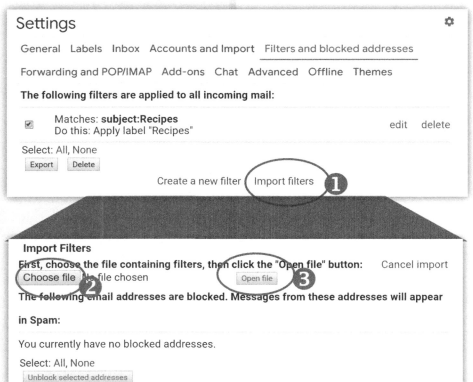

FIGURE 8.6 Importing filters

The screen will reload with the filters that were in the file. You can stop at this point or you can choose which filters you want to import. Simply click on the little check-boxes next to the filters you want added to your account and click on **Create filters**. If you want the filters to apply to all the emails that are already in your account, click on the little box next to **Apply new filters to existing email**.

Google will automatically create the labels that are needed by the new filters.

Blocked addresses

Blocked addresses are a type of filter which is why they are grouped together in the **Filters and Blocked Addresses** section of Gmail settings. It is a quick way of setting up a filter to send all email from a certain email address to spam.

Blocking an address

FIGURE 8.7 Blocking an address.

- From an opened email, click on the menu button (three vertical dots) on the top right above your email as seen in *figure 8.7*
- Look for **Block "x"** down the list, (in the illustration, this is Block "Ceri Clark"), and click on it
- You will be warned that all emails from this person will go to Spam. Click **Block**

All emails from this person will now go directly to spam. If you are expecting an email you can check your spam to see if there are any emails there or unblock the address which is explained in the following section.

Unblocking an address

There may be a time when you want to unblock an address you have blocked in the past.

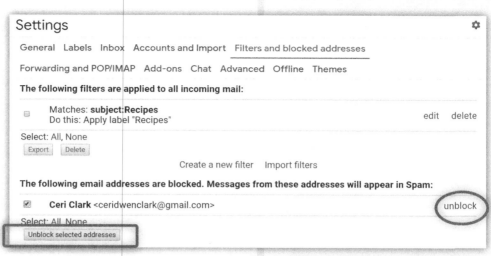

FIGURE 8.8 Unblock blocked addresses.

- First go to the **Gear Wheel**
- Click on **Settings**
- Choose **Filters and Blocked Addresses** and look down the page until you see **The following email addresses are blocked. Messages from these addresses will appear in Spam**
- Either click on **unblock** to the right of the blocked address or check the box(es) next to the blocked address(es) on the left and then click on **Unblock selected addresses**

Chapter summary

Filters are a powerful tool for organizing your emails. In this chapter we discussed what filters are, how to set them up, how to edit them and how to delete them. Blocked addresses are another form of filter which simplifies creating a filter that sends all emails from an email address to spam. The last item in this chapter showed how to unblock any email addresses that have been blocked.

08

Searching for, and in, Emails

●●●●●●●●●●●●●●●●

Searching for your emails is a breeze with Gmail. In the basic sense all you need to do is type in your search term in the search box and then click on the magnifying glass (or press Enter/Return) for the Google search engine to search all your email for you.

Google does accept Boolean searching, for example using AND & OR, and quotes, but for a simpler way of powerful searching click on the little arrow inside the search box. If you hover your mouse over the arrow, you will get a little message stating **Show search options**. These are shown in *figure 9.2*.

The beauty of these options is that you can not only search from a particular email address but from emails which have certain words in them. Here are some tips for searching.

Searching in your labels

You can search only within a label by clicking the arrows next to **All Mail** in the search options and selecting the label you want to look in.

If you just type in the search box, Gmail will automatically search all your mail, but you can search in just the email

What to expect in this chapter:

- Searching within your labels
- How to search for emails using an email address
- Searching your Sent emails
- Keyword searching
- Searching for emails with attachments
- Searching by size and date
- Sorting your emails by newest or oldest emails

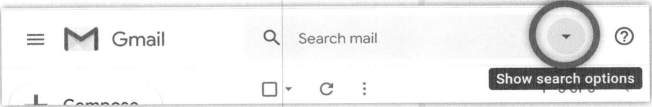

FIGURE 9.1 Advanced search options can be found by clicking the arrow inside the search box.

you sent. Also, if you are organized and assigned all your emails labels then you can search within just those. A possible scenario is that you may have a label for work related emails and another for personal. If this is the case you could just search in your personal emails if you needed to.

Combining a Label search with the other options such as subject, includes the words or doesn't have the words means you are less likely to come up with hundreds of irrelevant emails.

FIGURE 9.2 **Advanced search options**

Searching for emails from a certain person

This can be done in two ways, you can just put the email address into the search bar, or the way I recommend is to go into the advanced search and type it into the **From** field (less room for error).

If you are searching for emails from a company sometimes the best way to search is to only put the second half of the email address from the @ sign. For example enquiries@anycompany.com could be searched for by typing:

120

@anycompany.com

...in the **From** field.

This is useful because companies use many different email addresses and they may have sent you an email from different people and departments within the company. These could be sales@anycompany.com, orders@anyconpany.com, CustomerServices@anycompany.com or even no-reply@anycompany.com. You could be sent emails from vicky@anycompany.com to Dave@anycompany.com. The emails will usually all come from the same domain name which is the bit of the address after the @ sign. By typing @anycompany.com you are searching for all of these addresses and more in one fell swoop.

Searching emails you have sent to people

As above, you can type their email address straight into the search box or this time I recommend typing the email addresses into the **To** box in the advanced search. The searching tip for searching for all emails from a company as detailed above will apply to your sent email as well.

Subject searching

When you type in the subject box, it will only search the subject of your emails. If you want to search for say, Washington but you don't want all those emails with Washington in the body of the email, this is the way to go.

This is great if you are getting a lot of emails with the same subject and you want to delete them. For example, you can search for Annoying Company Newsletter in the subject box and all their emails will be found. You can delete them at your leisure.

Did you know...

> When you send emails try and make sure that the subject that you write is as descriptive of the content of your email as possible. Not only is this helpful for people receiving your email but when you want to find it again, Google will be able to find it easier if it has the right words in the subject.

09

Searching for emails using keywords (Includes the words...)

Whatever you are searching for, the **Includes the words** field can be indispensable and with the help of the other boxes you can really narrow down your search.

An example would be if you were searching for the holiday company that you had a holiday with last year because you want to book with them again but you have forgotten what they are called.

You can remember you went to Orlando but the holiday company just eludes you. Type in the box Orlando and (if you kept it) Google will find your receipt email which would have the name of the company on it.

Removing emails from the search

The box labeled **Doesn't have** is one of the most useful options in Gmail search. You may be getting lots of emails in your search which are irrelevant but the search brings them up with the words you have put in. Finding words in the erroneous emails which tells you they aren't relevant and putting them in this box when you search again will remove them from your search. Just make sure that the words you choose are not going to be in the emails you want!

Finding emails with an attachment

Ticking the box **Has attachment** will bring up results with only attachments. Gmail will also search within your attachments.

As an experiment I sent myself a document called Twinkle.
docx. The email subject had Twinkle in the name and
the content of the email simply stated Nursery Rhyme.
The attached document itself had the full nursery rhyme,
Twinkle, Twinkle, Little Star, typed out. I searched for star
in my Gmail and although star was only mentioned in the
actual document, Gmail put the email in the search results.

Searching through your Chats

Gmail will automatically search through your chats. If you
tick the box labeled **Don't include chats**, Gmail will only
search through your emails.

Searching by size

You can search for your emails by choosing greater than
or less than a certain size of email. If you regularly send
emails to a friend or colleague and they have sent you an
attachment but you've lost the email, you can search for
emails of a larger size to narrow your list.

Also, if you feel you are using too much space in your
Gmail account, you can search for all emails over a certain
size to find all emails with attachments. You can then
delete emails which you think you no longer need to
good effect. One email with an attachment can be worth
hundreds of emails without them.

Another alternative is that if someone has sent you a
document to your email that is large, you can save it
to your Google Drive. You could convert it to a Google
document format and delete the original. Information
kept in Google's own file types such as Google Docs and
Sheets do not count towards your space limits. If you are
desperate for space this is a viable way of saving space
without losing important documents.

Searching emails by date

The last option is to search within a time period. The

options are within 1 day, 3 days, 1 week, 2 weeks, 1 month, 2 months, 6 months, and 1 year of a date you can select by clicking into the box next to this option. For example 1 year of 1 April 2017.

Alternatively, if you want a longer time period, you can type into the main search bar in the format:

after:2012/4/1 before:2014/4/2

Sorting emails by newest or oldest

Lastly in this chapter there is a little known trick for sorting your emails inside Gmail.

On the top right of your Gmail account, Gmail lets you know how many email are on the page you are viewing and how many emails you have in total. If you click on these numbers you can click **Oldest** to sort your emails so that you see your oldest emails first.

FIGURE 9.3
Select **Oldest** and navigate using the arrows.

What this actually does is jump you to the page which has your oldest emails. It doesn't put your oldest emails on the first page by reordering them but instead takes you to the last page. If you click on **Newest**, it will jump you right back to the beginning. The arrows next to the numbers allow you to navigate through your pages of emails.

You can choose how many emails you have in your page by going to the **Gear Wheel** > **Settings** > **General** > **Maximum page size:**

Select the number of conversations per page here from 10, 15, 20, 25, 50 and 100 per page.

Chapter summary

Gmail has powerful search functionality and you can choose to use more than one option to really narrow down your search. Search options include emails to and from a particular email address, the subject, keywords, attachments, size and date. There are also options for removing erroneous emails using *Doesn't have keywords* and then sorting your emails so you see the oldest first. Whether you use one or more of these functions in a search, there is a combination that will help you to find what you need.

09

Changing the Look and Feel

• • • • • • • • • • • • • •

You've sent a couple of emails, told a few of your best mates about how great Gmail is but you're getting a bit bored with how it looks. This is the chapter to help you with this.

All of these changes can be made from **Settings**. This link can be found at the top right of the screen when you click on the gear wheel as illustrated in *figure 10.1*.

The Display Density

There are three options under **Display Density**. These are **Comfortable** (for larger displays), **Cozy** (again for larger displays) and **Compact**. Please see *figure 10.2* to see how each view compares side-by-side. They are designed to fit more or fewer emails depending on the size of the screen you are viewing your email on.

Space between emails

The space between each email is larger with Comfortable, less in Cozy and in Compact view there is the least amount of space between emails.

Attachments

The placement of the attachments affects how many emails you can fit on your screen at any given time without scrolling. In **Default** view your attachments will appear underneath your email. This doubles the space the email line takes up. In both **Comfortable** and **Compact**, an icon on the far right of the email line (just before the

What to expect in this chapter:

- What is display density and what each option looks like
- How to change your background with themes

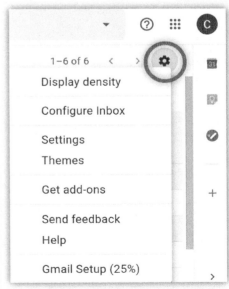

FIGURE 10.1 Location of Settings.

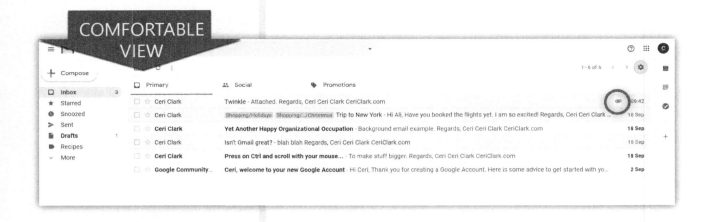

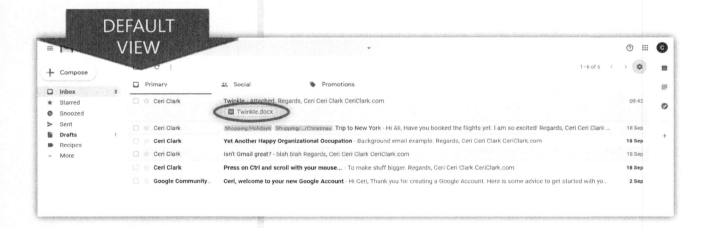

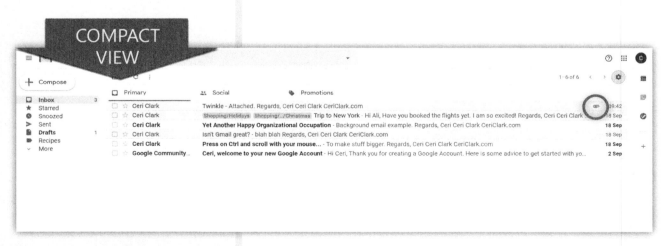

FIGURE 10.2 Attachment position in Density Display views.

date stamp of the email) lets you know that you have an attachment. See *figure* 10.2 for how this looks in practice.

Themes

To change the theme, choose **Themes** from under **Settings** under the gear wheel at the top right of the page. The themes can also be found as a tab at the top of the main settings page.

There are lots of themes to choose from and quite a few change automatically throughout the day, my particular favorite is the planets theme.

If you would like to use any of these themes, all you need to do is click on the square that represents them and then **Save** at the bottom. They should be applied.

There are a couple of themes that require you to let them know what country you are in but this is simply because the background picture changes according to the time of day (Mountains for example). It can be nice if you are stuck indoors with the curtains closed to know that it is sunset because your Gmail background changes!

If you want the original theme because you don't like the alternatives, choose the original, (the theme circled in *figure 10.3*), **Default** theme to go back.

Google has also given you the opportunity to add your own background from photos in your Google account. Click on **My photos** at the bottom left of the themes page to add them.

Try out the themes until you find one that you like. Sometimes a theme will make your navigation bar hard to see but you won't know until you try out a few. If there is one you particularly like but you are finding it hard to read the left menu, there are ways to make it clearer.

There are three options that appear when you click on a theme. These appear at the bottom right of the window and look like *figure* 10.4. These are **Text background**, **vignette** and **blur**.

More Images

Gmail

Mustard

Google

Zoozimps

?

My photos   Cancel   Save

FIGURE 10.3 Themes available

These options do not appear for every theme but when they do they can make all the difference for usability.

Changing the Text background

Within the text background options there is light or dark. This does not affect the navigation area but does the email pane. If you take a look at *figure* 10.5, the original shows a light text background while the second image shows how your emails will look with the dark background.

Vignette

Click on the vignette button at the bottom of the pop up (the theme settings page) to get a black fade edging to your picture. This can really make the text pop. Please see *figure 10.5* for how much of a difference this can make.

Blur

The last button to change your theme allows you to blur the image. *Figure* 10.5 shows the same background picture in all three iterations.

If you use the modification buttons on the bottom, it appears that you can only use the vignette or the blur; you cannot use both at the same time. You can however use the text background with either.

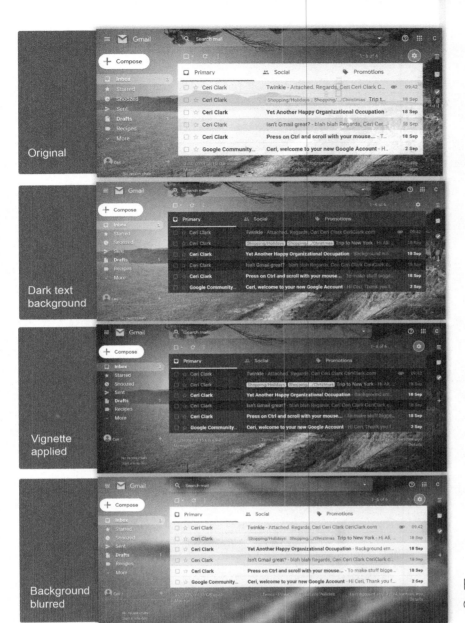

FIGURE 10.4 Buttons for adapting the theme.

FIGURE 10.5 Theme options.

10

Chapter summary

This chapter aims to give you a taste of how you can change the way Gmail looks to suit your personality. Change the density display to make it more comfortable to view and the theme to personalize it.

Gmail Settings

● ● ● ● ● ● ● ● ● ● ● ● ● ● ●

This chapter covers all the settings under the general tab in the first instance but then goes into detail about inbox, importing and exporting to other email accounts, forwarding and POP/IMAP, chat, web clips and offline. Labs, labels and themes have their own chapters.

The General settings tab

The number of general settings can seem quite daunting when you first see them. This section aims to dispel the apprehension of seeing all those settings in one page. To get to these settings click on the gear wheel at the right of the screen and click on **Settings** (*figure* 11.2).

Remember that if you make any changes you will need to scroll to the bottom of the page and click on **Save Changes** or the new setting will not apply.

Language

Choose the language appropriate to your region, for the US, US English is the default. UK users can choose the English (UK) option. If you communicate using Hindi, Arabic, or Chinese (or any other language that uses a different character set) then you will need to check the box next to **Enable input tools**. You should also check the box for right-to-left editing if your country's language requires this. Enable Input tools only works in the browser version of Gmail. Once it is enabled, you can get to it from the left of the gear wheel at the top right of your browser window.

Chapter 11

What to expect in this chapter:

- What is available in settings and how to use them
- Setting up your inbox view
- Accounts and Import, Forwarding and POP/IMAP
- Chat, Web clips and Offline

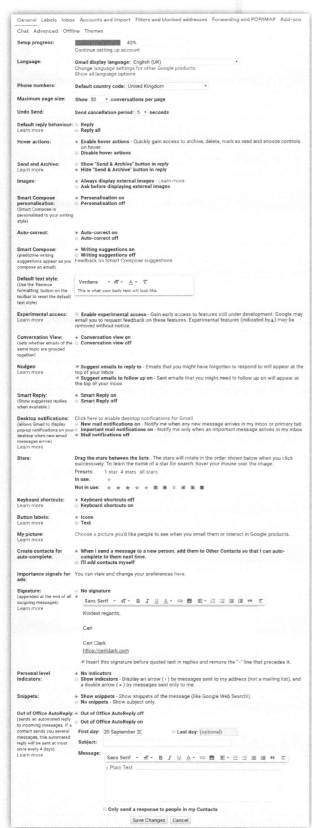

Phone numbers

This option is to allow you to use Google Voice. While it is only available in limited places at the moment the option to choose so many countries suggests that Google are planning to roll out Google Voice to more places in the future.

Maximum page size

This option depends on how much you want to scroll, the more conversations and contacts you allow on each page the fewer pages you will have to click through but it also means you will have to scroll more.

You can limit your emails on a page to: 10, 15, 20, 25, 50, 100 emails.

Undo send

This is an invaluable and highly recommended setting. Have you ever sent an email and instantly regretted it or spotted a spelling mistake just as you clicked send? Check this box and it will give you a grace period where you can click on **undo** so it will never get sent. You can set the grace period to 5, 10, 20 or 30 seconds.

Default reply behavior

This option asks if you want to automatically reply to one person or all people in your email. I would strenuously suggest that you choose **Reply**. You can always choose **Reply all** when you are typing the email but Gmail will automatically reply to just one sender email address if you click on just **Reply**.

I would not recommend **Reply all** as an automatic setting in any circumstances. It is easier to send an email again to people you have missed but very hard to make someone unsee an email!

It can seem very convenient to have a reply to all automatically done for you for every email you send. It means that no one would miss out on your emails if you are replying back, but if you are using your Gmail account for business purposes take the lessons learned from big business that this may not be the best idea. The news has been full in the past of emails sent to the wrong people by accident and then forwarded on to strangers. The type of email that you shouldn't reply to all will usually find their way half-way across the world before you can say *"Oh dear what have I done"*! It is best to think before replying and think twice before replying to all.

Hover Actions

Enable hover actions should be enabled by default. This option will save you a lot of time. When you hover over any email you will get a row of buttons that will appear which are **Archive**, **Delete**, **Mark as read** and **Snooze**. Please see *figure* 11.3 to see what these buttons look like. Rather than having to click next to an email and then choose these options from the top of the email list, you will be able to just click once when you hover over the email that you want to do these actions with.

If for any reason you do not want these buttons to appear when you are hovering your mouse over your emails then you can turn this off by checking the circle next to **Disable hover actions** in **Settings**.

Send and archive

Enabling this function will add a button and save you even more time! With one click you can send a reply to an email while archiving at the same time. Without this, you can reply as normal but the email will stay in your inbox until you archive it manually. I highly recommend this button!

Images

This refers to displaying images within emails. While it is

FIGURE 11.2 The settings button.

Tip!

Always click on **Save Changes** at the bottom of the settings page to make them apply.

11

FIGURE 11.3 Email options when you hover over an email.

nice to see adverts in all their glory, in the past, if an email slipped through which had harmful code in it, malicious code could have damaged your computer. Now the setting is really for saving bandwidth and avoiding adverts. If this is what you want, click on **Ask before displaying external images**. If this drives you up the wall, you can always change to the other option again later.

Choose from:

- **Always display external images**
- **Ask before displaying external images**

Smart Compose personalization/Smart Compose

Smart Compose personalization is related to a later setting called Smart Compose. Smart Compose is a feature that will give you suggestions for ending your sentence when you start writing it. If you ever had a friend who finished your sentences before you have even said them then you know the basic premise. On the one hand it saves you time, but on the other, it sometimes gives random suggestions that you didn't intend to say. The personalization option means that Gmail will try to learn how you write your emails and give suggestions based on what you have previously written. If you want these either click on:

- Personalization on
- Personalization off or
- Writing suggestions on
- Writing suggestions off

To use Smart Compose, as soon, as you see a suggestion that you agree with, press on tab and it will fill in the sentence for you including punctuation.

Auto-correct:

Auto-correct will correct your spelling mistakes as you go along, without the need for you to manually do anything. Don't rely on this as no spell check is a hundred percent right.

Default text style

If you always want to send emails with the same formatting, for example Arial font or larger text size, then you can make this happen automatically from here. There are four main options: there is the font (e.g. Arial, Times New Roman etc.), the size of the text, (Small, Normal, Large and Huge), the color of your text and finally you can remove all formatting to bring the text in all your emails to the basic Gmail offering. Set the text to how you want it and all new emails you send including replies will use this automatically.

Experimental access

Enable this if you want to try out new features as Gmail trials. Just remember to not get too attached to new functions as they may be discontinued at any time. You will however be one of the first to try out the new 'toys'.

Conversation view

You can turn this off or on here. I would recommend you keep this on as it means you keep all your email about one 'subject' in one place. However, if you like all your emails separated so you can see everyone's replies on individual rows in your message list on your email homepage then you can turn it off here as well.

Both styles have their advantages and disadvantages. On the one hand if you like to deal with things as they come in, then individual emails can be cathartic but make you feel like you have more work to do than you actually do. If you like to see all your conversations in one place, it can make your inbox look less cluttered and it will be easier to find what you need in one place. The downside of this method is that if you have different tasks in the one conversation, you can't dismiss (archive) the conversation until it is all completed.

Nudges

Gmail will remind you about emails it thinks you might have

forgotten. These are emails that might need a reply. Check the box next to **Suggest emails to reply to** for Google to remind you about emails that you haven't replied to yet. This is not always accurate but can be a safety net if you have a busy life and are liable to forget to reply. You can always just ignore the suggestions.

Choose **Suggest emails to follow up on** to remind you to keep track of important emails that you have sent.

Smart Reply

Similar to Smart Compose, Smart Reply, will try to save you time by giving you suggestions. If you leave it on you can always turn it off, if it doesn't meet your needs.

Desktop notifications

If you are using the Google's Chrome, Mozilla's Firefox, Microsoft's Edge or Apple's Safari browsers, then you can get notifications as pop ups to let you know when you have got new email. Your browser will prompt you to allow these notifications.

The options in Gmail are:

- **New mail notifications on - Notify me when any new message arrives in my inbox or primary tab.** This option will notify you of any new mail in your inbox but if you are using inbox categories then it will only let you know about new emails that are in your **Primary inbox**
- **Important mail notifications on - Notify me only when an important message arrives in my inbox.** You will only be notified of emails that have been marked important
- **Mail notifications off.** This will turn all desktop notifications off

Stars

Stars are used to help organize your email. For example if you star an important email that you need to deal with by next week, then you can search for just starred emails. Use this section to choose what stars will be available. Drag the stars and symbols from the **Not in use** row to the **In use** row with your mouse and click **Save changes** at the bottom of the page. To choose a different star, in your inbox click on the star symbol next to the email in the inbox. Keep clicking to get the different star and symbol options.

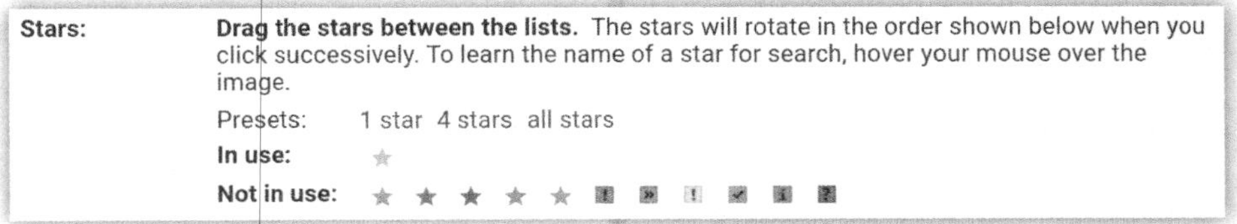

FIGURE 11.4 **Drag the stars and symbols from the Not in use row to the In use row to use them.**

Keyboard shortcuts

Turn these on or off depending on how much you want to use your mouse. I would recommend this is turned on so that you have the option to use shortcuts if you want to. A selection of shortcuts taken from the Google help pages are:

- To compose a message, type c, or Shift + c if you want it in a new window
- To return to the inbox type "u"
- To archive a message, type "e"
- To report spam, type "!"
- To bring up the label menu, type "l" (lowercase L)
- Add a Cc address to your email, type Ctrl + Shift + c (Mac: ⌘ + Shift + c)
- Add a Bcc address to your email, type Ctrl + Shift + b (Mac: ⌘ + Shift + b)
- To undo an action (it might not always work), type "z"

For all Google Gmail shortcuts, visit the Google help page at: http://support.google.com/mail/bin/answer. py?answer=6594

Button labels

If you find the icons too small or confusing, it is possible to change the navigation bar above your emails to have words instead of pictures. *Figure* 11.5 illustrates how the two views compare. The text view will take up more room in the Gmail specific navigation bar. You can make your browser bigger or smaller by clicking on Ctrl and

11

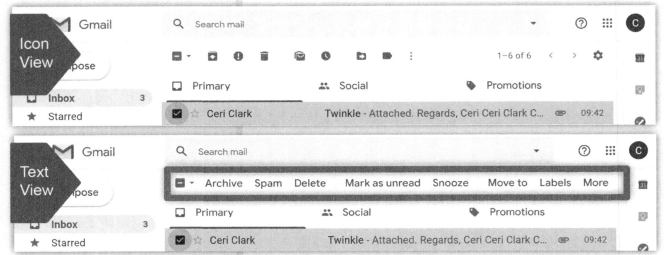

FIGURE 11.5 The difference between icon and text buttons.

FIGURE 11.6 Signature example.

using the scroll wheel on your mouse at the same time to compensate in Windows.

My picture

In this section you can change the picture you selected during setup. Clicking on **Change picture** (above your photo) brings up a window where you can search your computer for your favorite picture of yourself. You can always use your cat's picture if you prefer!

For more in-depth guidance on adding/changing your picture, please refer to the **Adding your profile picture** in *Chapter 3*.

Create contacts for auto-complete

This is a great time saver. Instead of adding contacts manually, Gmail will add them automatically when you send an email to someone. Of course if you send a lot of emails to people you are sure that you never want to contact again then using the **I'll add contacts myself** option would be better.

If you want to find these contacts in Google Contacts, they are in the **Other contacts**, located at the bottom of the left navigation column in Contacts. If you want them to appear in your main contacts list, just click on the **Add to contacts** button and it will move from **Other contacts** to your main list.

Important signals for ads

This setting is to show you what Google is using to target your adverts. When you click on the link you will be directed to a page which will show you what information Google is using and from where. You can choose what types of adverts are served to you and even what you don't want.

You can also opt-out of interest-based adverts. What this means is that you will still receive adverts but they won't be targeted and you can get anything. If you have to see adverts it can be better that it is something you don't mind seeing. There are plugins to browsers which will block adverts, even Google ones, but that is not in the purview of this book.

Signature

Your signature is how you end your email, it saves you having to type the same information time and time again. You can just add text, your name, address, phone number etc., or you can even add images. The formatting options are above the typing window as it is in composing emails or in your standard word processor.

Detailed instructions for adding and formatting a signature can be found in *Chapter 5 (Sending and receiving emails)*.

Personal level indicators

I would recommend turning these on, but if you don't plan on joining any mailing lists, then this is not important. This could be a good indicator of spam. You will find out if the email was sent directly to you and not to a generic mailing list address before you opened it.

If you are using your account for business purposes then this is useful as an email sent only to you could be an indication of whether you have to action the email.

The options you can choose here are:

> ### Did you know...
>
> You can have different signatures for all the different email addresses you have in Gmail.
>
> If you set up the **Send mail as** option in **Accounts and Import** then you can choose an option in the dropdown box (under No signature) to set up a different signature for each email address you can send from.

11

- **No indicators**
- **Show indicators** - Displays an arrow (›) by messages sent to my address (not a mailing list), and a double arrow (») will be by messages sent only to me.

Snippets

This option is a matter of personal preference. If you check your email in a public place then you may prefer to have this switched off. What it does is put the first line of your email viewable from the inbox. It can be a time saver as it tells you what is new in a conversation at first glance but it can also let other people looking over your shoulder know a little of what has been sent to you. The choice is yours.

Vacation responder/Out of office auto-reply

This section is very useful in a business context. It allows you to tell your contacts that you are not available when you are on holiday or if you are indisposed. If you want to use this for your holidays, remember to click on **Only send a response to people in my Contacts**. You don't want potential burglars knowing you are on holiday or spammers/hackers knowing you might not be checking your email!

You can schedule the message so it will be sent while you are away and automatically turn off when you are back.

Another possible (business) use is as an auto responder if you were to *not* include an end date. You can write a message such as *"Thank you for your email. Your message is important to us and we will get back to you as soon as possible."*

Again you can restrict this message to people in your contacts if you put phone numbers and other contact details in your signature that you may not want generally known.

The Labels tab

I have gone into more depth in *Chapter 7: Email organization with labels*, but if you have jumped to this section, basically think of them as folders but where one email can be in several folders/places at the same time.

This is the place where you can organize your emails by specifying what labels i.e. 'folders' you want to see in the left column. I would suggest you need the **Sent Mail**, **Drafts**, **All Mail** and **Trash/Bin** and add anything else as and when you need it.

The Inbox tab

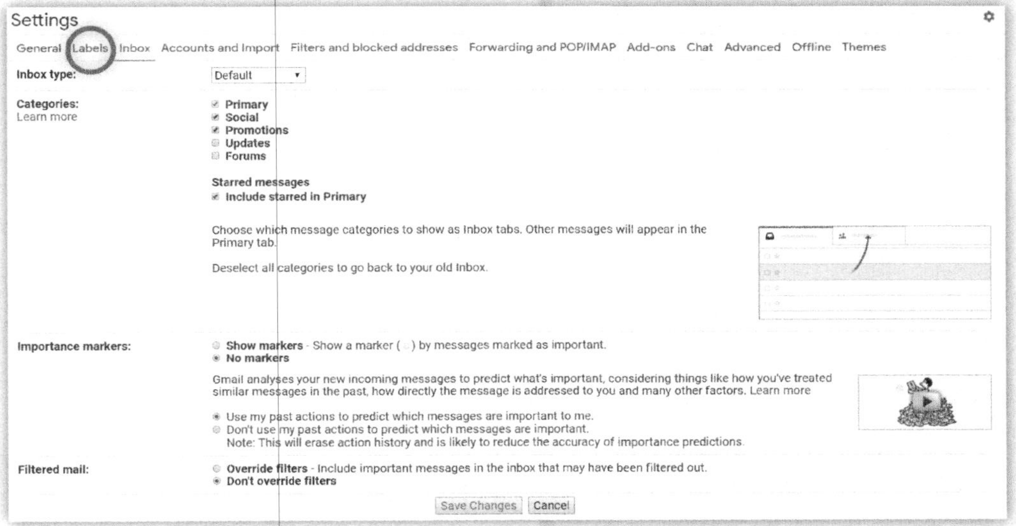

The inbox settings are Google's way of organizing your emails for you. If you don't want to use filters, using Google's Inbox feature can de-clutter your main inbox window

FIGURE 11.7 Inbox tab overview.

11

without any effort other than choosing which of their categories you want to use.

The first options that you will see are the inbox types. You can customize how your inbox is organized using these. The different inbox types will change what you see in this settings page. The inbox types are:

- Default
- Important first
- Unread first
- Starred first
- Priority inbox

Each option has their own particular look and functionality. Try them all out to see which suits you best. I will talk in more details about each type next.

Default

If you choose **Default** next to inbox type, then you can choose which categories you want to activate (if any). If you do choose default and categories I would strongly suggest that you also check the box next to **include starred in Primary**, simply for the reason if you have gone out of the way to star it or make a filter to do it then you clearly want to see it as a priority. You wouldn't want your starred email to be buried in social for example.

When you choose **Default** you can choose what Gmail category inboxes you want to implement. Here is a break down.

Gmail's category inboxes (tabs on the homepage)

Google has a set of category inboxes which can be used to automatically categorize your emails as they come in. They will appear above your message list on the homepage and all you need to do is click on the tab to see the emails.

You can activate or remove Gmail category inboxes (which appear as tabs above your message list) from two places:

> **Location 1. Gear Wheel > Configure inbox**
>
> **Location 2. Gear Wheel > Settings > Inbox (as long as Default is selected in the first option)**

To configure your inboxes, you need to use the inbox types detailed in the section in the **Inbox tab** located in the main Gmail settings, i.e. **Gear Wheel > Settings > Inbox**

The primary tab

Your primary tab, is the first tab you will see when you open your inbox. It should have all the emails that Google thinks are important to you. If Google cannot classify emails, then they will also go into here.

The social tab

Google will put any emails from social networks in this tab to stop them cluttering up your primary inbox. These can be from Facebook and Twitter to Goodreads.

The promotions tab

The promotions tab is for all those emails offering you deals on your favorite stores that you signed up for in the past. If you don't want these but you remember signing up in the first place then you can usually unsubscribe by going to the bottom of the open email to locate and click on the word **unsubscribe**. If you didn't sign up for the emails then feel free to mark them as spam. There are instructions for how to do this in *Chapter 4 Security*.

The updates and forums tab

The emails categorized as updates are usually confirmations, receipts, bills, and statements. Emails put into the forums category are usually from mailing lists or forums.

Important first

The **Important first** inbox type puts important emails at the top and everything else below. This has the benefit of only having the one inbox. However you will have to trust what Google considers important mail. Creating filters for emails you know are coming could affect this.

If you only have a few emails, then this could be the answer. If you have been using your Gmail account for a while and have consistently organized your email with filters and generally used your account, Google will be able to make more accurate guesses for what is important to you.

If you hover your mouse over the yellow arrow next to the check box in your email discussion, Google will explain why it thinks the emails are important. You can click on the

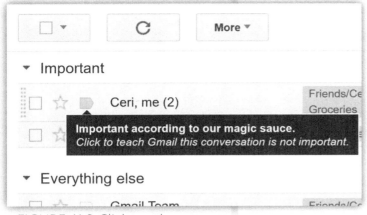

FIGURE 11.8 Click on the arrow to show it is not important.

arrow to let Gmail know it isn't important.

When the arrow is yellow it denotes that the email is important. Even if an email is not important the arrow is there but it has no color. If you want to mark an email important, click on the arrow and it will turn yellow.

The different options in the Inbox unread count didn't change the inboxes in the tests I undertook so I would leave these options as they are when you find them.

Unread first

The **Unread first** inbox type does what it says. Any email that you have not read yet will appear at the top of your inbox. Again, you will only have the one inbox to look through. This is a good way to use Gmail if you use your email with a task based approach (you assess an email and deal with it immediately or later). With this option you will see new emails first and can deal with these straight away. After this you can tuck in to the emails that you have read but that don't need immediate action.

The different options in the Inbox unread count didn't change the inboxes in the tests I undertook so I would leave these options as they are when you find them.

Starred first

FIGURE 11.9 Starred emails are grouped together unless they are marked as important.

All emails that you star or have starred by Gmail using filters will appear at the top of the list and everything else separated underneath. This option also means that you only have the one inbox to look through.

If you have a lot of starred emails, it could get a little annoying to scroll through lots of email before you get to new emails. However if you star emails you are working on or only have a few, then this could be a good option for organizing your email.

It is possible to prioritize your starred email by clicking on the star beside the email you want to mark important. If you keep clicking on the star you will scroll through the options you set in the general settings. As you can see in *figure* 11.9, Gmail will group the stars of the same type together. If any email are marked important then they will still rise to the top of the list.

The order that you have the stars in the settings will set the importance in the starred list. The first stars are the least important while the last star you drag and drop will become the most important.

Priority inbox

This leaves the Priority inbox. In this view items that Google thinks are most important will appear at the top. Click on **Priority inbox** next to the inbox type to activate it and then **Save Changes**.

Even though Google will try to prioritize your email, you can also dictate inbox sections by clicking on **Options** next to the appropriate section (see *figure 11.10* for more details).

If you click on **Options** or **Add section**, you will have the options in *figure* 11.10. You can choose the Gmail standard inbox settings or you can add your own section based on labels you have created. You can also choose how many emails will be displayed and whether you want to hide or remove a section.

When you click **Save Changes**, your inbox will instantly show the changes you made.

Your inbox can be customized further, once you have chosen the priority inbox. You can choose how it is laid out with the following sections:

- Important and unread
- Starred
- Empty
- Everything else

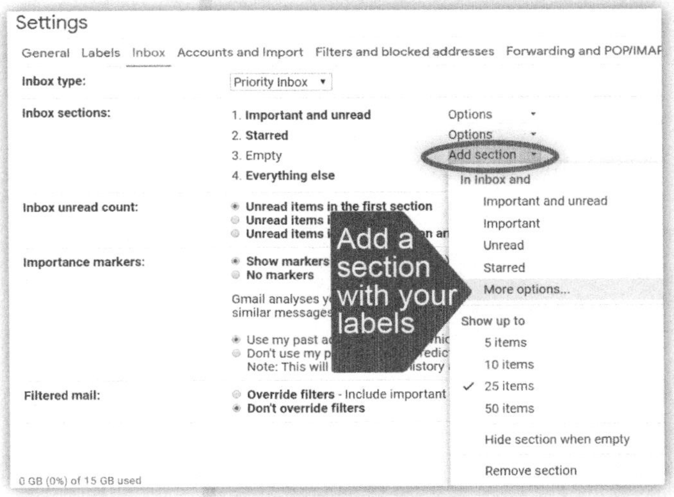

By clicking on **Options** to the right of these sections you

147

FIGURE 11.10 Prioritize with your own labels.

can change how many emails appear in each section. The third section can be the most powerful and interesting way of personalizing Gmail. Click **Add Section** and you can choose a label as a section under **More options**. This means that you can have all your emails about a certain subject right there in full view in your inbox. If you have set up filters so that your inbox is bypassed, you will see the newest five emails on the subject of your choice.

You can bypass filters by using the **Filtered mail** section of the inbox settings. This will include emails that Google feels is important to you even if you have filtered them out.

Accounts and import

This section is for changing your password, importing your old email from another provider, changing how your name appears when someone gets your email, granting access to your account and adding storage.

Change account settings (including password)

You should always have different passwords for different websites. However, Google allows you to have one password for all of its services. For the purposes of your password, Gmail, Google Drive, Google Docs, Google Sheets etc. *are all one website*. You will need to change this password from time to time. Perhaps it has been used on a different website such as a store and has been compromised, or the password just needs changing. Clicking on **Change password** allows you to do this. To get to this section go to:

Gear wheel > Settings > Settings > Accounts and import > Change password

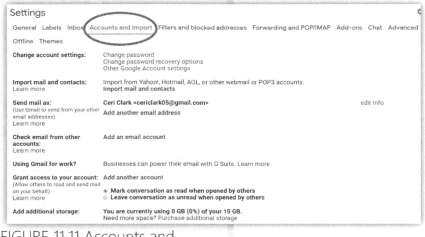

FIGURE 11.11 Accounts and Import Overview

148

If you forget your password you will need to have made sure that your recovery settings are updated. The second option (**Change password recovery options**) in this section will take you to a page where you can tell Google about a phone number or an alternative email address in the rare circumstance that you have forgotten your password. This is very important because if something happens to your account you will not be able to get in unless you set up the recovery options.

The **Other Google Account settings** points to a menu page where you can access your Google account settings which will affect all Google services including Google Drive, Docs, Sheets, Gmail etc. It is worth having a look around these pages even though they are not strictly Gmail related.

Import mail and contacts

Please see *Importing mail and contacts in Chapter 3. Getting started* for detailed instructions for how to import your emails and contacts from other email addresses you have previously owned.

You can stop the importing (if you took the option to import new messages daily for 30 days) by clicking on **stop** to the right of the email address or import from another address you may have by following the instructions again.

Send Mail As

You may have several email addresses which you may want to keep but only wish to send email from your Gmail account. This can be done in the **Accounts and Import** section under **Send mail as**. This will mean that you can choose to send from email addresses you already have access to from Gmail, but the recipient will think you sent it from somewhere else. It also means that all your sent email will be in the one place for ease of searching.

Send Mail As may not work for all your email accounts. For example, for this book I tested a Gmail and a Yahoo account for this feature. While the other Gmail account worked perfectly the first time, the Yahoo account refused

11

to work until I allowed **apps that use less secure sign-in** to access it. If you do try out these instructions and they do not work, you can use Gmailify which in effect does the same thing. When it is set up and you send an email from Gmail (selecting your yahoo account as the from address), when the recipient gets the email it will look like it was sent from your Yahoo account. This means that Gmailify is an alternative if **Send Mail As** does not work for a particular email. Please see **Check mail from other accounts (using POP3 & Gmailify)** in the next section for instructions on how to get to and use *Gmailify*.

As you would expect the email address you just created is already there. To add another one, click on **Add another email address** you own. A pop up will appear giving you a wizard to follow:

1. Enter your name and email address that you already own or have permission to access

2. Decide what name you want to be displayed in your recipient's email software against your emails. Tick the box (**Treat as an alias**), if you are emailing on someone else's behalf or one of your other email addresses and you want replies to go to the other inbox and not yours)

3. Type in your username and password from your other account and click on **Add account**

4. Next, verify your email address. Enter the verification code that Google has sent to your other email address. Google does not want unauthorized people sending from your other accounts. It also ensures that if someone tried to do this for your account without you knowing you are notified that someone is trying to access it. You or the person you are allowing access to your account will receive an email checking to see if they are okay with this. They or you need to click the confirmation link in the email address. If there is a problem with the link, there is a verification code as well. The easiest way by far is to click the link though. After you click on the link, click on **Confirm** and your two accounts are linked.

FIGURE 11.12 Step 1 is to type in your name and email address.

5. Once you have verified the access, log back in to your Gmail account. If you go back to your **Accounts and Import** section in the settings you will see **make default**, **edit info** and **delete**. Only click on **Make default** if you want this to be your primary address, the one that you want to receive and send emails with. Otherwise you will get the option of which email you want to use each time you compose an email

Make sure under the **When replying to a message** that you choose the **Reply from the same address to which the message was sent**. Otherwise, life can get very confusing for you and your recipient. They won't know where they should be emailing and you may give out an email address you wouldn't want a stranger, for example, to know about.

You are now set up. When you next compose a message in the **From** field where your email address appears, you can now select the new address if you so wish simply by selecting the little arrow to the right of the email address.

Check mail from other accounts (using Gmailify & POP3)

Gmailify and POP3 are other ways of sending and receiving emails from another account. Even more ways are to a) import your emails and contacts and either use your new email address as is, and b) use the **Send mail as** featured through Gmail.

Using POP3 to import email means that you can import the email from other email addresses you have just created or from another address to this one on a regular basis but all folders won't be the same on *every* device you use. If you send from a different device then the emails from that device won't be replicated in your webmail account for example. You won't have copies everywhere.

Gmailify means you can send email from your Gmail

If you or someone else is sending as an alias please be aware that the sent email will not be duplicated across accounts. This means that the email will not be in both sent items but will only appear in the email account you are emailing from, not the one you are pretending to email from.

11

Add another email address that you own

Send emails through your SMTP server

Configure your emails to be sent through yahoo.co.uk SMTP servers Learn more

SMTP Server: smtp.mail.yahoo.co.uk   Port: 465 ▾
Username: *Your Yahoo Username*
Password: •••••••••*<Your Yahoo Password>*
  ◉ Secured connection, using SSL **(recommended)**
  ○ Secured connection using TLS

Cancel   « Back   **Add Account »**

FIGURE 11.13 Type in your username and password from your other account.

151

Add another email address that you own

Confirm verification and add your email address

Congratulations, we've successfully located your other server and verified your credentials. Just one more step!

An email with a confirmation code was sent to *youremailaddress@yahoo.com*. [Resend email]
To add your email address, do one of the following:

| Click the link in the confirmation email | **OR** | Enter and verify the confirmation code |
| | | [_____] **Verify** |

Close window

FIGURE 11.14 Confirm that it is you setting up the link.

account but it will look like it was from your other account. The emails will be the same in your other account, e.g. be in the **Sent Mail** and your will get the great spam protection that Gmail offers.

On the other hand, you may as well just use Gmail on the web for convenience if you don't want to use Gmailify, IMAP, POP3 or Send Mail as.

If you do decide you want to use POP3, then please see the following tutorial. You can add up to five accounts.

Please note if you are importing emails using POP, you will need to make sure that it is enabled and configured from **Gear Wheel** > **Settings** > **Forwarding and POP/IMAP**.

Please take a look at the **Forwarding and POP/IMAP** section further along this chapter for more information.

Adding an Account

First, next to **Check email from other accounts**, click on **Add an email account**.

Type in your email address and then choose to link your accounts with Gmailify or import emails using POP3.

Follow the relevant instructions for Gmailify and POP3 below.

Gmailify instructions

Using Gmailify has the same first few steps as the POP3 option.

- Type in the email address that you want to import from and click on **Next** (*figure 11.10*)
- Click on **Link accounts with Gmailify** (*figure 11.15*).

152

- Click on the account you want to link
- Sign in to your other email account
- Click on **Agree**. You will see the following message:

> **You've been Gmailified!**
>
> **You can now manage your** *yourotheremailaddress* **emails from Gmail. Better spam protection and email categories will help keep your inbox clean.**

Your account should then be linked and you will be able to check this in the Gmail settings. To use your linked email account when you next compose a new message, click on the **From** box and choose the email address from the selection.

You can unlink at any time by going to **Gear wheel > Settings > Settings > Accounts and import** in Gmail.

POP3 instructions

Please note if you are importing from another Gmail account you will need to make sure that POP email is enabled from **Gear Wheel > Settings > Forwarding and POP/IMAP**. This is an important security feature as this setting could be used by hackers. Google has bypassed this by making sure you are the one to enable the feature.

- Type in the email address that you want to import from and click on **Next**
- Click on **Import emails form my other account (POP3)**
- Type in your username and password and select what you want Gmail to do to your emails and click on **Add Account**

Using Gmail for work?

Google does ask if you are using Gmail for work and refers you to their apps accounts. They do not guarantee anything with a free account. After all it is free and they are running a business. If you want more 'protection' then a paid apps system may be the way to go. Gmail can be sufficient for sole traders but you would need to read the terms and conditions of use to make a fully informed decision of what service you want to use.

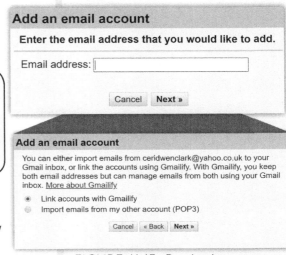

FIGURE 11.15 Beginning steps for adding an account.

11

Grant access to your account (Delegation)

Another interesting and useful feature is **Grant Access to your Account**. This should only be done where there is the utmost trust involved but if you have a family member who doesn't really use email but they still need an account then this is a great way to help them. Another possible use is if you are a couple and want to use one account for accessing services. Instead of setting up forwarding for the emails sent by your electricity supplier why not have a joint account to which you both have access? You can of course remove access by a click of a button if you need to regain control.

Add additional storage

When you have used your account for some time, you may feel you need more space. Click on **Purchase additional storage** for the latest prices and limits on offer by Google.

Filters and blocked addresses

Please see **Chapter 8 Filters and Blocked Addresses** for more information on this. If you just need to find them, go to the gear wheel on the top right of the screen >**Settings** > **Filters and Blocked Addresses**.

Forwarding and POP/IMAP

It is possible to forward all your email to another email address. For example if you would like your email to be forwarded to your work email address (or the other way around), then this is one possible way.

To find the options go to the gear wheel on the top right of the screen > **Settings** > **Forwarding and POP/IMAP** as illustrated in *figure* 11.16.

Forwarding

To add a forwarding address:

- Click on the gray box with the words **Add a forwarding address**. A pop up will appear asking you to add an address, type it in

- Click **Next**

- Click on **Proceed** and then **OK** and then go to the email account you specified

- Click on the link in the email sent to you from Gmail. A confirmation in a browser window will let you know you have been successful. If the link doesn't work, you will be able to use the code in the same email to confirm that the other email address is happy to receive the emails

POP download

POP mail is used for downloading into a desktop email application such as Outlook, Thunderbird, Postbox or MacMail. If this is a new email account, enabling POP for all mail if you want to use Outlook or another desktop client can be a good option. I would also recommend Archiving Gmail's copy in the drop down box. This means that when you visit the web version of Gmail you won't be overwhelmed with new email. You will know that it has been downloaded by the fact it is no longer in the inbox.

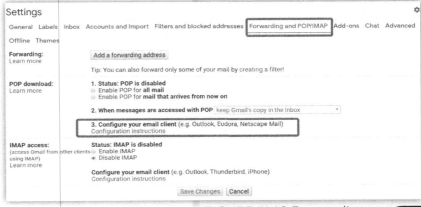

FIGURE 11.16 Forwarding and POP/IMAP

11

If you want to configure the settings on your particular email software, click on **Configure instructions** as seen in *figure 11.16*.

IMAP access

This is recommended over POP as instead of simply downloading your emails you can interact and sync it with both your email desktop application such as Outlook etc., apps on your mobile devices and the web version of Gmail. This means that if you move an email in Outlook to a folder it will appear labeled in Gmail as well as other ways of accessing your email and vice-versa.

Make sure IMAP is enabled by clicking **Enable IMAP** and then remember to save any changes you've made.

The key settings to remember for setting up your IMAP access on your device is imap.gmail.com using port 993 (with SSL) for the incoming server and the outgoing server should be smtp.gmail.com on port 587 (with SSL).

If you are using an apps account, then you will need the same settings. The device you are using may try to use the domain from your email address but ignore this and put the Gmail information in. For example don't let it put in imap.yourdomain.com, it should be imap.gmail.com.

For specific step-by-step instructions for using Gmail with Outlook, please check out **How do I add my Gmail account to Outlook** in *Chapter 17: Frequently Asked Questions*.

Add-ons

Add-ons are plugins that extend the functionality of Gmail. These are not made by Gmail and by adding these, you are giving third parties access to your account. They could, however streamline your working life from within Gmail, so it may be worth your while taking a look at some of these. Here is a brief description of some of the 100 add-ons available at the time of writing. The list of add-ons in Gmail will change over time, more will be added and others taken away. Some apps are only available in certain countries.

To uninstall any of the add-ons, go to the **Gear Wheel** > **Settings** > **Add-Ons** > **Manage** (the add-on) > **Options** > **Remove**.

Asana for Gmail Converts emails into tasks that can be worked on by a team to facilitate projects.

BuiltWith The BuiltWith add-on tracks technologies linked to the domains on emails you receive. This will give you information about the domain sending you emails.

Dialpad This is a phone service that works from inside Gmail using Google Voice.

Groove Gmail Add-on This application integrates your

Groove and Salesforce accounts with Gmail, connecting your CRM, inbox and calendar.

Hire This add-on is to help you in the recruitment process for your organization. It integrates with G-Suite tools such as Google Search, Gmail, Calendar, Docs, Sheets and Hangouts to streamline the hiring process.

MeisterTask for Gmail Use your MeisterTask account to turn emails into tasks and insert them into your project. The subject line and text content of the email will automatically be added to your task.

RingCentral for Gmail With your RingCentral account, you can see the online/offline status of your RingCentral contacts within your email threads in Gmail. From your emails, it allows you to take a look at their recent call history, make calls, and view and send SMS messages.

Smartsheet for Gmail Add-On Adds emails to spreadsheets. Add rows, comments and organize your attachments.

Sortd Gmail Add-on A light-weight CRM. This is a collaboration and organizational tool.

Streak CRM Add-on for Gmail Streak is designed for Sales, Recruiting, and Customer Support.

Trello for Gmail Converts your emails into tasks.

Wrike for Gmail Create and manage your tasks from your emails with Wrike.

Chat

If you enable this option then I would recommend you choose **Save chat history** so you have a record of what is said. You can always turn this off but if you need a 'paper trail' then this would let you know what was said and when.

Advanced (formerly Labs)

I would ignore this setting until you are completely familiar with the Gmail system. For more information on these, please see *Chapter 16: Advanced Options*.

Offline

Only enable this if you have an unsteady Internet connection or none for periods of time. Gmail is designed to be used online and works best this way.

Themes

There is more information on themes in *Chapter 10 Changing the Look and Feel.* However if you have jumped to this section you can change your theme by clicking on the picture you like in:

Gear wheel > **Settings** > **Themes**

Chapter summary

This is one of the largest chapters in this book as the settings have a wide ranging effect on Gmail and Google's other services. Many of the settings even have their own chapters in this book. Where information is discussed in more depth, the chapters are shown.

All the tabs within settings are explained within this chapter which include:

- General
- Labels
- Inbox
- Accounts and Import
- Filters and Blocked Addresses
- Forwarding and POP3/IMAP
- Add-ons
- Chat
- Labs
- Going Offline and
- Themes

Email Management

●●●●●●●●●●●●●●●●

Spending time setting up Gmail is only the beginning of keeping your email under control. If you have set up filters, labels and your settings correctly then you will only need to spend a few minutes each day going through what is important with only a few more minutes needed to deal with non-urgent matters.

Time management

To really get to grips with your emails, I would suggest spending 10 minutes of your time each morning to deal with your emails and an hour on a Monday or Friday morning to attend to new emails and keep them organized.

To make good use of your time, I recommend turning off email notifications. Before you say, "but I need to know when they arrive," do you? If you can schedule a time or times each day to check your mail, then you can give your emails the attention they deserve. You will be able to check when you are ready and not be at the mercy of your email.

Prioritize, prioritize, prioritize

I can't stress enough how important prioritization is for an organized inbox. Google gives you several tools for this, which includes filters but starring emails will prioritize emails within inboxes, whether created by Google or yourself.

Chapter 12

What to expect in this chapter:

- Strategies for time management
- Blending Gmail tools to best organize your emails

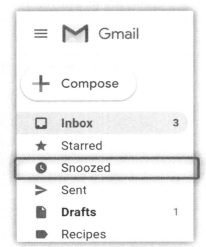

FIGURE 12.1 Location of your Snoozed emails.

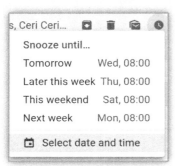

FIGURE 12.2 Snooze options

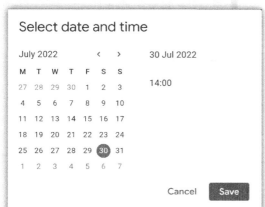

FIGURE 12.3 Choose a specific date and time in the future.

Starring emails

Star emails to be actioned. You can have different stars for how urgently the emails need to be dealt with. For example, an exclamation mark (this is still classed as a star), would be emails that need to be actioned within the next couple of days, a red star within the week, a blue star within the month and a yellow star to be dealt with by the end of 6 months. Anything that has to be sorted out immediately should already have been sorted out in your primary inbox.

If you can, set up filters that will automatically star email and sort them into the appropriate inbox. When you have dealt with your really urgent emails you will know that the less urgent emails will be there waiting and you will have a starting point for prioritizing further.

Snooze

The Snooze feature allows you to send an email away until you need to see or do something with it. You can even have it so that the email you want to snooze comes back repeatedly until you stop it. If you want to find your snoozed emails and it isn't back yet, just find the **Snoozed** link in the left menu. Press on the menu button (three horizontal lines) to see it on your mobile app.

1. Hover over an email, click on the clock symbol or select your email and choose the clock symbol from above the email list

2. Select from **Tomorrow**, **Later this week**, **This weekend** and **Next week** or click on **Select date & time**

3. You will need to pick a date and time if you chose the latter

4. Click on **SAVE**

On your mobile device, swipe your email left to snooze it. You will get the choice to snooze it to **tomorrow, later this week, this weekend, next week, select date and time** and you can select a particular date and time as well as place. The app will confirm that the email or reminder has been snoozed. Press on **Undo** and the snooze will be canceled.

Replying to messages

Knowing which emails you need to reply to can save you time. If you have been sent an email but it wasn't directed at you i.e. you were in the cc: box, the email is probably just for information. The sender will probably be very happy not to receive 200 messages from every recipient saying that they have received it.

You don't have to reply to every message that needs to be actioned straight away but you can use **Canned messages** to say thank you for your email (and that you will be dealing with it soon) using a filter to automatically send replies.

If you want to enable the canned response function, go to the cog or gear wheel on the top right of your Gmail screen, click on **Settings** then **Advanced**. Find **Canned Responses (templates)** and select **Enable** before clicking on **Save Changes** at the bottom of the page.

Now that Canned Responses are available on your Gmail account, start a new email and type in what you want in your canned reply into the email. This will become your template. You can use the usual formatting options, for example, bold, italics as well as including pictures and links. You can even include attachments. Remove any signature that you have set up in this email otherwise when you insert a new canned response you will get two signatures in the email.

On the bottom right of the email next to the picture of the trash can/bin, you will see a menu button. Select this and click on:

Canned responses > Save Draft as template > Save as new template...

A new window will load, prompting you to name your canned response. Choose a name that resonates with you.

Canned responses (templates)
Create a templated response by saving common messages using a button in the compose toolbar. Also automatically send templated responses using filters.

○ **Enable**
◉ **Disable**

FIGURE 12.4 Enable **Canned Responses** from **Advanced** in **Settings**.

12

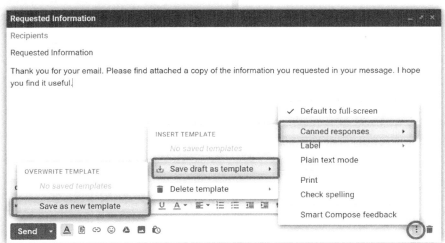

You might make a lot of these and you will want to be able to find it later. Click on **Save**.

If you made the canned message in response to a message, go ahead and click on **Send**. If you created the message from scratch to make a canned response to be used for later, delete the message you created. It will now be in your canned responses.

FIGURE 12.5 Create a canned response from a new message.

Replying with a Canned Response

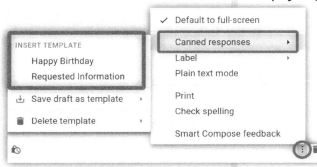

FIGURE 12.6 Where he templates are.

Click on **Reply** or start a new message. Go to the bottom right of your message and click on the menu button   next to the trash can/bin. Select **Canned Responses** and then choose a response from the list under INSERT TEMPLATE, that you want to reply with. *Figure 12.6* illustrates how to do this.

Editing/Overwriting a Canned Response

Unfortunately you cannot actually edit a canned response but you can overwrite it. Simply follow the steps to create a canned response as detailed above and then click on the name of the canned response in the list below **Overwrite template**. In short:

Canned responses > Save draft as template > Your template name to be overwritten

FIGURE 12.7 Where to delete a canned response.

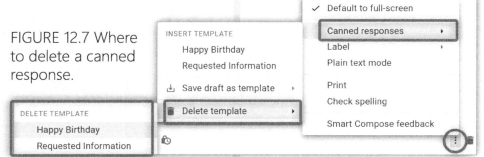

Deleting Canned Responses

Deleting a canned response is similar to overwriting one. Go to the menu button on the bottom right of a new email. Click on **Canned responses** and then **Delete template** and finally choose the canned response you want to delete under the light gray **DELETE TEMPLATE** as can be seen in *figure 12.6*.

Using filters to automatically send Canned Responses

If you have several canned responses, you can filter your emails so that when you get emails that meet certain criteria, they will get a canned response automatically.

In the following example I will walk you through how I would send canned responses to emails that I receive for review copies.

- Create your canned response (please see my instructions on how to do this earlier in the chapter)
- Go to the cog/gear wheel (top right of Gmail screen)
- Choose **Settings**
- Click on **Filters and blocked addresses**
- Scroll down and click on **Create a new filter** (bottom of screen)

For this example I typed in **Review** in the subject so that the filter will react to any emails that I get with Review in the subject. I then checked the box labeled **Has attachment**. You can just as easily put in email addresses.

- Click on **Create filter**

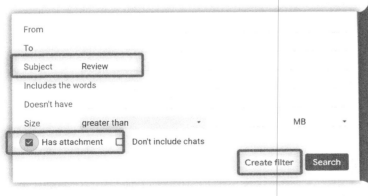

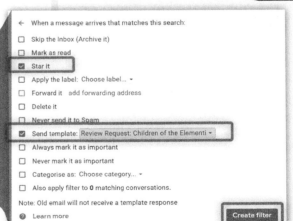

- On the next screen check the box next to **Send template** and choose the one you want to send for your

FIGURE 12.8 Creating a filter with a canned response.

search. At this point you can select other options like starring the emails so you can find and action them easier

In the above example I checked next to **Star it**. You can also **Always mark it as important**. Another option is to **skip the inbox** if the email needs acknowledgment but you don't need to do anything.

- Click on **Create filter**

Now any email that has review in the subject and also has an attachment will automatically get the canned response I selected.

Using the inbox tabs

The goal is to have only the important unread emails that you need to deal with in your inbox. Anything else should be in folders (labels) that you deal with when you have time.

Creating folders for your messages which do not have to be dealt with as soon as you open Gmail will mean that you will work on what matters first and then the rest in order of priority. While you can have several folders within folders for example, Newsletters, then Business Week Daily and possibly Reuters Money which could be Newsletters/BusinessWeekDaily and Newsletters/ReutersMoney, the aim is to quickly check these folders daily so you don't want to make work for yourself. I recommend having no more than three extra folders. Simplicity is the key. If you have too many folders and it gets too complicated, you just won't do it anymore. There are always far too many interesting things to do than dealing with your Gmail. Before I streamlined my email, my house received a regular lovely spring clean as a delaying tactic. My house is no longer as tidy but my email is now ultra organized!

The three labels/folders I would suggest are:

- Pending
- For Information
- Newsletters

The **Pending** folder will contain all the email that you need to deal with that are not important enough to be in the

Did you know...

If there are emails in the wrong tabs, then all you need to do is grab the email using your mouse and drag it to the appropriate tab before dropping it in it. You will be asked if you want all future emails from that address put into the new tab. I would recommend you do so unless the email you are dropping into it is a one-off.

Primary inbox, starred by importance.

The **newsletters** folder/label would have all your newsletters from different sources. Chances are you will not have time to read all the newsletters anyway as there are always more coming in than there is time to read. Just pick the most recent or that look the most interesting and delete the rest. Be honest with yourself, are you really going to read all those newsletters?

The **For Information** folder is for all email that you have been CC'd in. If you have been cc'd then the email was not sent to you directly. This means you can class it as not urgent because presumably whoever it was directed to is dealing with it. This means they can wait until you have time to look at them.

Your aim is that the above three folders should only have active emails in. If you only want to keep it in case you need it, file it somewhere. These folders are there to organize your mail not as storage. Set aside up to an hour on a Monday or Friday morning to sort emails out each week. If you follow all the advice in this book it could be reduced to as little as ten minutes. It will make you feel a lot better to finish the week or begin the week all organized!

Other Folders

Labeling is essential to keeping your emails organized in Gmail. Once emails have been dealt with and archived, you may want to get hold of them again. It will be a lot more efficient to find an email if you can search within a label as your Gmail account fills up.

Another reason to have other folders apart from having the inboxes as described earlier in this chapter is for family emails that you don't want distracting you during your working day.

Using filters with labels

I go into great depth on how to use filters in *Chapter 8:*

Filters and Blocked Addresses but if you only use filters with labels then you will still go a long way to organizing your mail. If you want to assign the label **Jobs** to all emails from your contact Jenny@WorkCorp.com, then go to:

the **cog/gear wheel** at the top right of the screen > **Settings** > **Filters and Blocked Addresses** > **Create a new filter**.

Type @WorkCorp.com (in case your contact from the company changes) into the **From** box and then click on **Create filter with this search**.

On the next screen check the box next to **Apply the label** and if you haven't already created the label, choose **New Label** where you can input the new name. Choose the label you want, **Jobs** in this example, (once it is created) and click on the box next to **Also apply filter to x matching conversations** before clicking on **Create filter**. This will then apply to all old emails already in your account and new email that you will receive in the future.

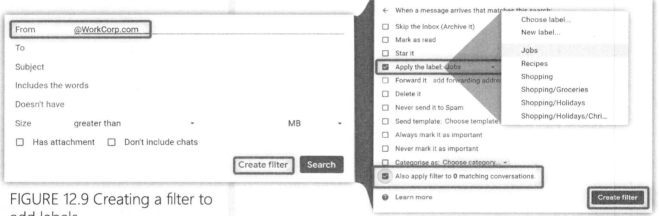

FIGURE 12.9 Creating a filter to add labels.

Setting up filters from related email in your inbox (Filter messages like these)

There is a quick way of creating filters straight from your inbox. This will save you an enormous amount of time.

- Check the box next to the emails that you want to filter,
- Click on **More**,
- Select **Filter messages like these**:

Gmail will populate the From field for you so any action you choose on the next screen will apply to any messages sent from the email addresses of the emails you originally selected.

- On the bottom right of the pop-up choose **Create filter**
- Choose what you want done with these type of emails. It will apply to all emails from that address. You can label, filter or even delete as soon as they come in
- If you want the action to apply to your existing emails, check the box next to **Also apply filter to x matching conversations**
- Click on **Create filter**

Unsubscribe from unwanted newsletters

You may have signed up to newsletters in the past that you may no longer want. You can unsubscribe manually using the instructions at the bottom of emails. This is not always a reliable method as there are some disreputable companies that don't always unsubscribe you.

If you definitely did not sign up to the email and there are no unsubscribe links in the email, click on the spam button at the top of the email.

Chapter summary

People can only ever give you advice on how to deal with your email. Organizing your email is a highly personal thing. What works for you does not necessarily work for someone else. You may prefer to have all your emails in a subject together as a discussion while another may want to turn this feature off (possible in Gmail) and have each email come in separately so you can see instantly what needs to be done.

It is possible you do not receive many emails at all, in which case I am very jealous, but this does make much of this chapter irrelevant. Maybe all you need is the Google inbox tabs or you are happy to turn them off and deal with

Did you know...

You can use **Filter messages like these** to delete a lot of emails from the same person at once. Check on an email in your inbox, Select the menu button above the email list, then **Filter messages like these** and then click on **Search**. You can then just delete all the emails in the search results.

FIGURE 12.10 Report spam to Google by clicking on this button.

12

emails as they come in. There is no correct way to deal with email only what works for you.

Organizing your email is a continual process, using the **Filter messages like these** option will make this easier but there will always be the odd email which doesn't fit into any category. Unsubscribing and the spam button are also important tools in your fight to keep your emails under control.

Using all of the tips in this chapter will not only save you time but will make you work more efficiently.

Chat

● ● ● ● ● ● ● ● ● ● ● ● ● ● ● ●

Gmail gives you the option to chat to your contacts. Chat has changed over the years and the new chat is based on Google Hangouts. The name may change over time to reflect this, so if Chat does disappear from your settings, it may have changed its name to Hangouts.

Sometimes you might want to get an answer quickly and if you see that your contact is online, it can be faster to open a text or video chat rather than send an email and wait for a response. If Chat is not visible at the bottom of the left navigation pane on the Gmail homepage you will need to turn on Chat first from the settings.

What to expect in this chapter:

- Turning on Chat
- Inviting contacts to chat
- Video, phone or text chat

Turning on Chat

The Chat function can be found in the left navigation bar on your Gmail homepage. You will need to invite someone to chat in the first instance but after that, your contact will be in the chat list.

1. Go to the **gear wheel** at the top right of the screen, this is the main settings button
2. Click on **Settings**
3. On the top row, select **Chat**
4. Turn chat on by choosing **Chat on**
5. Click **Save Changes** at the bottom of the screen

Inviting a contact to chat

The chat section of Gmail is on the bottom left of the Gmail screen, always available even when you are typing emails. If you can't see Chat and you know it is enabled,

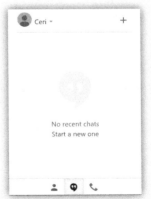

FIGURE 13.1 Chat is located at the bottom left of the Gmail homepage.

169

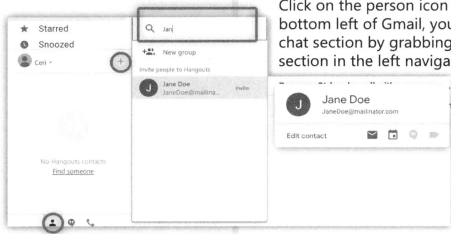

Click on the person icon (see *figure* 13.2) at the bottom left of Gmail, you may need to expand the chat section by grabbing the line under the **More** section in the left navigation bar and dragging up.

To add a contact, click on the person symbol at the bottom of the screen (the first button). Either click on **Find someone** or the button with the plus sign on it which is beside your profile picture in the chat section (they do the same thing).

FIGURE 13.2 Invite your contact to be able to chat with them.

Type your contact's name, email address or phone number in the search box. Google will look through your contacts in your Gmail account or contact them through the email address.

Before you can contact the person, they will be notified that you are trying to contact them for the first time. They will have to allow this before you can start chatting.

Accepting an invite

Click on the speech icon. The middle button on the bottom of the chat window. Please see *figure* 13.1 for what this looks like.

Invitations will appear at the top of the list with a picture of an open envelope. Click on this to get the invitation pop-up. Click on **Accept**.

Chat Overview

Chat can look different depending on what browser you are using. *Figure* 13.3 shows the active chat window in Google's Chrome while *figure* 13.4 shows what it looks like in Vivaldi. The Vivaldi version is the same as the last edition of Gmail which means Gmail is slowly replacing it with the new version as Chrome is the recommended browser. From now on I will refer to the Chrome version.

The active chat window will pop up when you click on your contact's name in the chat section of the left navigation bar on the Gmail homepage.

To start a text chat, start typing in the box at the bottom (see *figure 13.3 and 13.4*). You can add emoticons by clicking on the smiley face to the left of the box.

Attach an image by clicking on the square on the right of the box.

Above the conversation, you can click on the video camera icon to start a video call.

To chat to more than one person, select the person icon with the plus next to it or in the left navigation pane in the Chrome version.

If you want to have the chat in its own browser window, choose the pop out button on the top right, next to the minimize and exit buttons. This is useful if you are chatting to more than one person at a time.

Hamburger Menu button

This button (marked as Settings in figure 13.3) will give you the same options that you get when you click

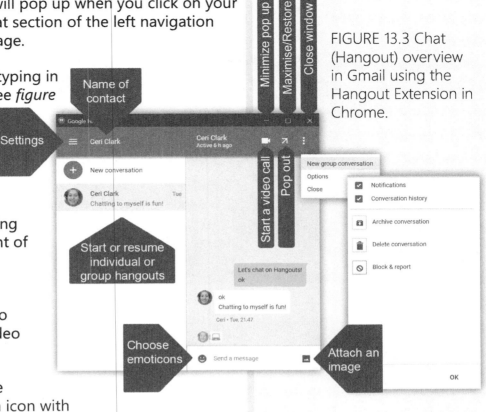

FIGURE 13.3 Chat (Hangout) overview in Gmail using the Hangout Extension in Chrome.

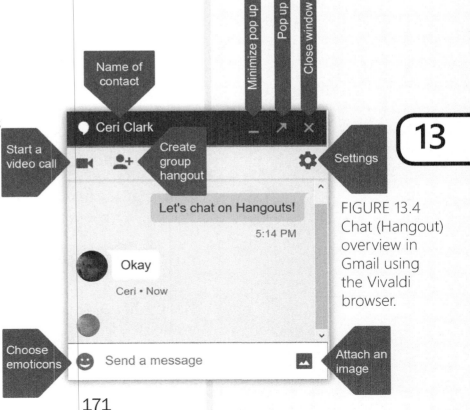

FIGURE 13.4 Chat (Hangout) overview in Gmail using the Vivaldi browser.

13

on someone's name in the chat window on the Gmail homepage.

From here, you can add or change your availability status, configure your notifications, hangout settings and other general settings.

Status

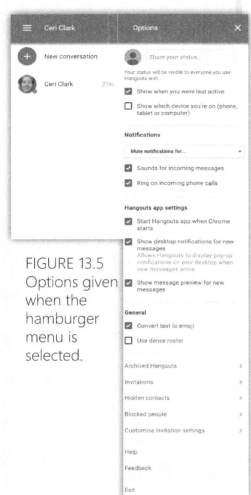

FIGURE 13.5 Options given when the hamburger menu is selected.

Type in your status whether busy, exploring a jungle or just chilling, This is next to your profile picture (if you have one) or otherwise the person icon as seen at the top of *figure* 13.5.

Beside your profile picture you can type in a status that you want your contacts to see. This can be busy, away from the desk or even a time frame such as, I will be back in ten minutes.

Directly underneath your status you can allow your contacts to see when you were last active, what device you are on and when you are talking to someone else.

The second option may not be a good idea as it may show you are out and about and not in your office or home. However, this information is only showed to people you are in contact with on Google hangouts so this may not be a problem.

Notification settings

The next options are notifications. This will mute your notifications for a period of time from one hour to one week. You are able to differentiate this option between muting your messages and/or phone calls.

Hangout app settings

This is where you can specify that Hangouts will open whenever you start Chrome. If Chat is an integral way that you communicate with people this may be a good idea but it could be annoying having windows open that you don't always use.

Allowing desktop notifications means that Google will try to get your attention with bleeps and the icon will flash in Windows. Chat will have to open in Chrome though.

Tick the box next to **Show message preview** for new messages, if you like to have an idea of what people are saying before you open the chat window fully. If you are busy, glancing to the bottom left of your Gmail screen will seem more efficient than having to do those extra clicks to see if it was worth taking the time now or later.

General

There are two settings under **General** at the time of writing. The first is to convert text to emoji. This means if you type :) then Chat will convert it to a smiley face.

The other option is to use dense roster. This is useful if you have lots of conversation on the go as they take up less space in your left navigation bar. They make your interface denser.

Use dense roster will tidy up your view of chat in the left navigation bar. It will remove avatars and recent messages giving a cleaner, less cluttered look.

Other Settings in the Chat hamburger menu

Click on the following links from the hamburger menu to find lists of:

- Archived Hangouts
- Invitations
- Hidden contacts
- Blocked people

Customize invitation settings.

Selecting **Recommended** under **Customize invite settings** will allow people who already have your contact details to send you a message directly. If they don't have any way of already contacting you then they must send you an invite. Using the recommended setting could save you from missing a message from a friend or colleague.

You can choose to let people contact you directly if they already have your email address or phone number. Alternatively you can choose to allow people with this information to either contact you directly or send you an invitation.

Bear in mind that people can guess your email address or phone (maybe get it from a hacked website on the Internet) and sometimes try to chat to you through Chat. These may be people you would rather not contact such as spammers or hackers. They may try to scam or just sell you something you don't want. I would recommend using the invitation option. If you recognize their name, profile picture or details, then you can always accept an invitation.

Menu button (three vertical dots)

New Group Conversation

This is self-explanatory, click on this to start a new group conversation. Start typing their names for Chat to go looking through Google Contacts (your address book) for you. Choose who you want to talk to and then click on **CREATE GROUP**.

Options

Options are where you can find your:

- **Notifications** Checking this will let you know that you have received a new chat message
- **Conversation history** Checking this means you can keep your old conversations
- **Archive conversation** Get rid of them temporarily but still be able to get at them
- **Delete conversation** Remove conversations permanently
- Block & report Stop people from contacting you

Archiving or deleting conversations

The menu button on the Chrome extension on the top right of the pop up will give you the options button. This allows you to archive or delete your conversation.

Deleting or archiving the conversation will only remove it from your own account. Delete the conversation if you want to permanently remove it. Archive the discussion if you want it to be available in searches in Gmail later.

Close

This closes your current conversation not Chat completely.

Searching your Chat history

Using text chat through Gmail does not mean you lose a record of your conversations with your contacts. As long as you do not delete your conversations then they are search-able within Gmail itself at the same time as you search for your emails.

When you find a relevant chat while you are searching your emails, if you click into the discussion, there is a button at the bottom of the conversation marked **Open Hangout**. This will open the chat window and you can resume the conversation.

Blocking contacts

If you would like the option of blocking a person you are chatting to, this could be particularly useful for ex-boyfriends/girlfriends, you can do this by the following method.

Click on **Ignore** at the bottom of the invite, you can then choose to **Report** or **Block** the person contacting you. Click **OK** for this to take affect.

You also do not have to accept invites to connect.

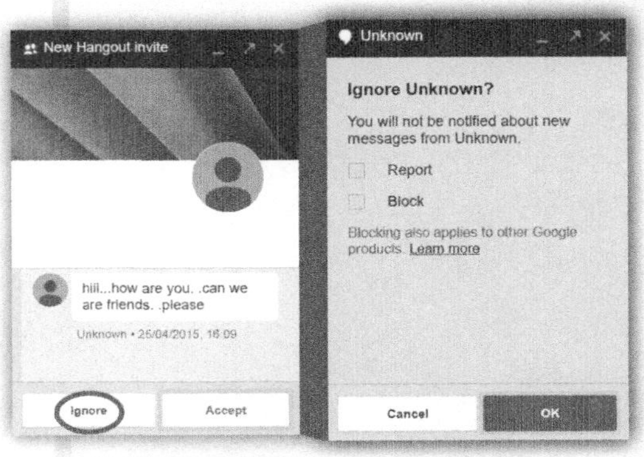

FIGURE 13.6 You can Block a contact by clicking on Ignore on the invite.

Video, phone or text chat

Whether you want to video, phone or text chat depends on the circumstances at the time you are trying to contact them. This could be anything from having a bad hair day, a work from home and forgot accidentally-on-purpose to take off my pajamas and wear work clothes day or more seriously, the other person is busy and you can type a message and you don't mind waiting for an answer. People will usually respond to chat messages a lot quicker than email.

If you click on the video icon then the hangout window will load. To call, click on the phone symbol and to text, just start typing.

Chapter summary

When you need to contact someone in a hurry through text chat or a phone call or you want a more personal way of communicating through a video call, Google's chat provides this through the integration of Google Hangouts into Gmail with the moniker Chat.

You cannot contact anyone without their permission, whether that is through them allowing you to contact them because you already have their phone number or email address or they have accepted your invitation to talk. If you do not want to connect with someone you can block or report them.

Chats can be deleted but if you keep or archive them then they are searched at the same time as your emails. There are numerous settings within chat which can be turned on or off depending on your needs. Chat can be a more immediate way of contacting friends, family or co-workers. You can let people know with the status option if you are busy or available to talk.

Google Tasks & Google Keep

●●●●●●●●●●●●●●●●

Google has improved Gmail by making it possible to use their Tasks and Keep services directly from Gmail. Google Tasks and Keep are great organizing tools that will make your life easier. Read on for getting the most of them using Gmail.

Google Tasks

Tasks are a great way of remembering lists of things to do. As long as you have access to the Internet you can add, edit and delete from your task list wherever you are. Whether on your smartphone or on your computer at home, use tasks to organize your life.

How to get to Google Tasks from Gmail

In Gmail, find and click on the Google Tasks symbol in the right navigation pane. If you cannot see the pane, there is an arrow located on the right of your screen as circled in *figure 14.1*. Click on it to make the Tasks icon visible in a list down the side. To collapse the list, click on the arrow again. Select the Tasks icon, (a tick on a blue background) to open the Tasks pane.

When you first open Tasks you will get a welcome screen. Click through this and you will be given the option to add a task. Click on Add a task (see *figure 14.2*) if you want to get started straight away. However before you do this, consider how you want to organize your tasks. You may want to have tasks under different lists. You could have a list for home and another for work and have different tasks under each. In a business or school scenario you might want to have different lists for different projects. The sky is

What to expect in this chapter:

- Getting the most out of Tasks
- Creating tasks
- Deleting tasks
- Organizing tasks
- How to get to Google Keep
- Google Keep Overview
- Making notes
- Archiving and deleting notes
- Pinning

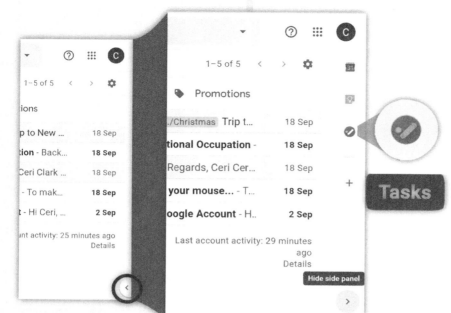

FIGURE 14.1 Tasks location

Creating a list

Creating a list is great for compartmentalizing your tasks for easy organization. Here's how to do it:

- Click on the arrow next to **My Tasks** (above + **Add a task**), as seen in *figure 12.2*

- Select **Create a New List**.

- Type in your title and click on **Done**.

Once you have created the Task you will be immediately be taken to the list and you can start making tasks but to find your Task list at a different time, click on the arrow next to **My Tasks** and choose the list and all the tasks you've added to it will load.

Deleting or renaming your list

Lists don't last for ever and you may want to delete them or re-purpose them by changing the name.

To either delete or rename your list, go into the list that you want to change or get rid of by clicking on the arrow next to **My Tasks** as circled in *figure* 14.2.

Next, look for the menu button (three vertical dots) beside + Add a task. Choose either, **Rename list** or **Delete list**.

Adding a task to a list

Before you add a new task, check that you are in the correct list at the top of the Tasks panel. If not, click on the arrow next to **My Tasks** and you can choose the right list.

To add a task, choose + **Add a task** the first time and then subsequently next to a circle as seen in *figure 14.3* and start typing. After you've made the first task you can then click on the + **Add a Task** button at the top of the pane to make the next task or just press enter to start another one.

If you want to add more details to a task (such as a due date) click on the pencil symbol (see *figure 11.4*) to the right of the task you've created and the page in *figure 11.5* will load. If you cannot see the pencil, hover your mouse over the task.

Click on the arrow on the top left of the Tasks pane to get back to your Tasks list. It will automatically save what you've changed.

In the details page you can:

- Change the title
- Add a description and other notes
- Change the list the task is under
- Add or change the date and time it's due
- Add a submenu

Change the title.

Alter your title here.

Add a description and other notes

Add a description or some notes to this section. If you want to do a list like a shopping list, adding a submenu is better as you can mark them as completed as you do them.

Change the list

Click on the arrow next to the list that is displayed and you will be given the option to change it to a list you have already made or create a new one.

Add or amend the date and time

Select **Add date** to bring up a mini-calendar where you

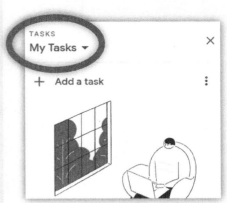

FIGURE 14.2 Add your lists first.

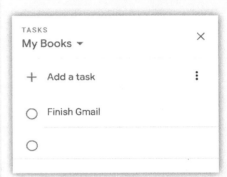

FIGURE 14.3 Add your first tasks.

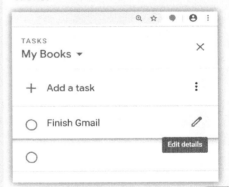

FIGURE 14.4 Edit a task.

14

FIGURE 14.5 Editing tasks options.

can choose what date you want to do the task by. The date you choose will appear in the list under the relevant task. You can also sort the list by date.

Adding in a date will also mean that your task will appear in Google Calendar on the date you have chosen. This means that if you use Google Calendar in Schedule mode, your day will already be organized for you.

When you choose your date and time you can also decide if you want to do it as a repeating task.

Add a submenu

This is where you can add mini-tasks that need to be done to complete the main task. For example if you are going shopping for groceries, you would add the individual items as subtasks. This will mean that as you maybe order the items online you can tick them off as you add them to your shopping cart. This could possibly be a great way to organize your Christmas presents! Add them through the year and tick them off as you buy them. Subitems will appear indented in the list.

If you have a project you could add items that you need to do to complete the project as a project management tool. *Figure* 14.6 demonstrates how this could be done.

Different parts of the project could be assigned to a task and this can be broken down further using a submenu. Each submenu item can be amended to add dates and notes. Simply hover over the submenu item to get the pencil icon and click on it to get the details page. In this page you can also move it to a different list.

The only downside is that you can only add one level of subitem. This means that you may have to make your strategy for dealing with your project simpler than you might otherwise do but with a bit of planning it is possible within Google Tasks. If you find that you need more sub-items and creating more lists is not an option or breaking it down to more initial tasks then you may need to use a more powerful task management tool.

Move items up or down

You can also move tasks by hovering over the tasks and 'grabbing' the tasks or subtask and moving it up or down with your mouse.

Tasks Menu

The tasks menu is located by +Add a task near the top of the Tasks pane as illustrated in *figure 14.7*.

Sorting by due date

If you have put dates to your tasks, see what you need to complete first by clicking on the menu button beside your list name.

You can choose to sort by your order or by date order.

Rename and delete list

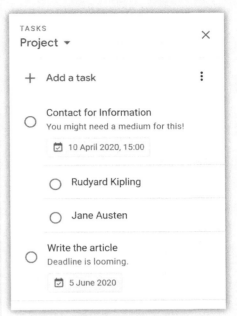

FIGURE 14.6 Using Tasks as a project management tool.

14

FIGURE 14.7 Location of Tasks menu

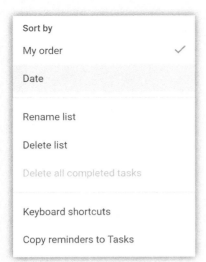

Sort by	
My order	✓
Date	
Rename list	
Delete list	
Delete all completed tasks	
Keyboard shortcuts	
Copy reminders to Tasks	

FIGURE 14.8 Task Menu options

Go to the list that you want to edit (click on the arrow next to **My Tasks** or the list you are in). Then, select the menu button as seen in *figure 14.7* and choose the action you want to take.

In this menu you can also delete all your completed tasks in one go. You can individually delete completed tasks by hovering your mouse over them and clicking on the trash can/bin symbol.

Completing a task

To complete a task simply check the box next to the subject. It will move to the bottom of the list and the text will have a line through it so you know you've done it.

Deleting or removing a task

To remove a task, click on the task and click on the pencil to bring up the details panel. Here select the trash can (bin) symbol at the top of the task window. Also see **Delete completed tasks** in the Tasks menu to remove completed tasks.

Print your tasks

Previously, it was possible to print tasks but with the new update, you will have to print them as part of your schedule in Google Calendar.

Here are some instructions to print your schedule in Google Calendar:

- Go to Google Calendar by clicking on the waffle menu at the top right of Gmail. It looks like a square made of 9 small squares.
- Next to the waffle menu in Google Calendar click on the drop-down menu and choose **Schedule**.
- At the top right of the screen click on the cog wheel and choose **Print**. You will be shown a Print preview.
- Choose your options and then press **Print** at the bottom of the screen.

Briefly the options available are:

- **Print range** (choose the dates you want to print from)
- **Font size** (how big you want the text to appear in your print out)
- **Orientation** (Do you want it portrait or landscape),
- **Show events that you've declined** (Shows ALL your events)
- **Black and white** (Takes away any color)
- **Print descriptions** (Adds extra information you've added)
- **Print end times** (Prints when you have to complete the event)
- **Print attendee**s (Who is going to any events you've set up)
- **Print your response** (If you've responded, these will be added to the print out).

View completed tasks

This is useful if you just want to see what you have completed/organized. Once you click on the circle to mark it completed a new option will appear below your tasks list called **Completed** with the number of tasks you have completed beside it.

To expand the list click on the arrow next to completed as see in *figure 14.9*.

Hover over the completed tasks to have the option of deleting them by clicking on the trash can/bin symbol or clicking on the tick to ping it back to the list above.

Clear completed tasks

Click on the trash can/bin symbol beside your completed task. To clear all the completed tasks in one go, select the menu button under the cross at the top right of the tasks bar and choose **Delete all completed tasks**.

Google Keep

Google Keep is a note-taking app that is available in Goo-

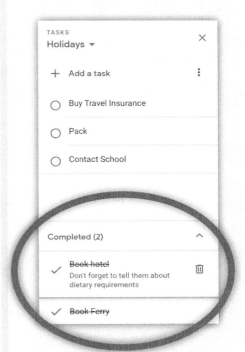

FIGURE 14.9 Where to find your completed tasks.

14

gle Calendar, Gmail and on Google apps on mobile devices. This means wherever you are, you can have easy access to your notes and lists. The nearest competitor to Google Keep is Evernote. However, Keep is simpler with powerful features that will make the choice of which to use an extremely difficult decision. Tip, I prefer Google Keep.

You may want to use Keep to save links from the web, to make and collaborate on lists, to make lists or make quick notes using voice (only in the mobile app).

How to get to Google Keep from Gmail

In Gmail, find and click on the Google Keep symbol in the right navigation pane. If you cannot see the pane, there is an arrow located on the bottom right of your screen as seen in *figure 14.10*. Click on it to make the Keep icon visible in a list down the side. To collapse the list, click on the arrow again. Select the Keep icon, (a light bulb on a yellow background) to open the Keep pane.

Google Keep will open in a pane as seen in figure 14.11. Google Keep is a simple note taking app but also powerful. The bottom of the pane tells you how else you can get to Google Keep. For example on Android and Apple devices, the web app (Google Keep website) and even a Chrome extension. The latter is particularly useful for saving websites in your notes. You can also get to Google Keep in Gmail as well as Calendar.

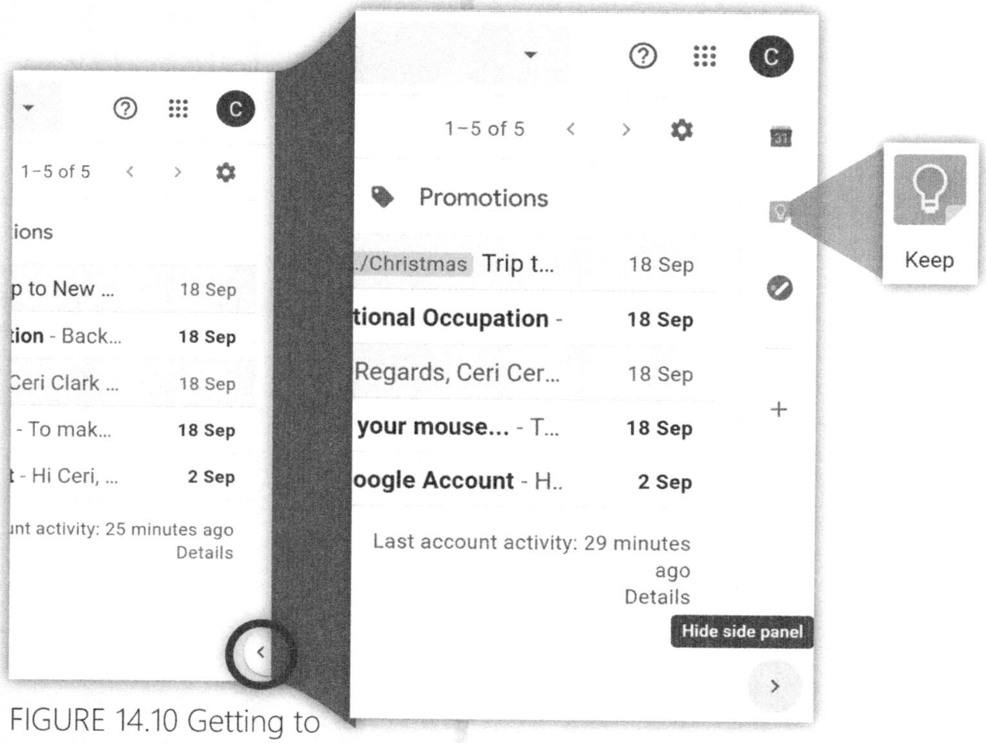

Overview

The top of the pane has three buttons.

Search

The beauty of Google Keep is that you can add labels to your notes making them easier to find. Search

FIGURE 14.10 Getting to Keep from Gmail

for text in your notes or labels. While you can search labels in Gmail you must add them in the Google Keep website. This may change in the future. When searching it is helpful to know that you can find what you need even if you only input a partial word.

Open in the Keep website

Click on this button and the Google Keep website will open in another tab. You will be able to use the more powerful features of Google Keep there such as collaboration etc.

Close Keep

Click on the **X** to close Google Keep and widen the Gmail view.

New List

Choose this to create a checklist. A checklist is where you can check items off the list and they are moved to a completed section, similar to Tasks.

Where to Find Google Keep

This is information on where you can go to use Google Keep. It misses out Google Calendar and Gmail. This may be because the functionality is limited compared to using the named destinations. This may change in the future.

Write a note

Start writing your note to yourself here.

Making Notes

There are two ways to make notes in Keep while you are in Gmail. They are useful in different ways. Notes can just be things to remember while a checklist can be useful

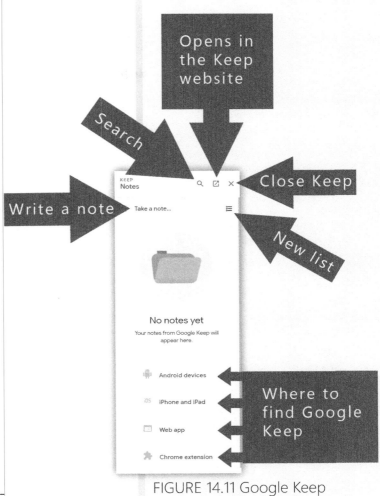

FIGURE 14.11 Google Keep pane overview.

14

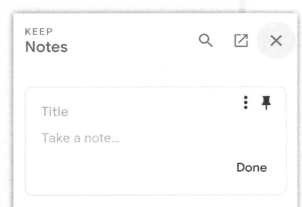

FIGURE 14.12 A blank text note.

for remembering to do things in a discrete list but also to share with people for say, shopping so that when someone gets an item it is removed and put in completed items wherever you see it. It is also useful for when you are reading an email and want to make notes about it as it is always on the right in Gmail.

A text note

Click on + **Take a note...** to start typing. The next figure shows how the box looks. This is the same box that you see whether you are creating it or editing it. The menu button (three vertical dots) gives you the option to archive or delete the note.

Type in the title then either press enter to go to the next box or click into it to write your actual note. Select **Done** and the note will appear in your list.

A checklist

Click on the button that looks like a bulleted list in the Google Keep pane to bring up the checklist notes box. Once you have finished, choose **Done** and the new note will appear in your lists.

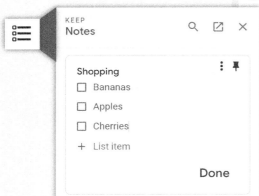

FIGURE 14.13 Creating a checklist.

Deleting and Archiving Keep notes

If you want to archive or delete any of your notes. Click into the note and press on the menu button (three vertical dots) and choose either **Archive** or **Delete**.

Pinning

FIGURE 14.14 Pin Symbol.

There will come a time when you have lots of notes but you have a few which you want to get to quickly but you may not want to search for them. This is where pinning can help you. Look for the pin symbol on the top right of the Note editing box (as seen in *figure 14.14*). Click on this and the note will appear above all your other notes in the Google pane as well as all the other ways you can access Google Keep.

Doing more with Google Keep

Google Keep is more than what you see in Gmail. If you go to the Keep website you will be able to set reminders, change the background color of your notes, collaborate and add images.

Admittedly, Google Keep within Gmail is very limited but, at a click of a button you have the full functionality available in the Google Keep Website. If all you want to do is view your notes, and make lists while looking at your emails, Google Keep in Gmail is adequate but if you want more, just click on the square with the arrow in it that appears at the top of the Keep pane.

Chapter summary

Tasks are a great way to keep track of life events or general tasks within Gmail. While using Tasks it is important to plan how you want to use it before adding tasks to get the most out of it.

Choosing lists to categorize your tasks will help to compartmentalize your tasks. This means you have three levels to organize your tasks. The list, the tasks and the submenu.

Checking the boxes next to your tasks will put lines through them and send them to **Completed** so you know they are done but you can always get them back or remove them forever.

You can add dates and times to your tasks which will add them to your Google Calendar where you can print them as part of your daily schedule.

While the best features for Google Keep are on the Google Keep website or the mobile apps, you can create basic notes and edit notes created in other places.

This chapter gives you an overview of both Google Tasks and Keep and explains what is possible for them in Gmail.

14

Gmail on Your Mobile Phone

● ● ● ● ● ● ● ● ● ● ● ● ● ● ● ● ●

With an ever growing number of new smartphones and tablets available there is no excuse to be without your email. Gmail is so simple to set up with an Android device. At the time of writing this book I have a Huawei Mate 9 so these instructions are designed with that phone in mind but the instructions should be similar across most Android phones and tablets.

Gmail should already be installed on your Android device. Browse your Apps list and find the (envelope) icon for Gmail. If it's not it is easily found in the Play Store by searching for Gmail. Your account will have already been set up when you set your Google account on your phone.

The screen when you launch the app will look like *figure 15.1*.

Overview

The homepage is deceptively simple. Direct from this page you can view your emails, compose new ones and type in the Search box to find your emails. You can browse your email and get to settings through the Gmail menu on the top left and clicking your profile picture will allow you to change your Google account settings (including your photo).

The Gmail menu

Tapping on the hamburger menu (three horizontal lines) will take you to the main Gmail menu. In this section you will find:

Chapter 15

What to expect in this chapter:

- An overview of the Gmail app
- Reading and writing emails on your Android device
- Searching your emails
- A look at the settings

View all your email from all your logged in accounts: **All inboxes** is from everywhere you are currently logged into on your phone. Therefore if you have an email address called dave@mailinator.com and davesmith@mailinator.com and you have selected the first email address and the

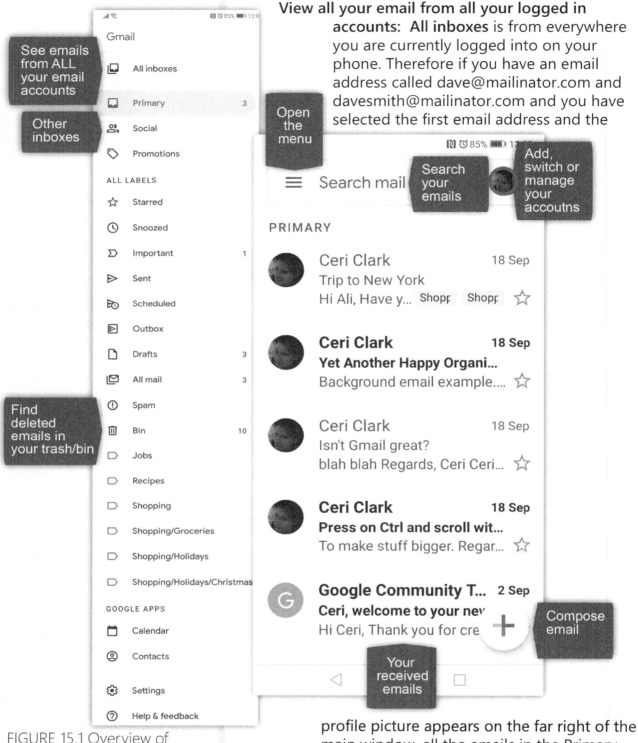

See emails from ALL your email accounts

Other inboxes

Open the menu

Search your emails

Add, switch or manage your accoutns

Find deleted emails in your trash/bin

Compose email

Your received emails

FIGURE 15.1 Overview of Gmail on your Mobile device.

profile picture appears on the far right of the main window, all the emails in the Primary 'tab' will be from that account. If you want to see all the emails from both accounts together, select **All inboxes**.

All labels: Labels included here are, **Starred**, Snoozed, **Important**, **Sent**, Scheduled,

Outbox, **Drafts**, **All mail**, **Spam** and **Bin/Trash**. If you can't find an email and you know you have not deleted it, look in **All mail**.

Your labels: Any labels you create will be under all the Gmail created labels/folders.

Google Apps: Shortcuts to Google Calendar and Google Contacts apps. If you don't have these already on your phone, you will be prompted to download them from the Google Play Store.

Settings: Your settings can affect all your Gmail account not just how you view them on your mobile. Take a look at the Android settings section for more information on these.

Help & feedback: Take a look at Google's own help pages here or give them feedback on their service.

The email window

Your emails will be displayed in the order Gmail received them and notifications will appear every now and again to let you know if any new email has arrived in your other inboxes (if they are activated). When a new email arrives in one of the Google inboxes, the inbox folder notification jumps to the top of the screen with the total amount of unread emails in the 'bar'. When a new email from the *Primary* inbox arrives it will appear above the other inbox emails, unless of course you get another email in one of your other inboxes and so on. This means your latest messages will always be at the top.

If you have the inboxes switched off in Settings the emails will appear in order of arrival.

Checking mail in the Gmail app

If your phone hasn't synced, press on your phone's screen and draw your finger down. A circling arrow will appear near the top of the screen to let you that Gmail is checking for new messages.

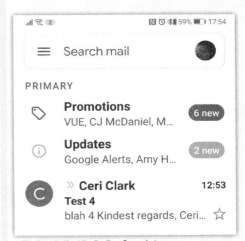

FIGURE 15.2 Refreshing the email list.

15

Composing mail in the Gmail app

The Gmail app now has the ability to schedule an email or enable confidential mode. This section will go into the options for sending an email.

Sending a basic email

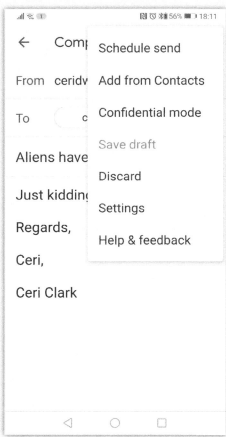

FIGURE 15.3 Extra options when composing an email.

1. Tap on the plus (+) symbol in the circle located on the bottom right of your device's screen
2. You can choose which email account you send from by pressing in your email address and selecting the one you want
3. Tap on **To** (the email address you are sending from will appear at the top. You can choose a different one if you have set more than one up in your phone's account options). You can speed this up by clicking on the menu button on the top right of your phone and choosing **Add from Contacts**
4. Type in the first few letters, if you have already sent an email to that person from your phone before, Gmail will suggest a person below where you are typing. Select the person by tapping on them
5. Add a subject
6. Type your message
7. (Optional) Press on the paper clip symbol to attach a file, including photos from your phone)
8. Tap on the arrow at the top right of the screen to send it

If you are not happy with your email you can click on **Discard** in the menu.

Scheduling your email

There may be a time when you need to send an email and you would rather send it in advance to arrive at a future date and time. This may be because you won't have time later or you are just forgetful like me.

While you are composing or replying to an email, press on the menu button on the top right of the screen and choose schedule send as seen in figure 15.3. The options in figure 15.4 will load on to your screen. These are Tomorrow morning, Tomorrow afternoon, Monday morning and Pick date & time.

The options will depend on the time of day your are setting up the schedule. If you don't like any of the options presented to you, press on **Pick date & time** and find something more suitable. While all times are in British Summer Time for me this will obviously depend on where you are currently residing.

Once you have chosen when you want it sent a confirmation message will appear giving you the option to undo.

If you change your mind about the email you can go into the **Scheduled** folder in the settings and remove it by going to:

- The Gmail app homepage
- Hamburger menu (Three vertical lines)
- Scheduled
- Click into your email
- Press on cancel send. The message will revert to draft.

You can delete the email by clicking on the trash can/bin on this screen or find it in drafts and do the same thing.

Confidential mode

Confidential mode severely restricts what your contact can do with the email. It can also make the email expire so they cannot read after a certain amount of time. Currently Gmail allows you to expire the email for 1 day, a week, a month, 3 months or 5 years. You can require a passcode for them to open the email. Once you have chosen your options, Press on **Save** and then send as normal. For more information on Confidential mode please take a look at *Chapter 5: Sending and Receiving Emails.*

The quick way for doing this is to:

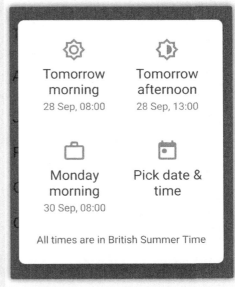

FIGURE 15.4 Scheduling options

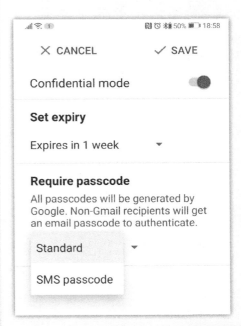

FIGURE 15.5 Confidential mode setting for your email.

- Type your email
- click on the menu button on the top right of the screen
- Choose **Confidential mode**
- Make sure the toggle is switched on
- Set your desired expiry period
- Choose **Standard** or **SMS passcode**
- Click **Save**
- Press Send arrow at the top of the email

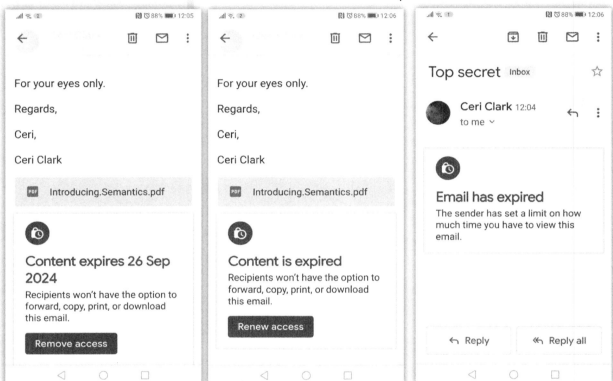

FIGURE 15.6 Confidential mode set to expire an email, removed access, and how it looks to your contact when it has expired.

Removing access

When you send something to the wrong person by mistake or you just want to remove access for any reason, if you have enabled confidential mode you can remove the access to the email from your sent items. This is how to do it:

- Find the email in your sent items.
- Choose the hamburger menu on the top left of your phone's Gmail homepage and press on Sent.
- Find your email and then press on **Remove access**.

They will no longer be able to read it, but they will still be able to read the subject heading as can be seen in *figure*

194

15.6.

To restore the access again follow the steps above but click on **renew access** instead.

Replying to and forwarding mail in the Gmail app

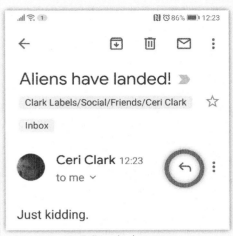

FIGURE 15.7 Reply button.

The arrow pointing left will allow you to reply to an email.

- Open an email
- Press on the arrow pointing left (circled in *figure 15.7*) on the right of the screen beside your contact's name and fill in the boxes as necessary

Pressing on the three vertical dots will give you the option to **Reply all**, **Forward**, **Add** or **Remove star**, **Print** (the message), **Mark unread from here and block people from** sending you messages. Press on any of these options for them to take affect.

FIGURE 15.8 **Press the three vertical dots for more options.**

Snoozing emails

Snoozing can remove emails from your inbox until you need to deal with them. Long press on any email i your inbox, press the menu button on the top right and then press on Snooze. Choose how long you want to snooze for. See *figure* 15.9 for the options available. Choose **Select date and time** for more control.

Find your snoozed emails again before the appointed time by going to **Snoozed** via the hamburger menu on the top left of your phone's screen from your phone's Gmail homepage.

Browsing your email using Labels

- Tap on the top left of the Gmail app (three lines)
- Scroll down to the label you want

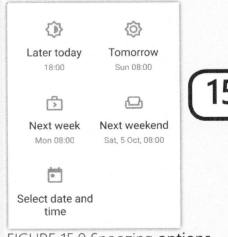

FIGURE 15.9 Snoozing **options.**

15

- Tap the Label you want to go in

Search your email

- Tap into the search box on the top of the screen
- Type in your search term and tap on the magnifying glass on your keyboard (or return depending on your keyboard). You will get a list of emails with the search words in them. For tips on searching Gmail please see *Chapter 9: Searching For, and In, Emails*

Settings

You can get to the settings by tapping on the hamburger menu (three lines on the top left of the main screen).

On the top right of the homepage screen you will find your profile picture. Here you can manage your Google account and even change your profile picture. This is particularly useful for that selfie you have stored on your phone.

General settings

There are several settings within this section which, once set, will apply to all your Gmail accounts that you use with the Gmail app.

Below is a closer look at the options in the main window but you can get a couple more by clicking on the menu button (three vertical dots). These options are:

Under the menu button in Settings

Manage accounts

This takes you to your phone's settings.

Clear search history

Clears your search record.

Clear picture approval

Stops pictures showing in your emails which you may have approved previously. This will stop all pictures showing automatically so you would have to go and approve them all again if you just wanted to stop getting pictures from one sender!

Help & feedback

Access help from Gmail and provide feedback on their service.

Gmail default action (Archive and delete options)

This setting will determine if your email will be deleted when you swipe or archived. I always choose archive as it is easier to find the emails if they are mistakenly archived than if they are deleted.

Conversation view

If you are using IMAP, POP3 or an Exchange account, you can group emails within conversations. This is great for keeping related emails together.

Conversation list density

As with the website view you can choose default, comfortable or compact view.

15

Swipe actions

This is a great time saver. If this setting is activated, swipe your finger to the left or right on the email you want to archive or delete depending on how you set the previous option and it will go. You will have the option to undo for a couple of seconds if you made the gesture by mistake.

Default reply action

This option will allow you to choose **Reply** or **Reply all** as a standard action when you press on the arrow to reply.

I do not recommend that you have this setting on. Replying to all is very dangerous if you are in a hurry. The email may go to people you do not intend it to. You can always choose to Reply all to each message as you reply, but having a blanket settings could cause problems.

Auto-fit messages

If you have messages that don't wrap easily, this option will shrink it so it fits in the window. You can then zoom in to read the text.

Auto-advance

When you archive or delete you can choose here whether you want to go to a newer or older message or go to the conversation list.

Open web links in Gmail

When this is turned on, you will open websites in the Gmail app. With this turned off Chrome will load if you have it installed. I prefer to have this turned off which means that I can continue to look at Gmail while browsing the Internet. I found this useful when needing to refer to some information on a web page. When the web page is opened in Gmail I have to leave the page to view any emails.

Action confirmations

- Confirm before deleting
- Confirm before archiving
- Confirm before sending

These options are self-explanatory. If you want Gmail to ask whether you are sure that you want to delete, archive or send your message then turning this on will help you.

Email settings

These settings apply to the email address you specify.

Manage your Google account

Click here to manage your Google account from your mobile device. You can also get to this by pressing on your profile picture from your phone's Gmail homepage via the Gmail website.

The options here are:

- Update your profile photo.
- Personal info
- Data & personalization
- Security
- People & sharing
- Payments & subscriptions

These are your Google settings and apply to all Google services from Calendar, Drive to the Play Store.

Press on your profile photo to be given the option of changing the photo.

The personal info section is for what you want shared with the world. You can also see who you've blocked, if you are sharing your location and where you can manage your Google activity. For some of these settings you will be redirected to a browser on your mobile device. I would advice that you use a computer when changing these

15

important settings.

Data & personalization deals with your privacy option. Get your privacy check up here.

For more information on *Security*, take a look at *Chapter 4: Security*. This is where you can change your password and manage your other security options.

People & sharing gives you links to organizing your contacts, see and manage who you have blocked, manage your location settings and choose what others see about you.

Payments & subscriptions include payments for Google products. This could be from one off payments at the app store or if you have subscriptions through Google Play.

Other information in this section include what language you have chosen for your account, How much storage you have in your Google account, deleting Google services like Gmail. To delete Google services you will be redirected to the Internet which is a good idea as you don't want to press on this by accident!

The areas in the tabs are not set in stone. Some items are in several places. Having a browse around to familiarize yourself where things are is a must to keep on top of your Google security and privacy.

More general settings (on an email account basis)

Inbox type

By choosing this option you can make the *Priority inbox* your default inbox. I would recommend you do this only after a couple of months of using your email and you are sure that Google is tagging the right emails as important.

Your default inbox will show you emails as they come in but you can change this to show important first, unread first, starred first or of course your priority inbox.

Inbox categories

This is where you choose which inboxes you want the emails to be filtered by in your Gmail. These are **Primary**, **Social**, **Promotions**, **Updates** and **Forums**. You can also drag all your starred emails in to the primary inbox here as well, no matter how old they are.

Notifications and Inbox sound & vibrate

Control if and how you get notifications with this setting.

Manage labels

This is where you can turn on syncing for individual labels. It is not for creating/editing or deleting labels.

Default reply action

Choose from **Reply** or **Reply all**. Choosing **Reply** is usually best as you can control who gets to see your emails.

Mobile Signature

The Signature you created on the web version of Gmail does not apply on your smartphone. You must create another one here. There are no formatting options for your signature on the mobile version of Gmail.

Conversation view

This is where you can make sure that all emails with the same subject are grouped together as a conversation. If this is not enabled all emails will appear individually by the time they came in. This means you will have to search for the rest of the conversation if they aren't included in the email as sent.

15

Smart Compose

This is auto-correct for emails. Google will suggest text as you write. This can save you time.

Smart reply

Gmail will suggest replies when it can if you have this turned on. It can save you time.

Vacation responder/Out of office auto-reply

You can set up a vacation/holiday responder here. If you do set one up I would advise that you check the button for it to work with your contacts only. Burglars have been known to break into houses when they know the owners are on their vacation/holiday.

Nudges Reply and follow up

You can choose to enable the email options to reply to or follow up old emails. They will reappear in your inbox another time suggesting that they may need a reply or follow up.

Inbox tips

Select this is you want unsubscribing tips.

Sync Gmail and days of mail to sync

If you are going to use this app, you need to sync your Gmail but you can choose how many of those emails you want on your phone by choosing how many days of your messages you want on there.

Download attachments

Choose whether you want attachments to be auto-downloaded.

Images

This is where you can get Gmail to ask before showing you images in your email or to always show them. It is best to have the setting on **Ask before showing**. There are a couple of possible reasons for this:

- A spammer can use an image to see if your address is real. When you open an email, images are drawn from across the web. Spammers can record that it has been seen. The spammer can then sell your email or try to send emails to him/herself knowing that there is a possibility the spam message could be read.

- Another reason could be that in the past viruses were hidden within images. This has for the most part been stopped as Google will block those they know about and spammers/hackers have now moved on to other means of harm or easier targets but there is still the possibility. If you only allow images to be shown from trusted sources then this threat is pretty much eliminated.

Adding another email account

You can add another account in two places in your Gmail app; the first is by pressing on the menu button on the top left of the screen on the main window (your main email list) for the **Settings** and then pressing on **Add account** or you can click on your profile picture on the top right of the main window and choose **Add another account**.

In each location you will be given the option to choose Google, a Gmail address or Personal (IMAP/POP), Yahoo, outlook etc. In each case follow the on screen instructions.

15

Chapter summary

Over the years the Gmail app has become more versatile. You can do a lot with the app but there are still limitations where you are redirected to the website. This is a good thing as it is easy to press a button by accident on a touch screen and losing access to emails, files and everything else on a Google account would be disastrous if it wasn't done this way.

This chapter gives an overview of the Gmail app, how to compose emails, where Gmail has placed your labels and where and what the settings are. When you are not at your desktop or laptop, Gmail on your mobile device has everything you need.

Advanced Options

Formerly Google Labs, Advanced includes experimental features that Google are testing. They may disappear at any time or if they become popular, appear as standard options later.

I'm going to go through the advanced options that are available at the time of writing. To find these, click on the gear wheel at the top right of Gmail and then go to **Settings** > **Advanced**

Remember to click **Save** at the bottom of the page every time you make any changes or they won't take effect.

Chapter 16

What to expect in this chapter:

- What are the Advanced Options?
- What can you do with Gmail using these?

Templates

These used to be called Canned responses. They can save you time by automating your email. Please see *Chapter 12: Email management* for more information.

Auto-advance

This is great for busy Gmailers. If you are tired of going back to the inbox just to get to the next email then enabling this lab will mean you automatically go to it after you delete, archive or mute the email you are reading. When it is enabled you can choose whether

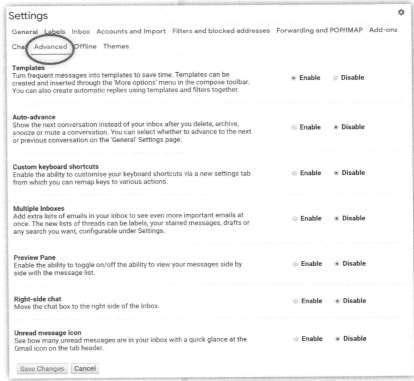

FIGURE 16.1 Advanced options.

to go to an earlier or later conversation.

Custom keyboard shortcuts

Change or make your own keyboard shortcuts, simply enable this tool (clicking save changes at the bottom of the page) and then go to **Gear wheel** > **Settings** > **Keyboard Shortcuts**. The new option will appear at the top of the Settings page once you have enabled it and clicked on **Save Changes**.

See figure 16.1 for the options available. You can choose the keyboard shortcut in the second box.

- Compose (c)
- Compose in a tab (d)
- Search email (/)
- Back to threadlist (u)
- Newer conversation (k)
- Older conversation (j)
- Select conversation (x)
- Toggle star/Rotate between superstars (s)
- Remove label (y)
- Mute conversation (m)
- Report as spam (!)
- Delete (#)
- Previous message (p)
- Next message (n)

- Reply (r)
- Reply in a new window (R)
- Reply all (a)
- Reply all in a new window (A)
- Forward (f)
- Forward in a new window (F)
- Search chat contacts (q)
- Go to Inbox (gi)
- Go to Starred conversations (gs)
- Go to Sent messages (gt)
- Go to Drafts (gd)
- Go to All mail (ga)
- Go to Contacts (gc)
- Go to previous page (gp)
- Go to next page (gn)
- Move focus to toolbar (,)
- Select all conversations (*a)
- Deselect all conversations (*n)
- Select read conversations (*r)
- Select unread conversations (*u)
- Select starred conversations (*s)
- Select unstarred conversations (*t)
- Update conversation (N)
- Remove label and go to previous conversation (])
- Remove label and go to next conversation ([)
- Archive and go to the previous conversation (})
- Archive and go to next conversation ({)
- Undo last action (z)
- Open 'more actions' menu (.)
- Mark as read (l)

- Mark as unread (U)
- Mark unread from the selected message (_)
- Mark as not important (-)
- Open keyboard shortcut help (?)
- Archive (e)
- Open 'move to' menu (v)
- Open 'label as' menu (l)
- Expand all (;)
- Collapse all (:)

- Snooze (b)
- Open conversation (o)
- Focus last mole (ESC) or (Shift+ESC)
- Mark as important (+) or (=)
- Go to next inbox section (`)
- Go to previous inbox section (~)
- Go to Tasks (gk)

Action	Key(s)	
Compose	c	or
Compose in a tab	d	or
Search email	/	or
Back to threadlist	u	or
Newer conversation	k	or
Older conversation	j	or
Select conversation	x	or
Toggle star/Rotate between superstars	s	or
Remove label	y	or
Mute conversation	m	or
Report as spam	!	or
Delete	#	or
Previous message	p	or
Next message	n	or
Reply	r	or
Reply in a new window	R	or
Reply all	a	or
Reply all in a new window	A	or
Forward	f	or
Forward in a new window	F	or
Search chat contacts	q	or
Go to Inbox	gi	or
Go to Starred conversations	gs	or
Go to Sent messages	gt	or
Go to Drafts	gd	or
Go to All mail	ga	or
Go to Contacts	gc	or
Go to previous page	gp	or
Go to next page	gn	or
Move focus to toolbar	,	or
Select all conversations	*a	or
Deselect all conversations	*n	or
Select read conversations	*r	or
Select unread conversations	*u	or

Action	Key(s)		
Select starred conversations	*s	or	
Select unstarred conversations	*t	or	
Update conversation	N	or	
Remove label and go to previous conversation	]	or	
Remove label and go to next conversation	[	or	
Archive and go to the previous conversation	}	or	
Archive and go to next conversation	{	or	
Undo last action	z	or	
Open 'more actions' menu	.	or	
Mark as read	I	or	
Mark as unread	U	or	
Mark unread from the selected message	_	or	
Mark as not important	-	or	
Open keyboard shortcut help	?	or	
Archive	e	or	
Open 'move to' menu	v	or	
Open 'label as' menu	l	or	
Expand all	;	or	
Collapse all	:	or	
Snooze	b	or	
Open conversation	o	or	
Focus last mole	ESC	or	Shift+E:
Mark as important	+	or	=
Go to next inbox section	`	or	
Go to previous inbox section	~	or	
Go to Tasks	gk	or	
Add conversation to Tasks	T	or	
Go to Label	gl	or	
Show menu	hm	or	
Show Archived Hangouts	ha	or	
Show Hangout requests	hi	or	
Focus on the Conversation list	hc	or	
Open phone	hp	or	

Save Changes   Cancel

- Add conversation to Tasks (T)
- Go to Label (gl)
- Show menu (hm)
- Show Archived Hangouts (ha)

- Show Hangout requests (hi)
- Focus on the

16

FIGURE 16.2 Keyboard shortcuts as they appear in Gmail..

Conversation list (hc)
• Open phone (hp)

Multiple inboxes

This tool can keep your emails organized if you do not use the recommended Gmail inboxes. You can choose to have lists of email such as by label, archived or keyword. Once enabled go to the Multiple Inboxes in settings (**Gear wheel** > **Settings** > **Multiple Inboxes**) to set your preferences.

Some examples of new inboxes:

• Label:Shopping – This will show emails which have had the label Shopping applied to them. Substitute Shopping for one of your labels.
• is:unread – This will show only unread messages
• is:starred – This will show only starred messages
• is:sent – This will show emails that you've sent

Please note if you have enabled Google's inbox categories, you must go to inbox in settings and uncheck all the inboxes you can, otherwise it will not work.

Warning, check to see if the settings button is on the top right of your screen when you enable Multiple inboxes. If it is no longer there, go back using your browser buttons and re-enable the Gmail inboxes. You don't want to be left without the ability to get to the settings options!

Preview pane

Do you miss the preview pane in Outlook and other traditional email programs? This option allows you to get the familiar style inside Gmail. When you check a box in your list view you will be able to see the contents of the email in the new Preview Pane.

Once you have enabled the preview, you need to use the drop-down button on the top right of the screen and choose vertical or horizontal view as seen at the top of the next figure. Grab the edge of the pane between the message list and the preview pane with your mouse to

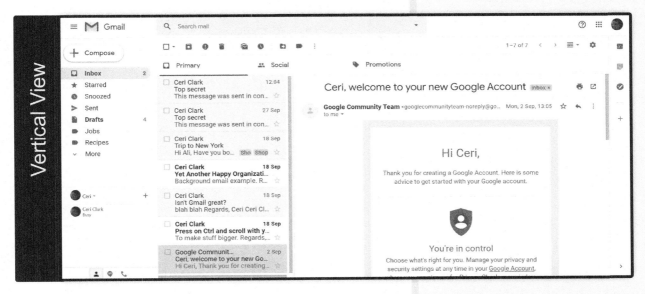

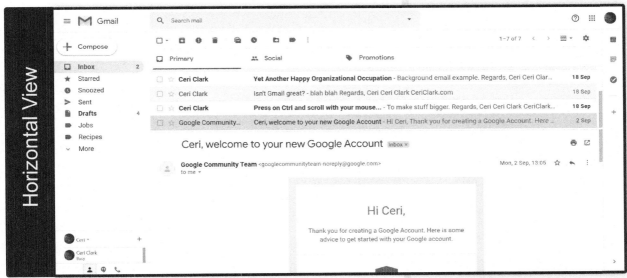

make it bigger or smaller.

FIGURE 16.3 Preview pane options.

Right-side chat

As is suggested by the title you can move the chat from the left column to the right with this option.

FIGURE 16.4 Unread emails displayed in the browser tab.

Unread Message Icon

Are you constantly flicking between tabs on your browser to see if you have any new emails? This lab can solve this problem but only if you use Chrome, Firefox or Opera. It will put a little unread message count number on the tab where you have your email open so you can just glance up rather than having to open the tab all the time.

Chapter summary

Google has extended Gmail with experimental options available under **Advanced** in the settings. They were originally called labs and plenty of functions that were labs in the past are now integrated functions inside Gmail. For example, you can now undo a sent email. In a previous edition of this book, that lab appeared in this chapter. There are only seven 'labs' now but they are worth looking at. They can change the way you work and make you more efficient while you are working. The labs discussed in this chapter are:

- Auto-advance
- Templates (formerly Canned responses)
- Custom keyboard shortcuts
- Multiple inboxes
- Preview pane
- Right side chat
- Unread message icon

Frequently Asked Questions

● ● ● ● ● ● ● ● ● ● ● ● ● ●

What is the address to login to Gmail?

https://mail.google.com or https://gmail.com

Help I've lost my password, what do I do now?

You've been on holiday or have had better things to do than check your email. You've opened up Gmail and you can't remember your password. Please use the following instructions to get your password sent to you:

1. Go to https://mail.google.com if you are not already on the login screen. Click on **Forgot password?** Click **Next**. If your password is correct you will be let in. If it isn't...

2. Click on **Try another way**

3. Choose to have Google send a verification code to the spare email address you nominated on your account. If it is correct you will be let in. If you don't have one...

4. Click on **Try another way**

5. Type in the phone number you nominated on your account. If it is correct you will be let in. If you didn't give a phone number...

6. Click on **Try another way**

7. Type in the month you created the account. If it is correct you will be asked to type in an email

What to expect in this chapter:

- How to get to Gmail
- Recovering or change a password
- Do you need a particular browser
- How to print emails from Gmail
- Using or removing the extra inboxes in Gmail
- How to remove people in a Reply to all before it is sent
- Increasing the size of the text in your browser
- Adding images to email
- Adding Gmail to Outlook

address you have access to...

8. Type in an email address, if Google doesn't recognize it, you will be refused access

Where do I go to change my password?

Go to **Settings** > **Account and Import** > **Change password**.

Do I need a special browser to use Gmail?

Gmail runs on most browsers including Internet Explorer, Firefox, Chrome and Safari. If something doesn't work, try another browser. The recommended browser is of course Google's own browser, Chrome.

How do I print email?

This is easy. Enter the email you want to print. Click on the arrow next to reply at the top right of the email and select **Print**.

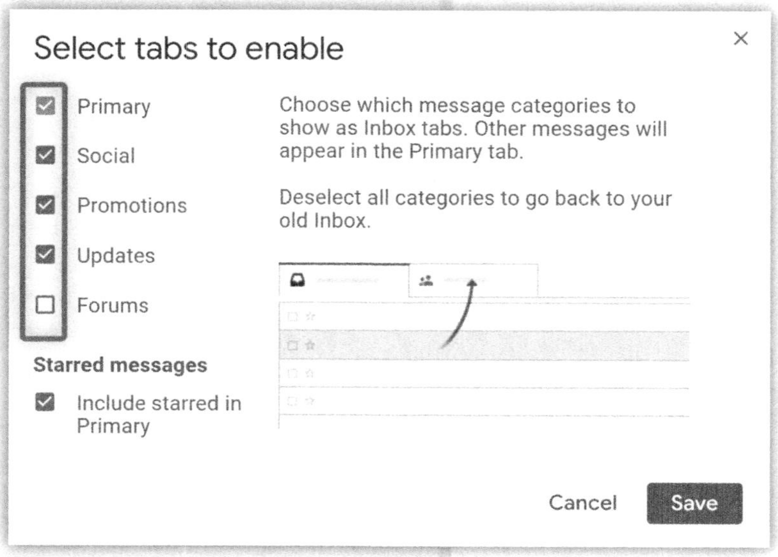

Select tabs to enable ✕

☑ Primary
☑ Social
☑ Promotions
☑ Updates
☐ Forums

Starred messages
☑ Include starred in Primary

Choose which message categories to show as Inbox tabs. Other messages will appear in the Primary tab.

Deselect all categories to go back to your old Inbox.

Cancel   Save

FIGURE 17.1 Uncheck the inboxes you don't want and click **Save**.

How do I remove the 'extra' inboxes like updates, social and promotions?

The easiest way to do this is to click on the **gear wheel** and choose **Configure inbox**.

In the page that loads, uncheck all the tabs you can (you won't be able to get rid of the Primary inbox as it is the main one). Once you click **Save,** all your tabs will disappear leaving you with the one inbox.

The other way to turn off the other inboxes is to go to the **gear wheel** on the top right of your screen then **Settings > Inbox**.

In the **Categories** section, uncheck all the boxes bar Primary and then click on **Save Changes** at the bottom of the screen.

How do I remove email addresses when I Reply to All?

The way to remove email addresses when you reply to more than one person is to click on the email addresses to expand them and click on the x beside each address to remove them one-by-one.

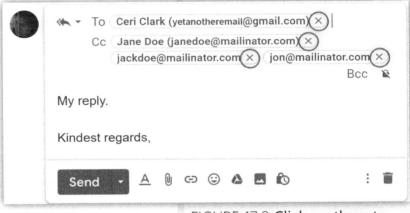

- Open the email.
- Click on the menu button (three vertical dots)
- Select Reply to all
- Click on x more (x is the number of contacts that the message was sent to)
- Click on the x next to the names you want to remove

FIGURE 17.2 **Click on the x to remove an email address.**

How do I increase the size of the text in my browser and my Android phone?

To make text bigger in in any browser by pressing down on the Ctrl key and then pushing away on your scroll wheel to make the page bigger or closer to you to make it smaller.

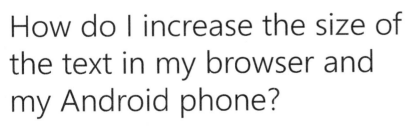

On your Android device you can make the text size bigger by changing them in your phone's main settings. These can be found at **Settings** > **Display** > **Font size** and you can also pinch and zoom inside emails.

How do I add images to my emails?

There are three ways to add images to an email. One way you can add them is by adding them as an attachment. Click on the paper clip as seen in *figure* 17.3, browse for the image on your computer and click open. The file may take a few seconds to load.

FIGURE 17.3 **Click on the paper clip to attach files, the drive icon to send a link to share files or the picture icon to add pictures inside the email.**

The second way to add an image is to click on the Google Drive icon ad choose a file in your Drive. You can then send a link in your email to the file in your drive. This will save you space in your email as you will already have it in Google Drive and it won't be in Gmail. Also if someone replies and sends the file back to you, they will still only be sending you the link to the file in your Drive so there won't be multiple copies bouncing around taking up valuable storage space.

The third way is to click on the icon that looks like a picture. The third circled icon in *figure* 17.3. Once clicked the instructions are the same as if you are adding a profile picture, please take a look at *Adding your profile picture* for more detailed instructions on how to do this.

How do I login when someone is already signed in?

If you allow a visitor to login in to their Google account on your computer and the person forgets to sign out of their account when they leave, you may have problems signing in.

If this or a similar situation happens to you, first sign out for them by going to the account section at the top right of the screen.

Click on their profile photo or initial in the circle and click on **Sign out** at the bottom of the drop down.

Choose your name in the list. If it does not appear, select **Use another account** and login as normal.

In the past I encountered a glitch and I was unable to login as it would just revert to the other account I was trying to log out of. If this happens to you, remove the account and then log in to the one you want by clicking on **Remove an account** at the bottom of the list. Click on the '-' sign in the circle and confirm that you want it removed from the browser. You can always add it again later if you want to.

A way to avoid this is to have your visitor use a different browser from the one you usually use. There are several to choose from including Microsoft Edge, Mozilla Firefox, Opera, Vivaldi, or Safari (on Apple devices).

How do I add my Gmail account to Outlook

Adding Gmail to Outlook has simplified considerably over the years but there are still three steps you need to do to add your account to Outlook. If you have the recommended 2 step authentication enabled as set out in the Security chapter of this book, then the three steps are necessary but you may be able to leave out the app specific password section if you do not have it enabled.

The steps are:

- Enabling IMAP on your Gmail account
- Getting your App Specific Password and
- finally adding the account to Outlook

The sections below will go into the process for these one by one.

17

Step 1: Enable IMAP

- From the Google Homepage, click on the Cog wheel and select **Settings**
- Choose **Forwarding and POP/IMAP**
- Click on **Enable IMAP**
- Scroll to the bottom and choose **Save Changes**

Next, you will need to get your app specific password.

Step 2: Getting an App Specific Password

FIGURE 17.4 Select your Google Service and the method you want to get it through.

- On your Gmail homepage, click on your profile picture then choose **Manage your Google Account**
- On the left choose **Security**
- In the main window, under **Signing in to Google**, click on **App Passwords**
- You may be asked to login to make sure that the person accessing your Google account is you. If it does, login and click **Next**
- To get your Gmail into your Microsoft Outlook on your computer choose these options by selecting them in the dropdown menus, e.g. Mail and Windows Computer
- Click GENERATE
- Copy the app password that Google has generated so that you can add it to Outlook.

Step 3: Adding Gmail to Outlook

FIGURE 17.5 Copy the app password as shown in the pop up.

- Open Outlook
- Click on the **File** tab in the top left of Outlook
- Select **Add Account**
- Type in your name, email address
- In the password field put in your app password that you copied in Step 3
- Click **Next**
- **Click Finish**

Chapter summary

This chapter covers questions that I have been asked, these are:

- What is the address to login to Gmail?
- Help I've lost my password, what do I do now?
- Where do I go to change my password?
- Do I need a special browser to use Gmail?
- How do I print email?
- How do remove the 'extra' inboxes like updates, social and promotions?
- How do I remove email addresses when I Reply to All?
- How do I increase the size of the text in my browser and my Android phone?
- How do I add images to my emails?
- How do I log out if someone else is already signed in?
- I want to access Gmail through Outlook, how do I do this?

If there are any questions you would like answered about Gmail that you think should be in this guide, visit http://www.CeriClark.com and have a look at my contact page. I will update the e-book with new additions to the FAQ and the paperback when the next edition is written.

FIGURE 17.6 Click on **Add Account** after you selected **File** in Outlook.

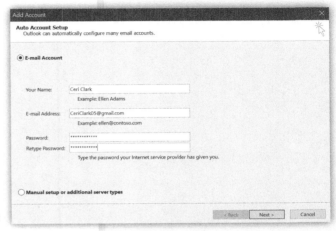

FIGURE 17.7 Add your Gmail details and click Next.

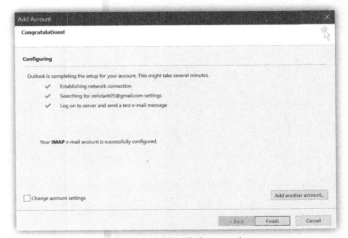

FIGURE 17.8 You have successfully added your account, click Finish!

17

Google Calendar

● ● ● ● ● ● ● ● ● ● ● ● ● ● ●

Google's Calendar application is another service that is closely integrated with Gmail, as such this chapter will go into the basics and some tips that will show how Calendar can make your life easier.

Calendar is the name of Google's calendar offering but you can have several distinct calendars within Calendar and within those have your events. The events are organized by areas of your life (calendars). This could mean you have two (or more) calendars. For example, you may have family, personal and work calendars. Organizing your life this way means that you can show or hide these calendars allowing you to see all aspects or only one in one place at different times. While at work you may not be interested in your family events like school trips and vice-versa, you won't be interested when organizing your family life that you have a meeting on Monday morning. However at a different time you want an overview of everything in which case you would view all your events and calendars as one big calendar. Also you can share your calendars with other people and you may only want to share your meetings with colleagues, not your dentist appointments. Google Calendar is very powerful and gives you a lot of control over how you share this information, as long as you plan before you add your events so you can choose to share calendars while keeping your privacy. This section is an overview of how Calendar can work for you.

How to get to Google Calendar

Google's Calendar service is available on your computer

Chapter 18

What to expect in this chapter:

- How to get to Google Calendar and a calendar overview
- Multiple calendars, the benefits and how to create, delete, use, edit and print them
- Changing the calendar view and appearance
- Sharing calendars including importing and exporting calendars
- What are flairs and how to use them
- How to set up and use goals, reminders and tasks in Google Calendar

FIGURE 18.1 Using the app launcher to get to Calendar.

and your mobile device whether it is a phone or a tablet.

Getting to Calendar from your computer

Going directly there

Type in the following Internet address in your browser to go directly there on your computer:

https://www.google.com/calendar

Sign in with your email and password. If you are already logged in to any other Google service, you will not need to sign in again.

Navigate to Calendar from the app launcher

FIGURE 18.2 Moving the Calendar icon in the App launcher.

You can also get to Calendar using the App launcher. This is the button with nine squares located on the top right of your browser window when you are on any Google page. It is in the shape of a square as shown in *figure 18.1*. Click on the Calendar symbol and you will be taken to the service.

If you use Google Calendar a lot, you can move the Calendar icon in the app launcher and move it to any location within it.

1. Ensure you are signed into any Google website
2. Click on the button with nine squares located on the top right of your browser window. This is also known as the App launcher button or a Waffle
3. Grab the Calendar icon with your mouse and drag it up to where you want it to be. In the example in *figure 18.2*, I have put it as the first icon but you can just as easily put it anywhere in the list

Google will remember this and it will appear at the top of every Google page where you are logged in.

Getting to Calendar from your mobile device

Google's Calendar app is available on Apple's iOS and Android's Gmail as well as on computers. Navigate to your mobile device's app store to download the app. Once you have done this, open up Calendar from your app list.

Calendar Overview

This section will give you an overview of the calendar homepage as illustrated in *figure 18.3* on the next page.

Toggle menu on and off

Remove or bring back the left hand menu by clicking on the three horizontal lines button.

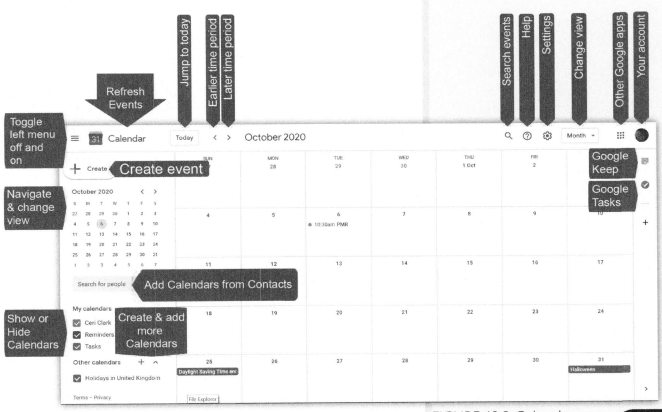

FIGURE 18.3 Calendar overview

18

Refresh events

If you cannot see any events you expect to see in your calendar or you are viewing somebody else's calendar, click on **Google Calendar** at the top of the page to refresh the events shown on the page.

Jump to today

Click on **Today** to jump to today from anywhere in the calendar.

Earlier or later time period

These arrows will let you move the main calendar view earlier or later. If you are viewing a week then you can go one week earlier or later, if you are viewing a month, it will go to the previous month or the next month and so on.

Search events

Clicking on the magnifying glass will bring up the search box on the top of the page. As with the Gmail website and emails, search your events by typing in this box. Advanced options are available by clicking on the arrow next to the box.

Change view

View your Calendar with several different predefined views. These include:

- Day
- Week
- Month
- Year
- Schedule (Agenda)
- 4 days

Extra options which modify the above views on the same drop-down:

- Show weekends
- Show declined events

These are the most popular ways to view your calendar but you can have custom views by highlighting a custom range on the month calendar in the menu on the left. This will be detailed more further in this chapter.

Settings

The gear wheel will take you to Calendar specific settings.

App launcher (other Google apps)

When you press on the squares (on the top right of your screen), you will be given the option to go to other Google services like Docs, Slides, Drive and Maps etc. You can add more apps to the initial list and re-arrange them as you prefer them laid out. For example, you may use Sheets and Docs more than any other Google service. The icons can be moved around so they appear at the top.

Your account

Here you can change your account options, find out about Google's privacy policy and update your Google settings. This is where you can add or change your profile picture and manage your security settings for Google.

Left navigation menu

There are a few options in this navigation menu, here is a quick breakdown of what is possible from here.

Toggle the left menu off and on

The hamburger menu (three horizontal bars) is the means to see the left menu. If you cannot see the menu, click on the hamburger menu. If you want more space to see your calendar, press it again.

Create an event

The button with the plus button will allow you to create new events in your calendars.

Navigate and change view

Click and drag on any date to any other date and you will create a custom date view in the main window. This allows you to see a complete week at the end or the beginning of a month or a set number of days not catered to in the predefined view list.

Clicking on any date will bring up that date in the main calendar window.

Search for people

This is where you can add a calendar from a friend or a colleague. Type in your friend's name and it will search for them in Contacts. When you see the right name, click on them to add the calendar. Above the search box their name will appear with an **x** next to them. Click on this to remove their calendar. Click into **Search for people** and start typing more names to add even more calendars. Adding calendars this way is temporary, if you refresh the page, they will disappear. To add them in a more permanent way, add them through Other calendars. You will need your friend's permission to view their calendar and they will add you to their calendar. You will then be able to see the calendar.

Adding and Other Calendars

Adding your own or other people's calendars is now under **Other calendars**. Select the cross next to **Other calendars** to, subscribe to a calendar, create new calendar, browse calendars of interest, add using a URL or

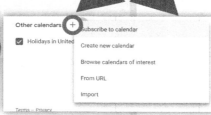

Click on the + to add new calendars

Click into the boxes to show/hide calendars

Other calendars + Subscribe to calendar
Holidays in United Create new calendar
Browse calendars of interest
From URL
Import

Terms – Privacy

FIGURE 18.4 Adding a calendar

224

Import from a file. Please take a look at **Having multiple calendars** later in this chapter for more detail.

Showing or hiding your calendars

In *My* or *Other calendars* you can check the boxes next to a calendar to show or hide events in the main calendar window. You can also remove calendars or change the color of calendar events by hovering over the calendar and clicking the three vertical dots for more settings. Please note removing is not the same as deleting. You will need to make sure that you click on **Delete** at the bottom of the settings page when you press on the menu button next to the calendar. Pressing the **X** just removes it from the list and anyone who you have shared it with will still be able to see it.

Have multiple calendars

Google Calendar gives you the option of having many calendars. This is useful for having a personal or business calendar or you could have project calendars in a business scenario. Each member of your family could have their own calendar but you could view all the events as if they were in one calendar. The advantage of having multiple calendars is that you can turn off calendars temporarily to get a cleaner, uncluttered view if you need to. You could for example turn off your family calendars and just show the project you are working on during work hours. Google Calendar is very versatile.

Any tasks you make in Gmail will appear in your calendar when you check the box next to **Tasks** under your calendars in the left menu bar.

Adding calendars

As mentioned earlier you can create multiple calendars but you can also add other people's calendars. All the events will appear side by side in the main calendar window and you can show or hide events on a calendar basis.

Adding Calendars

There are five ways to add a calendar to Google Calendar. These are:

- subscribing to a calendar,
- creating new calendar,
- browsing calendars of interest,
- adding, using a URL or
- Importing from a file

These are in the order as they appear when you click on the + by Other Calendars.

Subscribing to a calendar

Subscribing is adding a calendar from someone else which already exists.

To do this either click on **Search for People** and then search for the person in your Contacts to add their calendar or Click on the + sign next to **Other Calendars** and choose **Subscribe to calendar** as seen in *figure* 18.4. Search for your contact's name which Google will pull from Contacts and select it when you see it.

Once you select the name you are looking for it will appear under Other Calendars and you will be able show, hide the calendar in your main Calendar window or remove the calendar. Needless to say, you will not be able to delete someone else's calendars.

Creating a new calendar

To create a new calendar that you own, click on the + next to **Other calendar**. Select **Create new calendar** and the settings page will load for adding a new calendar.

Type in your calendar's name, a description of the calendar and make sure that the time zone reflects the calendar's needs. If a project is done internationally but most of the participant's are in one country then it makes sense to make it the time zone of that country.

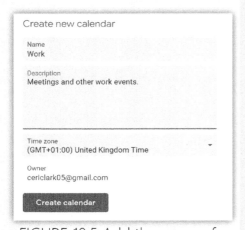

FIGURE 18.5 Add the name of your new calendar, what it's for and the most relevant time zone for the calendar.

Click on **Create calendar** and your calendar will be created.

To get back to the calendar homepage click on the arrow next to **Settings** at the top left of your screen.

You have a few seconds to click on **Configure** at the bottom of the screen. You will always be able to configure your calendar from the menu on the calendar homepage (hover over the calendar to get the menu button for the settings option) but if you want to get it right from the beginning then click on configure just after you've created it.

Browsing calendars of interest

There are a few ready-made calendars that Google has created which are pre-populated with events that you might find useful. If you do add them, you can always either unsubscribe or show/hide them to suit your needs. At the time of writing these calendars are available:

Holidays

- Christian Holidays
- Jewish Holidays
- Muslim Holidays
- Orthodox Holidays
- Regional holidays

Sports

- American Football
- Baseball
- Basketball
- Cricket
- Hockey
- Rugby

Other

- Phases of the Moon

Select any one of these and they will appear under your **Other Calendars** on the bottom left of your Calendar window.

Adding, using a URL

If you are given a URL for a calendar or you get the URL from a webpage you can add it to your calendar by clicking on the + sign next to **Other calendars** and selecting **from URL**.

This is someone else's calendar so you won't be able to delete it but you can remove/unsubscribe or hide it so you can't see it anymore.

Importing from a file

Please see **Sharing Calendars** further in this chapter.

Configuring your calendar

You can get here by clicking on **Configure** that appears at the bottom of the screen after you have created the calendar or you can navigate to here by:

Calendar homepage > **Hover over the calendar that you want to share** > **Menu button** (three vertical dots) > **Settings and Sharing**.

Please see the Settings section of this chapter for more information on how to configure your calendars.

Deleting calendars

Deleting a calendar is possible from the calendar settings page. You cannot delete another person's calendar but you can unsubscribe from them. If you hover over the calendar you want to remove, click on the **X** that appears and it will be unsubscribed from. If it does not belong to you, the calendar can be brought back by adding it again and it will appear under **Other Calendars**.

If you own the calendar you unsubscribe from, you cannot get it back. Also, this is true for deleted calendars.

To permanently delete calendars:

- Hover over the calendar in the left navigation bar
- Click on the menu button and choose **Settings and sharing**
- Scroll to the bottom of the main screen and select **Delete**

Color-code your calendars

When viewing your calendars, it is really helpful to color-code them so that you can see at a glance what events are due on a date or even over a month. You can color-code events but also calendars so that they have a certain color by default. This would be very helpful if you have personal and work calendars. You will be able to see immediately if you have a personal appointment during a work day. You would also be able to see at a glance what could possibly be rearranged. Event colors do priorities over calendar colors, so if you set an event to be a particular color, the calendar color won't show up on it.

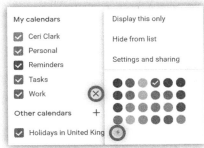

FIGURE 18.6 You can select even more colors by choosing the + underneath the color chart.

To color-code your calendars:

- Hover over the calendar in the left navigation bar
- Click on the menu button and choose the color you want

You are not restricted to the colors available when you click on the menu button. By clicking on the plus sign underneath the color chart you can choose any color, including black.

Density and color

Head over to the gear wheel on the top right of your screen to choose **Density and color**. It should already be set to responsive which means it will pick the best 'look' for how big your screen is and the modern color scheme. Toggle between the options to find a combination you like.

Your default calendar

Your default calendar is the first calendar you have when you first open Google Calendar. It will have the name you opened up your Google account with. Events will be put in

18

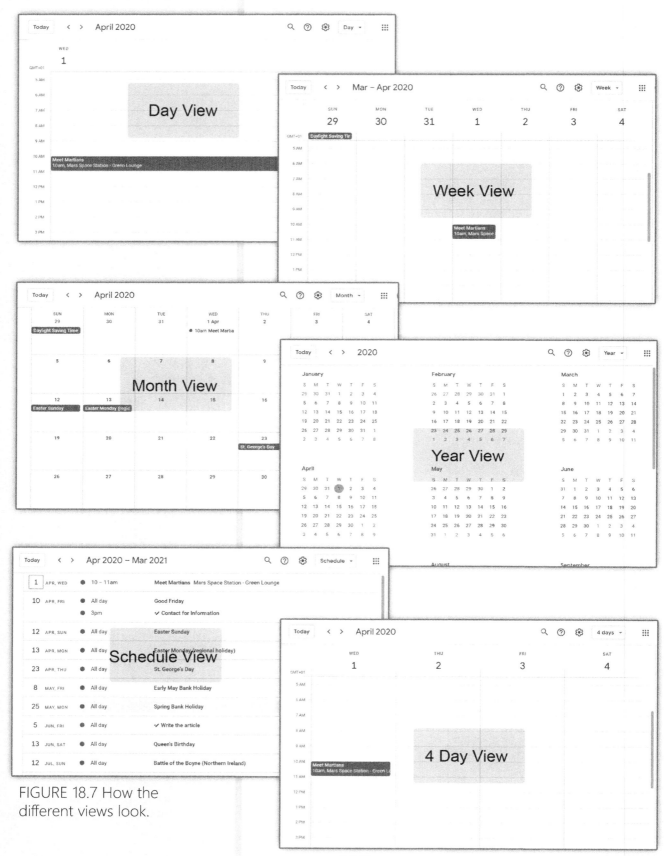

FIGURE 18.7 How the
different views look.

this calendar unless you choose another calendar. You can change the name and other settings on this calendar by hovering over it in the left hand menu and choosing the menu button (three vertical dots) and selecting **Settings and Sharing**. You cannot delete this calendar. If you press delete it will only get rid of all your events.

Calendar appearance

There are several ways to view your calendars. You can zoom in to one day, a week, a month or zoom out to see a whole year.

Change the view

The options for viewing your calendar range from a day, week, year, your agenda (schedule) and 4 days. Click on any of these options to change how your calendar home page looks. Please see *figure 18.7* for how these look.

There is also a custom view where you can highlight a date range from the month view in the menu and the homepage will change to reflect this. If you want a three or six day view, or maybe you want to see what your appointments will be over the next two weeks. Click on the date and drag to the end date you want to see for a custom view. The new date range will appear on the homepage.

Show or hide weekends

During your work week you may not want to be distracted by the glorious plans you have for the weekend, even if it is just binge watching the latest Netflix original.

As in *figure 18.8*, click on the time period you want and select **Show weekends** to remove the tick. This will remove weekends from your view. To bring it back click on **Show weekends** again.

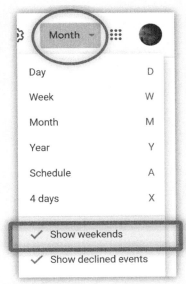

FIGURE 18.8 In the view dropdown menu, click on Show weekends to see them.

18

Show declined events

As illustrated in *figure 18.8*, at the bottom of the list, click on **show declined events** to remove the ticks and to remove declined events from the current view. Click on the option again to show them again.

Create events

When you have your calendars all set up, it is time to add an event.

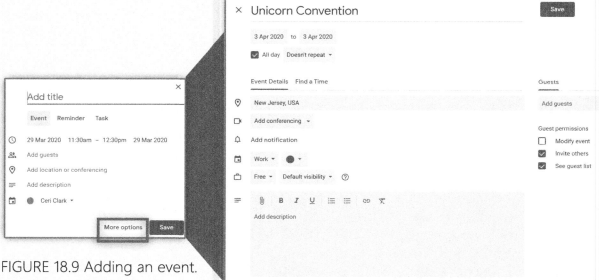

FIGURE 18.9 Adding an event.

Using the + Create button

Click on the **Create** button with the plus on it at the top left of the screen in the navigation menu to go to the Create pop up.

To get all the options available, please click on **More options** on the pop up.

The title (the Subject of your event)

In the pop-up (or event page) type in your title. Be as descriptive as you can but as brief as you can. To help

Google has created some flairs (background pictures) for certain events that are triggered by keywords. I will go into more depth with these in the Flairs section. For example Dinner with James Smith will bring up an image of a laid table.

Date

Next, click into the date and choose the date you need from the drop-down calendar (month view).

Time

Next to the date, choose the start time and the end time. Notice the Time Zone next to the times? Click on this and it gives you the option of having a separate time zone for the beginning and end of your event. This is particularly useful if you are taking a flight and you are leaving in one time zone but arriving in another!

Location

You can put a location next. It accepts zip/postal codes and you will be able to click on it and go to Google Maps if you do this. However, if you don't need the location on your calendar (you can still put it in the description) then you can have a flair as your background picture if you have one. If Google has a picture of your location on Google Maps it will put the image into your event after it is submitted to make it easier to see. Google Map images take precedence over Flairs.

At the time of writing these pictures appeared when you click on an event in a browser on your computer but they appear in your event list on a mobile device. If you want to use background pictures, your decision on what you want to use will be determined by how you view your calendar.

Add conferencing

Add a Google Hangout to your invitation by choosing this

233

18

option from the drop-down list.

Notifications

Choose whether you want a notification or an email before the event. You can have several of these. You can have an email at the beginning of the week to remind yourself that there will be an event. Another one on the day and a notification just before the event in case you get distracted.

Which calendar?

If you have more than one calendar, you can choose which one to put your event in. This is useful if you have shared your calendars with certain groups so they will be automatically updated with your event without having to send an invitation. If there are changes to your events, check the calendar before you go to it in case the date, time or location has changed. Even if you have not been sent an update, changes will be reflected in your calendar. This is unique to Google Calendar as other calendar applications require you to be sent updates for changes to be applied to attendee calendars.

Busy?

If you say you are busy, then it will show up when someone else is trying to schedule you.

Description

Put as much or as little information as you want in here. Bear in mind that others may be reading the description so you may or may not want to put personal information in your descriptions.

Inviting guests

Inviting guests is an important feature of Google Calendar.

You can give them permissions to change the event and you can even find mutual agreeable times for meetings.

Optional attendance

When you hover over your guest's name on the right of the page you will see a little icon of a person. Click on that and you can choose to make that person's attendance optional. Click on the icon again to make their presence a requirement.

Guest permissions

When you invite someone to your event, it appears in their calendar. You can choose whether they are allowed to modify the event, invite others or see the guest list. This only applies to other Google users. If they are outside the Google system they will have to download an iCal file and load it into their calendar manually.

Find time (scheduling event times to suit everyone)

Under the time and date information beside the **EVENT DETAILS** you will find **FIND A TIME**. Click on this and you will be able to see when your guests are available. Of course this only works if your invited attendees are Google Calendar users themselves and that they have agreed that you can see their calendars.

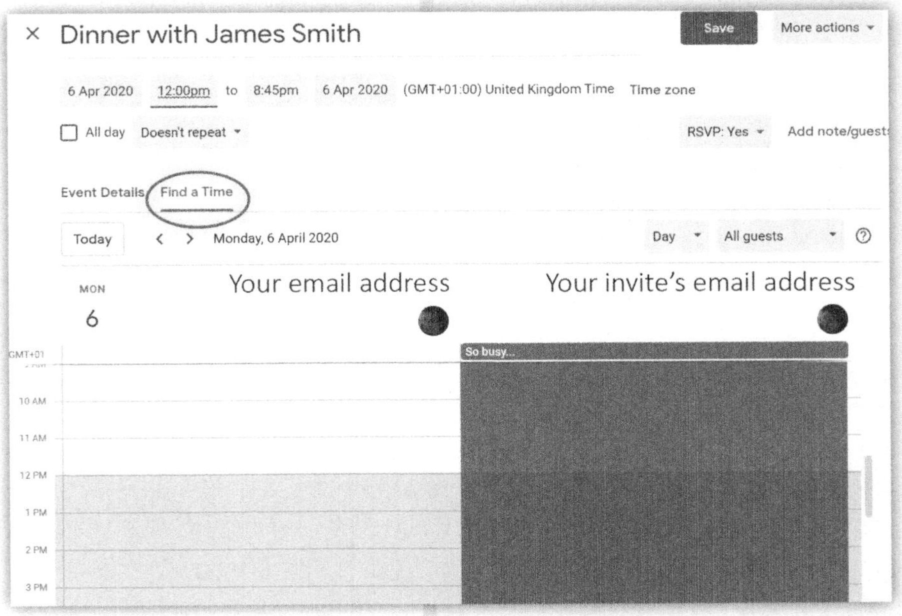

On the right you can add guests and toggle their calendars on and off. Choose a date and time where you are all free.

When all the details are filled in to your satisfaction click

FIGURE 18.10 Find a mutual agreeable time for your meeting using **FIND A TIME**.

18

235

FIGURE 18.11 An invitation sent by email.

FIGURE 18.12 Example event card.

on **SAVE** at the top of your screen by the title of the event and your event will not only be created but invites will be sent to your guests.

By typing into the Calendar

Click into a date in your calendar and type as if you were talking to a personal assistant, for example, **Dinner with Dave**. Click into the dates and times to change them. You can edit the event by finding it on the date and clicking on the entry and then the edit button (pencil in circle).

Responding to an event

If you have been sent an invitation by email, select your response from the buttons presented in the email. The options are **Yes**, **Maybe** and **No**. The button will change color but nothing will happen but it will show you are going within the event in the calendar.

You can also accept an invitation from the calendar entry itself.

Click on the entry in your calendar homepage and you will see at the bottom of the pop up '**Going?**' On the right next to this it will say **YES**, **NO** and **MAYBE**. Choose the option that suits your schedule.

You can see who else is going if you are the organizer or if your organizer has allowed you to, as can be see in *figure 18.12*.

If the attendee does not respond they will show up as not responding in Google Calendar.

Please be aware that these steps may not apply to your attendees who are outside of the Google system and use different Calendar applications. They will get the email but they may not be able to accept the invitation because they don't have a Google account that will allow them to do so. They will have an ICS file which they will put into their own Calendar system but it may be completely separate. Any changes you make will have to be sent to them as an update so they can manually add the file to reflect changes to their calendar. However, if they are in the Google system, it will happen automatically.

Flairs

Flairs are pictures that Google has created to illustrate Calendar entries. A typical example can be seen in *figure 18.13, 18.14 and 18.15*. Typing in certain keywords will bring up pictures. There is no definitive list of these flairs as more are added all the time and some maybe taken away but here is a list compiled from forums on the Internet on what has worked for many people. Some flairs will only work for certain countries and there may be more that have not been found (as there are lists for different countries).

All the images belong to Google and are copyrighted so shouldn't be used outside of Google Calendar. They are shown in this book for educational use.

The words in bold below are categories within the larger categories I have listed. The keywords after the colon are the flair names. These were tested at the time of writing and appear as images in the figures on these pages.

Communication and Media

book club: book club

cinema: cinema, movies

communication: reach out to, write letter, send invitations

reading: reading, newspaper, ebook

Did you know...

Please be aware that if you have already accepted an invitation to an event, the date, time and location may change without you being notified.

Your event will be updated automatically in your calendar but you will not be emailed or otherwise notified unless an update is specifically sent.

This is also true if your attendees use a different calendar such as Outlook for example. They will be notified by email and they will have to load a file into their calendar application to get the updated information.

If you want your attendees to know of changes you make to your events, make sure you click send updates when you save the changes.

Education and Learning

computer science: learn to code, coding time, hackathon, Rails Girls, Railsgirls, Hour of Code, Codecademy, Computer Science, Programming in Python, Programming in Java, Web Development, Web Programming

graduation: graduation

languages: Arabic Class, Arabic Course, Bulgarian Class, Bulgarian Course, Catalan Class, Catalan Course, Chinese Class, Chinese Course, Croatian Class, Croatian Course,Czech Class, Czech Course, Danish Class, Danish Course, Dutch Class, Dutch Course, English Class, English Course, Farsi Class, Farsi Course, Filipino Class, Filipino Course, Finnish Class, Finnish Course, French Class, French Course, German Class, German Course, Greek Class, Greek Course, Hebrew Class, Hebrew Course, Hindi Class, Hindi Course, Hungarian Class, Hungarian Course, Indonesian Class, Indonesian Course, Italian Class, Italian Course, Japanese Class, Japanese Course, Korean Class, Korean Course, Latvian Class, Latvian Course, Lithuanian Class, Lithuanian Course, Norwegian Class, Norwegian Course, Polish Class, Polish Course, Portuguese Class, Portuguese Course, Practice Arabic, Practice Bulgarian, Practice Catalan, Practice Chinese, Practice Croatian, Practice Czech, Practice Danish, Practice Dutch, Practice English, Practice Farsi, Practice Filipino, Practice Finnish, Practice French, Practice German, Practice Greek, Practice Hebrew, Practice Hindi, Practice Hungarian, Practice Indonesian, Practice Italian, Practice Japanese, Practice Korean, Practice Latvian, Practice Lithuanian, Practice Norwegian, Practice Polish, Practice Portuguese, Practice Russian, Practice Slovak, Practice Slovenian, Practice Spanish, Practice Swedish, Practice Thai, Practice Turkish, Practice Ukranian, Practice Vietnamese, Russian Class, RussianCourse, Slovak Class, Slovak Course, Slovenian Class, Slovenian Course, Spanish Class, Spanish Course, Swedish

Class, Swedish Course, Thai Class, Thai Course, Turkish Class, Turkish Course, Ukranian Class, Ukranian Course, Vietnamese Class, Vietnamese Course

music class: piano, singing, music class, choir practice, flute, orchestra, oboe, clarinet, saxophone, cornett, trumpet, contrabass, cello, trombone, tuba, music ensemble, string quartett, guitar lesson, classical music, choir

Food and Drink

bbq: bbq, barbecue, barbeque

beer: beer, beers, Oktoberfest, October Fest, Octoberfest

breakfast: breakfast, breakfasts, brunch, brunches

coffee: coffee, coffees

cooking: cooking

dinner: dinner, dinners, restaurant, restaurants, Family meal

drinks: cocktail, drinks, cocktails

lunch: lunch, lunches, luncheon

Health and Grooming

dentist: dentist, dentistry, dental

haircut: haircut, hair

manicure: manicure, pedicure, manicures, pedicures

massage: massage, back rub, backrub, massages

Hobbies, Leisure and Sport

american football: football

art: painting, art workshop, art workshops, sketching workshop, drawing workshop

badminton: badminton

baseball: baseball

18

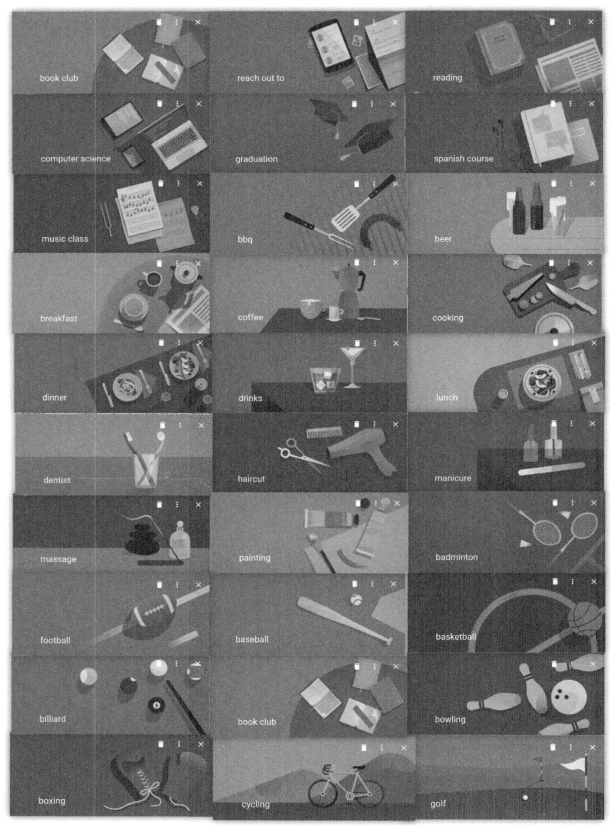

FIGURE 18.13 Flairs

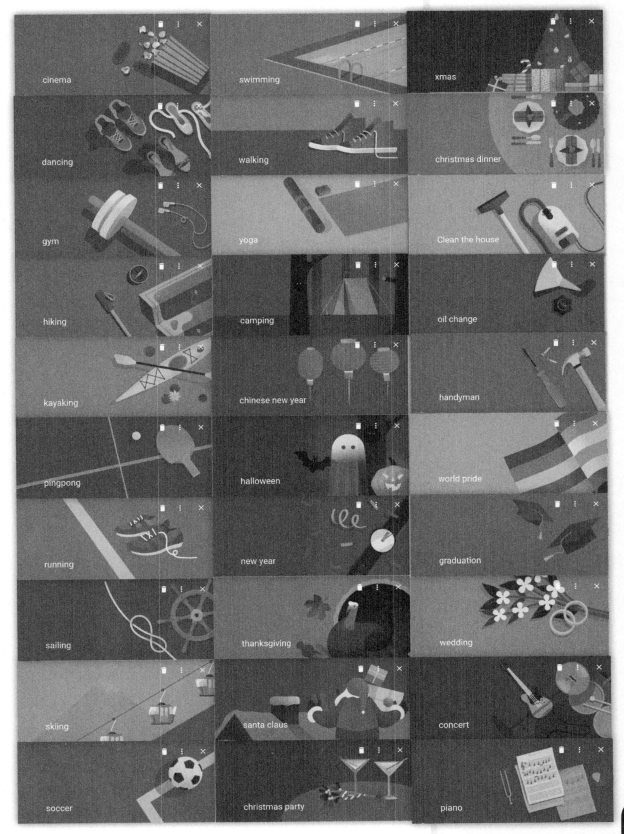

241

FIGURE 18.14 More Flairs

18

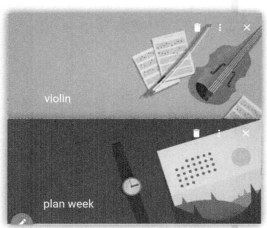

FIGURE 18.15 Even more Flairs

basketball: basketball

billiard: billiard

bookclub: book club, reading

bowling: bowling

boxing: boxing

cinema: cinema, movies

cycling: bicycle, cycling, bike, bicycles, bikes, biking

dancing: dance, dancing, dances

golf: golf

gym: gym, workout, workouts

hiking: hiking, hike, hikes

kayaking: kayaking

pingpong: ping pong, table tennis, ping-pong, pingpong

running: jog, jogging, running, jogs, runs

sailing: sail, sailing, boat cruise, sailboat

skiing: skiing, ski, skis, Snowboarding, snowshoeing, snow shoe, snow boarding

soccer: soccer

swimming: swim, swimming, swims tennis: tennis

walk: going for a walk, walking

yoga: yoga

Holidays and Travel

camping: camping

chinesenewyear: chinese new year, chinese new years, chinese new year's

halloween: halloween, helloween, hallowe'en, Allhalloween, All Hallows' Eve, All Saints' Eve

newyear: new year, new year's, new years

santa: Santa Claus, Father Christmas

thanksgiving: thanksgiving

xmas: christmas, xmas, x-mas, boxing day

xmas meal: christmas dinner, christmas lunch, christmas brunch, christmas luncheon, xmas lunch, xmas luncheon, x-mas dinner, x-mas lunch, x-mas brunch, x-mas luncheon, christmas eve dinner, christmas eve lunch, christmas eve brunch, christmas eve luncheon, xmas eve dinner, xmas eve lunch, xmas eve brunch, xmas eve luncheon, x-mas eve dinner, x-mas eve lunch, x-mas eve brunch, x-mas eve luncheon

xmas party: christmas party, xmas party, x-mas party, christmas eve party, xmas eve party, x-mas eve party

Household

clean: cleaning, clean the house, clean the apartment, clean house, tidy up, vacuum clean, vacuum cleaning

oilchange: oil change, car service

repair: fridge repair, handyman, electrician, DIY, electrician

LGBTQ

pride: christopher street day, dyke march, gay parade, gay pride, gayglers, gaygler, lesbian march, lesbian parade, lesbian pride, euro pride, europride, world pride, worldpride

Life Events

graduation: graduation

wedding: wedding, wedding eve, wedding-eve party, weddings

Music

concert: concert, gig, concerts, gigs

instruments: piano, string quartett, singing, saxophone, orchestra, oboe, music ensemble, music class, tuba, trumpet, trombone, guitar lesson, flute, cornett, contrabass, classical music, clarinet,

You can add an iCal Calendar to your Google Calendar and it will continually update without you doing anything.

If you are using Microsoft Outlook, you can add an iCal Calendar as an internet calendar and it will update your Calendar with details as they change. What is really happening with Outlook is that it is looking at the internet periodically and downloading (and loading) the file so you don't have to.

choir practice, choir, cello

violin: violin, violins

Planning

plan my day: plan week, plan quarter, plan day, plan vacation, week planning, vacation planning

One flair can be used to illustrate many activities. Even though you may have chosen a keyword to make one appear, if you have set a location for your event and Google has an image for that place, it will supersede the flair keywords.

Delete and get your events back

If you want to delete your calendar events, click on your event and then click on the trash can (bin) symbol that appears at the top of your pop up. In your Google Calendar app, you need to press on the menu button on the top right of the event to delete it.

Once deleted your events are stored in the trash (US)/bin (UK). You can restore deleted event entries up to 30 days after you removed it. In Calendar, go to the **Gear wheel** at the top of the screen and press on **Trash** in the US or **Bin** in the UK. On the far right of your event entry you can restore it (arrow pointing left) or delete it forever (trash/bin symbol).

If you want to permanently delete **all** events in your trash, go to:

- In Calendar, go to the **Gear wheel** at the top of the screen
- Press on **Trash** in the US or **Bin** in the UK
- Click on Empty Trash/bin

Settings

There are two ways to get to the settings:

From the top of the screen, click on the **Gear wheel** and choose **Settings**. The other way is to click on the menu button from the calendars in the left menu, please follow these steps:

- Hover over the calendar you want to share or update and click on the menu button (three vertical dots)
- Choose **Settings and sharing**

The method of getting to Settings will determine where in your settings the page will load.

On the left you will see **General**. These are the options that will appear if you go to the top of the page and select the **gear wheel** and then **Settings**.

General Settings

You can scroll down the main window to get to any of these sections or click on the headings in the left menu. You can collapse the general settings in the left menu by clicking on the arrow next to **General** in the menu.

Language and region Select your region to get the correct language. In the US, deleted items will be in the trash and in the UK it will go in the bin, etc.

Time zone You can set a secondary time zone here. More information is in the Time zone section of this chapter.

World clock Show more than one clock across the world.

Event settings When you create an event, calendar will suggest time periods. You can also always set the guest permissions so that you don't have to set it a particular way each time you make an event.

View options If you only use this as a work calendar and you only work week days, you can set the Calendar so it only shows the week days. Other options include; show declined events, reduce the brightness of past events, view calendars side by side in Day View, start the week, on Saturday, Sunday or Monday, what time period

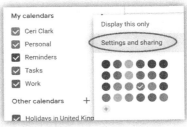

FIGURE 18.16 How to get to your Calendar's settings.

you want to see when you load Calendar and if you want an alternate calendar, in a different language.

Events from Gmail Add events automatically from Gmail.

Keyboard shortcuts Check the box if you want to be able to use keyboard shortcuts.

In the left menu under General you will see **Add Calendar**.

Add Calendar options

Subscribe to Calendar Add someone else's calendar from here

Create new calendar Create a new calendar from here.

Browse Calendars of Interest Browse calendars that are already set up which include holidays, sports, phases of the moon and a calendar that contains week numbers.

From URL If you have the URL of an iCal Calendar, this is where you add it.

Import & export

Please see *Importing and exporting your calendars* later in this chapter.

Calendar specific options

Calendar Settings These are what you initially set in the calendar information, (name, description and time zone).

Auto-accept invitations Do you want to allow people send you invitations which automatically appear in your calendar?

Access permissions Here you set the calendar to be seen by the public? You also can set it so that they see the detail or only if it is free or busy.

Share with specific people You can let only certain people see your calendar.

246

Event notifications This is your default notification for all events on the Calendar you are configuring. How soon before your event do you want to be notified? Would you like it to be a notification or an email? You can always change these when you make or edit an event. This just saves you time if you use the same notifications for most or all your events.

All-day event notifications Choose the way you want to be notified of all day events here.

General notifications How do you want to be notified for new events? This could be when someone sends you an invitation or when they change, cancel, respond, (where guests respond to an event for which you can see the guest list and your daily agenda), or receive an email with your agenda (every day at 5am in your current time zone).

Integrate calendar This is where you get the code to share the calendar or embed it in to a website.

Remove calendar Here you can unsubscribe from a calendar or delete it entirely.

Under the gear wheel there are a few extra settings which are:

- **Trash (Bin in the UK)** Go here to see events that you have deleted to either remove them completely or restore them.

- **Density and color** Choose whether you want the calendar to respond to the size of the window or be compact and if you want modern or classic colors.

- **Print** Print out the calendar you are viewing from here. Please take a look at Printing your calendar for more information on this.

- **Get addons** As with Gmail, Calendar has several additions to improve your experience. At the time of writing the addons that work with Google Calendar are: Zoom for Google Calendar, Cisco Webex, GoTo Meeting, UberConference for Google, RingCentral for Google Calendar, Blue Jeans Meeting, Vonage Conference for Google Calendar and Jitsi Meet for Google Calendar. How to use these are beyond the remit of a Simpler Guide but check them out if you are using services by these companies already.

18

Embedding your Calendar in a website

Embed your calendar is a feature for your websites. Embed the code to let people know events. These events will be public and would be useful if you want to let people know where you are if you are a musician, author or someone who sells craft items at fairs. This could be an elegant solution for letting people know what you are doing in your professional life. Just remember to have a separate calendar for this. You don't want the general public knowing about your dentist appointments!

- Hover over the calendar you want to share and click on the menu button (three vertical dots).
- Choose **Settings and sharing**.
- Either click on **Integrate calendar** in the left menu or scroll down to the section.
- Click on the code under **Embed code** and right-click to copy it.
- Embed it in the code of your website.

Time zones

If you are traveling to a different time zone, you can get Calendar to set a beginning and end time in different time zones. If you work with anyone in another time zone or don't want to wake up a friend or a family member in a different country by accident, knowing the local time is a must. Get Google Calendar to show you the other time zones to avoid any mishaps.

To get to the time zone options:

- Click on the **gear wheel** on the top right of the screen
- Click on **Settings**

Google will show you your local time zone in Calendar so it is important to set the correct time but it will also show you the local time when you are traveling to another time zone.

248

In **Settings,** change the options in **Language and region,** **Time zone** and **World clock**. Make sure all these sections are set to get the benefit of the time zone options.

Sharing Calendars

Sharing your calendar will help your friends, family or co-workers to organize your events. They will not only see when you are available but they will be able to use the scheduling option in Google to create events that will suit everyone who needs to go.

Sharing your calendar by invitation

You can share your calendar by inviting people in the settings.

- In the left navigation menu, hover over the calendar you want to share and click on the menu button (three vertical dots)
- Click on Settings and sharing
- Scroll down to share with specific people.
- Click on **Add People**
- Add an email address or start typing a contact's name and choose their name when you see it
- Decide which permission you want your invitee to have
- Click **SEND**

Your contact will get an email and they can choose to add your calendar to their calendar by searching for your name in the **Search for People** section of Google Calendar.

Adding by subscribing your calendar to Outlook

You can add your Google Calendar to your Microsoft Outlook software by subscribing to your Google Calendar. This will mean that when your Google Calendar will update so will your Outlook every time you open it.

- Go to the gear wheel on the top right of Google Calendar

18

- Choose Settings
- Scroll down to Settings for my calendars (it will be on the left)
- Click on the Calendar you want to share.
- Click on Integrate Calendar
- Look for Secret address in iCal format in the main window, right click on the URL and copy it

- Open Outlook
- Open the Calendar
- In the Home tab, click on Open Calendar
- Click on From Internet
- Paste the URL you copied in Google
- Cllick on OK

Your Google Calendar will now appear on the left

FIGURE 18.17 From the Calendar you want to share, click on Integrate Calendar, then find Secret address in iCal format then copy the link.

next to your other calendars.

Importing and exporting calendars

Add or export calendar or event information using the import and export options in Google Calendar. This section covers the option for adding a friend's calendar or sharing your calendars with them.

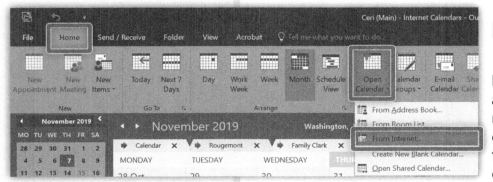

FIGURE 18.18 Find **Open Calendar** and **From Internet** in the **Home** tab.

Importing

Reasons for importing a calendar could be to move from a different calendar application or to see someone else's events in a file that they have given you. These are the steps to import a calendar from a file into Google Calendar.

- In the left menu, look for **Other calendars**. Click on the plus next to this
- Choose Import from the menu that loads as illustrated in figure 18.18
- Browse your computer for the file you want to import and click **Open**
- Click on **Import**

The events will appear in your calendar. You can also get to **Import** from the settings under the gear wheel. It will be at the top of the settings page when you click on **Import & export**.

Exporting

Your reasons for exporting your calendars could be to share your calendar with other people but you might also want to download and keep the ICS file for back up purposes. Use the subscribing option above if you want the recipient to get updated information.

- Go to the **gear wheel** on the top right of Google Calendar
- Choose **Settings**
- Select **Import & export**
- Choose **EXPORT**. All your calendars will be exported in a single Zip file
- Choose where you want the file to be saved on your computer and click **Save**. You can rename it to make it easier to find if you wish
- Unzip the file (in windows right-click and choose **Extract All**)
- Each calendar will be in a different file with an ICS ending. Choose which calendars/files you want to share or backup and download the file

Keyboard shortcuts

To turn this option on, scroll down to the bottom of the **Settings** page and check the box next to Keyboard shortcuts.:

- Click on the Gear wheel on the top right of the screen

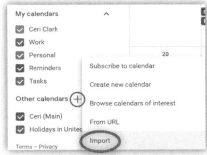

FIGURE 18.19 Find the Import option by clicking on the plus next to **Other calendars**. The plus sign has been added to the above image for clarity (it's actually hidden behind the menu).

251

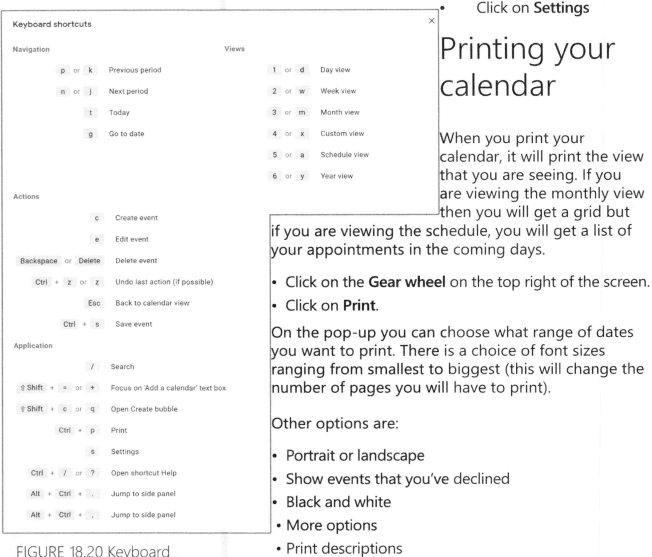

Keyboard shortcuts   ✕

Navigation

p or k	Previous period
n or j	Next period
t	Today
g	Go to date

Views

1 or d	Day view
2 or w	Week view
3 or m	Month view
4 or x	Custom view
5 or a	Schedule view
6 or y	Year view

Actions

c	Create event
e	Edit event
Backspace or Delete	Delete event
Ctrl + z or z	Undo last action (if possible)
Esc	Back to calendar view
Ctrl + s	Save event

Application

/	Search
⇧ Shift + = or +	Focus on 'Add a calendar' text box
⇧ Shift + c or q	Open Create bubble
Ctrl + p	Print
s	Settings
Ctrl + / or ?	Open shortcut Help
Alt + Ctrl + .	Jump to side panel
Alt + Ctrl + ,	Jump to side panel

FIGURE 18.20 Keyboard shortcuts.

- Click on **Settings**

Printing your calendar

When you print your calendar, it will print the view that you are seeing. If you are viewing the monthly view then you will get a grid but if you are viewing the schedule, you will get a list of your appointments in the coming days.

- Click on the **Gear wheel** on the top right of the screen.
- Click on **Print**.

On the pop-up you can choose what range of dates you want to print. There is a choice of font sizes ranging from smallest to biggest (this will change the number of pages you will have to print).

Other options are:

- Portrait or landscape
- Show events that you've declined
- Black and white
- More options
  - Print descriptions
  - Print end times
  - Print your response

Click **PRINT** to send it to your printer.

Goals (Only on your mobile device)

When you use the Google Calendar app on your mobile device you can choose to set goals. This could be a gym visit. If you feel you can't do the gym visit, Calendar will reschedule for a more suitable time.

- On your Calendar app, press the circle with the plus sign in it on the bottom right of your screen
- Choose Goal
- Select from the list: Exercise, Build a skill, Family & friends, Me time and Organize my life
- Narrow down your option
- How often?
- For how long?
- Best time? Morning, afternoon, evening or anytime
- For most skills, Calendar will schedule a time, but for exercise, connect to Google Fit

When all the steps are done Calendar will suggest a time, you can readjust this to a different time but you don't have control over the time. It will search your Calendar for free times. You can however snooze the events if you are not ready on a particular day.

One more word of warning. You cannot choose a start date. Be ready to do the goal you are setting as Calendar will schedule the first 'event' for tomorrow!

Reminders

Reminders can be viewed and made in Calendar. To view them, make sure that the checkbox is selected in the left navigation menu.

Create a Reminder

Reminders can be viewed and created in Google Keep and Google Calendar. These are the steps for creating them in Google Calendar:

- Click into a date (or time frame if you are in day mode)
- Choose **Reminder**
- Alter the time and dates if necessary and choose whether you want the reminder to repeat
- Click on Save

At the time of writing, flairs did not work with Reminders. If you want to edit your reminder, click on it and choose

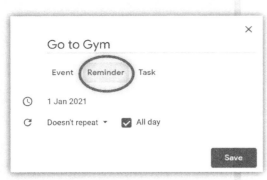

FIGURE 18.21 Click into a date and time and choose **Reminder.**

FIGURE 18.22 Mark your Reminder as done.

the pencil symbol that appears on the card.

You can add Reminders to your tasks menu by importing them at the bottom of the Tasks pane when it is opened. Simply, click on the Tasks button on the far right (the tick) and click on Import your **X** reminder.

Remove reminders

Find the reminder you want to remove, select it and choose **Mark as Done.**

Tasks

Tasks are available in Google Calendar as well as Gmail. To view them, make sure that the checkbox is selected in the left navigation menu in Google Calendar.

Viewing Tasks

Click into the box next to **Tasks** to view them in the calendar. You can also see your tasks as a list on the right of the Calendar screen. If you cannot see it, click on the Tasks icon (a circle with a tick in it) that you can click on to make the list visible. To collapse the list, click on the **X** at th top right of the Tasks pane.

Creating, editing and deleting tasks is the same as if you are in Gmail. Please see *Chapter 14: Tasks & Keep* for more information on how to do these.

Chapter summary

With a mix of events, reminders, tasks and goals, Google Calendar aims to supercharge the way you organize your time. This chapter gives you an overview of what is possible and how to achieve certain functions within the service. Google Calendar integrates with Gmail which gives it a place in this book.

The beginning of this chapter covered how to get to

Google Calendar using the address bar and the app launcher which appears in ever Google service where you are signed in.

Next was a calendar overview which covered the main features from the calendar homepage and how to navigate it.

Multiple calendars are an essential feature of Google Calendar, allowing you to separate your life into calendars so that you can turn events on and off by category. Turn off your personal calendar to concentrate on your work appointments for example.

Adding calendars, configuring them and your default calendar are all detailed next along with how to add a friend's calendar. Color coding your calendars allow you to see at a glance what you have planned for the day, week or month. Choosing a density and color will personalize your calendar even further.

Changing the view of your calendar can help you to focus on what needs to be done. Only looking at what needs to be done a day or a week can affect how you work. Taking a macro or micro view of your life can help you to plan how to want to spend your time. The calendar appearance section details how to show or hide weekends and show declined events.

A chapter on Google Calendar wouldn't be complete without a section on creating events and of course responding to them once you have been extended an invitation.

Flairs are pictures that Google have created to illustrate certain events. Typing keywords into your event title will make these pictures appear. In the flairs section of this chapter, there is an index of the keywords and images that go with each keyword. Drill down the categories to find the keyword that best illustrates your event and it will show when you click on your event and on your calendar entries on your mobile device.

Another section discusses deleting events and how to get them back.

18

There are two ways to get to the settings in Google Calendar. The settings section gives you an overview of what is available and how to use them.

If you would like your calendar to be public there is no better way than to embed your calendar into your website. Take a look at **Embedding your Calendar** in a website for more information on how to do this.

The next section goes into how to individualize Google Calendar for your time zone and how to view different time zones within Google Calendar. Features include how to set a beginning and end time to an event which start and finish in different time zones as well as seeing different time zones from within the left menu.

Sharing calendars through inviting people and also Importing and exporting calendars are shown and the keyboard shortcuts available for Google Calendar are detailed. The gear wheel is where you go to print your calendar.

Another feature which hooks into Gmail and Calendar in this chapter discusses how to create and remove reminders and how you can use tasks in Calendar.

Glossary

	2-step verification	A security feature where two items are needed to log in to a website. This is usually a password and some other form of identification such as a code from a mobile device.
A	**Address bar**	The box at the top of your browser where website addresses show, for example https://gmail.com
	Address book	Similar to an old-style book where addresses were written in a book but held electronically in Gmail.
	Adobe Flash	This is software which operates in browsers that is created by Adobe to view interactive elements on a webpage.
	Android device	These are smartphones and tablets which run on Google's operating system, Android.
	App	Short for application, these are small programs which run on mobile devices such as smartphones and tablets
	Archive	Archiving emails means in the strictest sense that the label inbox has been removed from an email and is no longer in your inbox. You can find any email in All Mail unless it has been deleted.
	Attachment	This is a document, picture or anything that can be 'attached' to an email.
B	**Browser**	This is a computer program that allows you to view webpages.
C	**Captcha**	Also known as word verification, this box, usually containing letters or numbers is used to prove that people submitting to a website are not robots. Captcha can also be images.
	Chat	In Gmail, this can be talking using text or your webcam.
	Contacts	People you have connected with by Gmail or Google+.

Text file which contains simple information such as exported contact information. This type of document can be opened in text or spreadsheet applications.

CSV

A number of emails grouped together with a common subject.

Discussion thread

Google's free online storage of files and photos. It is also the place where you can create free spreadsheets and documents.

Drive

D

This is a feature where you can download some data or a document that can be saved on your computer which can then be used on a different account or application.

Export

E

An application on your computer which allows you to find files, folder, and software on your PC. This is called Finder on Macs.

File Explorer

F

A feature of Gmail that sorts your email by predetermined elements. This can be for example filtering your email so all emails from a certain address will go into a finance folder (label).

Filters

The symbol located on the top right of Google pages that will take you to the settings for that service.

Gear wheel

G

A unit of computer storage. At the time of writing Google gives you 15 Gigabytes of space. This is roughly equivalent to 200,000 emails.

Gigabytes

The free email service provided by Google.

Gmail

There are good or bad hackers but for the purposes of this book, I refer to those nefarious people who have devoted their lives to harming you or others by breaking in to computers and websites.

Hackers

H

Hangouts refer to connecting to people by both instant messaging (text chat) and video chats with webcams.

Hangouts

	Hashtags	These are words preceded by the # symbol. For example #cooking is a hashtag.
	Homepage	The start page of a website, also known as the main page.
I	Icon	A picture or symbol which when pressed takes you to another webpage or function (such as a Google Hangout).
	Images	Photos, pictures and graphics.
	Import	This is a feature where you can upload some data or a document to a web service like Gmail or Google+.
	Inbox	This is an electronic folder which holds your emails. Traditionally your inbox was one folder where all your emails first arrived. Gmail now provides several inboxes which sort your emails into categories.
K	Kindle	This is a device which uses the AZW or Mobi e-book formats.
L	Labs	Google Labs are experimental features that Google are testing. They may disappear at any time or if they become popular, appear as standard options later.
	Labels	Labels are what folders are in other programs. You assign a label to an email to sort them. Click on a label to find other emails of the same type.
	Lastpass	This is a service from lastpass.com where you can store all your passwords in the cloud which is protected by one password and 2-factor authentication for extra security. Use this service to generate a different password for every website you sign up to but you will only have to remember the one.
N	Nested label	A nested label means that a label will appear under another in the label list.

A string of letters and numbers which can be a phrase or random which allows you access to a website or service.	**Password**	**P**
A computer that runs the Windows operating system.	**PC**	
This is where criminals will try to get your personal information from you by sending emails that appear to be from people or organizations you trust. This can be usernames, passwords and/or credit card information.	**Phishing**	
In the context of this book this is your information held by Google.	**Profile**	
Schemes designed to commit fraud.	**Scams**	**S**
Text that finishes off an email. This is usually your name but can include your address, email address, phone numbers and images.	**Signature**	
Irrelevant, unwanted and unasked-for emails.	**Spam**	
The subject of your email should be a short description of the contents of the email.	**Subject**	
See 2-step verification	**Two-factor authentication**	**T**
URL is short for Uniform Resource Locator. It is a quick way of saying web address.	**URL**	**U**
Get rid of emails you no longer want by following the instructions at the bottom of emails to unsubscribe from future messages.	**Unsubscribe**	
A unique piece of information used as a means to identify you to Google.	**Username**	
This is a way of sending contact information in the form of a document. Import vCards to Gmail to fill in details of a contact.	**vCard**	**V**

W

Webcam

Webcam A video camera which will enable you to talk face-to-face in Google Hangouts.

Word verification

See Captcha

Index

A

Address book

Advanced, formerly Labs

Android phone, see Gmail app

Appearance

Attachments

B

Blocking

C

Calendar

About Ceri Clark

Ceri Clark is a full-time author and mother. She was a Librarian with over eleven years of experience in corporate, public and private libraries culminating in a Library Manager position at the ill-fated English Audit Commission.

Following the closure of the library (and the future demise of the organization) she began to utilize her skills for searching, writing and advising with her Simpler Guides Series. Find out more about Ceri Clark at cericlark.com.

Simpler Guides

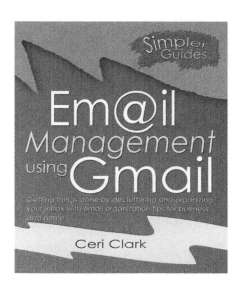

Books for Children

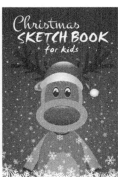

Just add Passwords...

Disguised password book series - different sizes, different designs.

     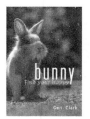

   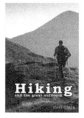  

Discover even more password books and journals with Ceri Clark's new pen name, Penny Quill.